RACISM

RACISM

CHALLENGES TO BEING CHURCH

EDITED BY
Cardinal Peter Turkson AND
Emmanuel Katongole

FOREWORD BY
Bishop Edward K. Braxton

Paulist Press
New York / Mahwah, NJ

Cover image by RysaVector/Shutterstock.com
Cover and book design by Lynn Else

Library of Congress Cataloging-in-Publication Data
Names: Turkson, Peter, 1948– editor. | Braxton, Edward K., other.
Title: Racism: challenges to being church / edited by Cardinal Peter Kodwo Turkson.
Description: New York; Mahwah, NJ: Paulist Press, [2025] | Includes bibliographical references. | Summary: "This book is a collection of papers on racial relations in Scriptures, Church, and society"—Provided by publisher.
Identifiers: LCCN 2024019986 (print) | LCCN 2024019987 (ebook) | ISBN 9780809157068 (paperback) | ISBN 9780809188833 (ebook)
Subjects: LCSH: Racism—Religious aspects—Catholic Church. | Race relations—Religious aspects—Catholic Church.
Classification: LCC BX1795.R33 R34 2025 (print) | LCC BX1795.R33 (ebook) | DDC 282.089—dc23/eng/20240807
LC record available at https://lccn.loc.gov/2024019986
LC ebook record available at https://lccn.loc.gov/2024019987

ISBN 978-0-8091-5706-8 (paperback)
ISBN 978-0-8091-8883-3 (ebook)

Published by Paulist Press
997 Macarthur Boulevard
Mahwah, NJ 07430
www.paulistpress.com

Printed and bound in the
United States of America

CONTENTS

FOREWORD

Bishop Edward K. Braxton

As a Catholic bishop in the United States, I have studied, spoken, and written about racial divide in this country for many years.[1] I know the benefits of seeing this complex and challenging issue from new perspectives. This volume on racism, with unique chapters written by authors with a deep connection to Africa, brings new and valuable insights to the conversation about "race," "racism," "prejudice," "ethnicity," "culture," "education," "Scripture," and "religion" from the moving viewpoint of their remarkably diverse life experiences, disciplines, concerns, and areas of scholarship. Each writer brings outstanding academic erudition and profound concern about the racial divide to bear on his or her topic. The following thirteen chapters may be particularly important for those American and European readers who do not frequently study works by African authors, or authors with long life experiences in Africa. Reading these pages about the racial divide in Africa and in the United States will engage readers in a serious dialogue with the authors with whom they may not always agree but from whom they will glean fresh perspectives.

While the tragedy of human enslavement has been a global phenomenon, the history and consequences of enslavement in the Americas, and more specifically in the United States, remains a topic of intense contemporary discussion and scrutiny. Individuals seeing the nomination of their political party as candidates for the presidency of the United States have been pressed to answer questions on this topic. Here, I present a brief overview of the transatlantic slave trade, the *Dred Scott v. John F.A. Sandford* decision, and the gradual awakening of the conscience of the Catholic Church concerning the grave sin of racism as a backdrop to the chapters that follow.

The racial divide in the United States is the product of the transatlantic slave trade. The capturing, selling, and buying of enslaved free human beings from West Africa has been called America's original sin. The transatlantic slave trade consisted of Europeans capturing, purchasing, and enslaving free African children, women, and men and transporting them across the Atlantic Ocean to the Americas. These free human beings, who were sold for profit, were uprooted from their homelands, families, cultures, economic resources, languages, and religious traditions, and introduced into an alien culture where they were treated as beasts of burden to power the economic engines of the plantations in the Americas.[2] At least 12.5 million African people endured the Middle Passage across the Atlantic Ocean, between 1517 and 1867. Many perished on these hellish voyages. Those who lived suffered the harshest treatment, fell victim to diseases, and lived in a state of paralyzing fear about their unknown fate.

Perhaps as many as 10.7 million survived this ordeal. Millions ended up in forced labor on sugarcane plantations in Brazil and in the Caribbean. Approximately 3.5 percent were brought to British North America and the United States. It is estimated that at least 395,000 African people ended up in North America. Additionally, the Royal African Company brought seven thousand African people directly to Virginia between 1670 and 1698. The practice of using enslaved free African people spread rapidly on the plantations of the South. No fully accurate record exists of the many forms of abuse suffered by these victims of human arrogance and hatred. This is particularly true of the sexual abuse of women.

The moral evil and mortal sin of the transatlantic slave trade have had a fundamental impact on almost every aspect of the economic, social, political, educational, and religious life of the United States. The fact that the Catholic Church in Europe and in the United States did not mount a vigorous opposition to this unspeakable horror in fidelity to the gospel of Jesus Christ is one of the most shameful episodes in the history of the Church. Most European-American Christians today do not have an adequate understanding of the ongoing impact of this sordid history on what is euphemistically called "the race problem" in America. If the Church had aggressively condemned human slavery as the very opposite of the teaching of Christ that all people should love God with their whole being and love their neighbors as they love themselves, the Church might have had the moral clarity and courage to condemn vigorously the unspeakable moral evil of Adolf Hitler and the Nazi Party in Germany when they almost succeeded in their efforts to destroy the Jewish people in the Holocaust between 1933 and 1945.

Could there be a flaw at the foundation? Could the transatlantic slave trade, the history of racism, the ongoing manifestation of the racial divide that we are witnessing in the United States today, and the issues addressed in the chapters of this volume be a result of a foundational flaw born of moral blindness due to wrong choices made by "people of faith" who should have known better? Robert B. Taney, a Catholic, rose to prominence under President Andrew Jackson and was eventually appointed chief justice of the Supreme Court. On March 6, 1857, he wrote the majority opinion in the seven-to-two *Dred Scott v. John F.A. Sandford* decision in what is generally considered to be the most odious and shameful ruling in the Supreme Court's history. He declared that people of African ancestry living in America had absolutely no legal standing before the court and could not sue for their freedom because they were nothing more than the property of their "owners." It is stunning to think that a Catholic, who surely knew Jesus's teaching to love our neighbors as ourselves and who knew from Jesus's teaching of the Good Samaritan that every human being is our neighbor, could have penned these words:

> The question is simply this: Can a negro [*sic*], whose ancestors were imported into this country, and sold as slaves, become a member of the political community formed and brought into existence by the Constitution of the United States, and as such become entitled to all the rights, and privileges, and immunities, guaranteed by that instrument to the citizen? One of which rights is the privilege of suing in a court of the United States in the cases specified in the Constitution.
>
> It will be observed, that the plea applies to that class of persons only whose ancestors were negroes [*sic*] of the African race, and imported into this country, and sold and held as slaves. The only matter in issue before the court, therefore, is, whether the descendants of such slaves, when they shall be emancipated, or who are born of parents who

> had become free before their birth, are citizens of a State, in the sense in which the word citizen is used in the Constitution of the United States....
>
> They had for more than a century before been regarded as beings of an inferior order, and altogether unfit to associate with the white race, either in social or political relations; and so far inferior, that they had no rights which the white man was bound to respect; and that the negro [*sic*] might justly and lawfully be reduced to slavery for his benefit. He was bought and sold, and treated as an ordinary article of merchandise and traffic, whenever a profit could be made by it. This opinion was at that time fixed and universal in the civilized portion of the white race. It was regarded as an axiom in morals as well as in politics, which no one thought of disputing, or supposed to be open to dispute; and men in every grade and position in society daily and habitually acted upon it in their private pursuits, as well as in matters of public concern, without doubting for a moment the correctness of this opinion.
>
> Yet the men who framed this declaration were great men—high in literary acquirements—high in their sense of honor, and incapable of asserting principles inconsistent with those on which they were acting. They perfectly understood the meaning of the language they used, and how it would be understood by others; and they knew that it would not in any part of the civilized world be supposed to embrace the negro [*sic*] race, which, by common consent, had been excluded from civilized Governments and the family of nations, and doomed to slavery. They spoke and acted according to the then established doctrines and principles, and in the ordinary language of the day, no one misunderstood them. The unhappy black race were separated from the white by indelible marks, and laws long before established, and were never thought of or spoken of except as property. (See 60 U.S. 19 How. 393 393, 1856)

Many southerners thought Chief Justice Taney's opinion definitively resolved the issues concerning the status of enslaved free human beings before the law. Instead, it was met with widespread outrage and fueled the fires that led to the Civil War. Eventually, the Emancipation Proclamation (1863), the Civil Rights Act (1866), and the Thirteenth, Fourteenth, and Fifteenth Amendments to the United States Constitution (1868) nullified Taney's infamous ruling, giving human beings of African ancestry full citizenship (on paper only!), thus making them, for the first time, African Americans!

Nevertheless, this ruling by the first Catholic chief justice, which seems glaringly false today, created a flaw at the foundation of the country's relationship to people of color. It is not possible for us to know how the clear teaching of Jesus Christ to love our neighbors as we love ourselves escaped Justice Taney and the six justices who concurred with him, unless we consider the possibility that they simply could not conceive of Dred Scott as their neighbor because of his African heritage. He was not really a person, only property.

Unfortunately, there were, within the horizon of possibilities of the Catholic Church, firmly held opinions that made Taney's decision possible. There was a "flaw at the foundation" that, sadly, was supported by teachings at the highest levels of the Catholic Church. We learn from history—and credible historical documents suggest—that one of the first extensive shipments of human beings from West Africa in the transatlantic slave trade was probably initiated at the request of a Roman Catholic bishop, Bartolomé de las Casas, who later regretted his position and worked to improve the plight of the African and indigenous peoples.

Moreover, between 1573 and 1826, the Catholic Church placed books critical of enslaving free human beings on the Index of Forbidden Books. The Church excommunicated Capuchin missionaries because they urged that enslaved free African people in the Americas should be given their freedom. Blessed Pius IX, within whose pontificate (1846–78) the Dred Scott decision was handed down, wrote, "Slavery itself...is not at all contrary to the natural and divine law, and there can be several just titles of slavery, and these are referred to by approved theologians and commentators of the sacred canons.... It is not contrary to the natural and divine law for a slave to be sold, bought, exchanged or given."[3]

Prominent American bishops (including John Hughes, New York, 1842–1864; Francis Kenrick, Baltimore, 1851–1863; St. John Neumann, Philadelphia,1852–1860; and Anthony O'Regan, Chicago,1854–1858) did not vocally condemn the Supreme Court's *Dred Scott* decision.

Indeed, historian John Strausbaugh, writing about Archbishop Hughes, observed that the archbishop's position was that as long as slavery was legal in the South, owning slaves was not a sin. He did not admire President Lincoln and found no place in his heart for people of African ancestry. Strausbaugh notes that, as the conflict between the abolitionists and the Irish workers intensified, antiabolitionist forces in New York would "scare workers with terrible predictions that if the millions of enslaved blacks in the South were freed, they'd flood into northern cities and take away all the work."

> With the flood of Famine Irish into the Lower East Side in the 1840s and 1850s, the immigrants' struggle to set themselves apart from blacks and be accepted by whites turned mean and hard. The Irish now developed a fierce strain of anti-black and anti-abolitionist sentiment. Clinging desperately to their low-level jobs, Irish workers hated the abolitionist movement they feared would unleash millions of freed black workers to flood the city and replace them.

Hughes said that if the president's goal in the Civil War was to end slavery, then Irishmen "will turn away in disgust from the discharge of what would otherwise be a patriotic duty."[4]

Clearly, the transatlantic slave trade was a flaw at the foundation of the United States that had a tragic impact in Chief Justice Taney's decision, *Dred Scott v. John F.A. Sandford*, another flaw at the foundation.

In 2013, 156 years after Taney's decision, the critics of Chief Justice John Roberts, only the third Catholic chief justice, penned the infamous Supreme Court decision, *Shelby County v. Holder*, which struck down section IV of the Voting Rights Act. This decision ruled that states, municipalities, and counties with a history of disenfranchising voters based on race were no longer required to submit changes in their election laws to the Department of Justice. This decision effectively gutted the Voting Rights Act.

After that, legislators in Georgia passed many new voting restrictions and nineteen other states enacted thirty-four similar laws. President Biden spoke out forcefully against any efforts to restrict voting rights. The president urged citizens and the members of both parties to take the necessary steps to win the approval of two bills—the Freedom to Vote Act and the John Lewis Voting Rights Advancement Act—that could turn back some of the most difficult restrictions passed by state legislatures in 2021, by setting minimum requirements for early voting and for what forms of identification are accepted at polling places, and by easing the voter registration process. These bills have not become law.

On June 29, 2023, the Supreme Court spoke again. Chief Justice John Roberts, writing for the majority, by a vote of six to two, in *Students for Fair Admissions v. Harvard*, 600 U.S. 181 (2023), a landmark decision, ruled that affirmative action in college admissions is unconstitutional, thus reversing the lower court ruling. The court held that race-based affirmative action programs in college admissions processes violate the Equal Protection Clause of the Fourteenth Amendment. In this ruling, along with *Students for Fair Admissions v. University of North Carolina*, the Supreme Court effectively overruled *Grutter v. Bollinger* (2003) and *Regents of the University of California v. Bakke* (1978), which validated some affirmative action in college admissions provided that race had a limited role in decisions.

Catholic Chief Justice Roberts has been sharply criticized for rulings that seem tainted by the flaw at the foundation of Catholic Chief Justice Roger Taney's decision in 1857.

The flaw at the foundation of practices and policies of the United State that continues to influence American life and the life of the Catholic Church is *not* a flaw in the Gospels, the clear teachings of Jesus Christ, nor in the mystery of the incarnation—"And the Word became flesh and lived among us " (John 1:14). For the Church, the flaw emerged, in part, because of the Eurocentric development of Church history with little regard for Asia and almost no regard for Africa. Thus, when Europeans wrongly thought they "discovered" America, they brought the biases, prejudices, and ignorance of a Eurocentric Church with them, and acting, at times, as if there was no culture other than European culture. Most Europeans arriving in the Americas had little or no knowledge of African people, whom many regarded as "savages." While they may have believed that people of color needed to be baptized to be "saved," they did not believe that they were equal in dignity and value as their European American counterparts.

Fortunately, over time, individual Catholics and some religious communities of priests, brothers, and sisters began to oppose racial bias and recognize that all people are made in the image and likeness of God. They worked to overcome the racial divide with groups like the Catholic Interracial Society. This awareness gradually found expression in the following teaching documents of the United States Catholic bishops:

"Discrimination and Christian Conscience"—A statement of the U.S. Catholic Bishops, November 14, 1958.

"On Racial Harmony"—A statement by the Administrative Board, National Catholic Welfare Conference, August 23, 1963, that reaffirms the U.S. Catholic Bishops' official position against racial discrimination and segregation.

"Brothers and Sisters to Us"—A pastoral letter on racism, U.S. Catholic Bishops, November 1979.

"We Walk by Faith and Not by Sight: The Church's Response to Racism in the Years Following"—25th Anniversary Executive Summary, 2004.

"Reconciled through Christ" (*Reconciliados en Cristo*)—A publication that explores the reconciliation and greater collaboration between Hispanic American Catholics and African American Catholics, U.S. Conference of Catholic Bishops, February 1997, 2013.

"Open Wide Our Hearts: The Enduring Call to Love" (*Abramos nuestros corazones: El incesante llamado al amoarta*)—A pastoral letter against racism, developed by the Committee on Cultural Diversity in the Church of the United States Conference of Catholic Bishops (USCCB), November 2018.

The extraordinary scope, breadth, and depth of some of these documents has led some commentators to say that the Catholic Church does not need to write more. The Church simply needs to do more. And one thing the Church still needs to do is to make sure the contents of these documents are known and studied in every diocese, parish, catholic school, and seminary. As one bishop said, "The Church is far more effective in disseminating its teachings on the sin of abortion than it is in disseminating its teachings on the sin of racism."

Knowing the truth of this statement, I include here key paragraphs from two of the most important of these documents, "Brothers and Sisters to Us" and "Open Wide Our Hearts." Some readers of this volume may be seeing these texts for the first time.

"BROTHERS AND SISTERS TO US":

> Racism is an evil which endures in our society and in our Church...We are convinced that the majority of Americans realize that racial discrimination is both unjust and unworthy of this nation....
>
> We do not deny that changes have been made, that laws have been passed, that policies have been implemented. We do not deny that the ugly external features of racism which marred our society have in part been eliminated. But neither can it be denied that too often what has happened has only been a covering over, not a fundamental change....
>
> This new economic crisis reveals an unresolved racism that permeates our society's structures and resides in the hearts of many among the majority. Because it is less blatant, this subtle form of racism is in some respects even more dangerous—harder to combat and easier to ignore. Major segments of the population are being pushed to the margins of society in our nation. As economic pressures tighten, those people who are often black, Hispanic, Native American and Asian—and always poor—slip further into the unending cycle of poverty, deprivation, ignorance, disease, and crime. Racial identity is for them an iron curtain barring the way to a decent life and livelihood. The economic pressures exacerbate racism, particularly where poor white people are competing with minorities for limited job opportunities. The Church must not be unmindful of these economic pressures. We must be sensitive to the unfortunate and unnecessary racial tension that results from this kind of economic need....
>
> Racism is a sin: a sin that divides the human family, blots out the image of God among specific members of that family, and violates the fundamental human dignity

of those called to be children of the same Father. Racism is the sin that says some human beings are inherently superior and others essentially inferior because of races. It is the sin that makes racial characteristics the determining factor for the exercise of human rights. It mocks the words of Jesus: 'Treat others the way you would have them treat you.' Indeed, racism is more than a disregard for the words of Jesus; it is a denial of the truth of the dignity of each human being revealed by the mystery of the Incarnation....

Today in our country men, women, and children are being denied opportunities for full participation and advancement in our society because of their race. The educational, legal, and financial systems, along with other structures and sectors of our society, impede people's progress and narrow their access because they are black, Hispanic, Native American, or Asian....

The structures of our society are subtly racist, for these structures reflect the values which society upholds. They are geared to the success of the majority and the failure of the minority. Members of both groups give unwitting approval by accepting things as they are. Perhaps no single individual is to blame. The sinfulness is often anonymous but nonetheless real. The sin is social in nature in that each of us, in varying degrees, is responsible. All of us in some measure are accomplices. As our recent pastoral letter on moral values states: "The absence of personal fault for an evil does not absolve one of all responsibility. We must seek to resist and undo injustices we have not ceased, least we become bystanders who tacitly endorse evil and so share in guilt in it."

"OPEN WIDE OUR HEARTS":

Consistently, African Americans have been branded, by individuals, society, and even, at times, by members of the Church, with the message that they are inferior. Likewise, this message has been imprinted into the

U.S. social subconscious. African Americans continue to struggle against perceptions that they do not fully bear the image of God, that they embody less intelligence, beauty, and goodness.

This reality represents more than a few isolated stories; it was the lived experience of the vast majority of African Americans for most of our national history. We acknowledge with gratitude the religious orders whose charism embodied evangelizing and caring for those who were marginalized and unwelcomed. We recall the bold witness of the Divine Word Missionaries, the Oblate Sisters of Providence, Sisters of the Holy Family, the Josephites, the Franciscan Handmaids of Mary, and the Blessed Sacrament Sisters. Likewise, countless individuals—Daniel Rudd, Thomas Wyatt Turner, Sr. Thea Bowman, and Dr. Lena Edwards to name a few—worked tirelessly against the prevailing current of racism to share the Catholic faith with persons of African descent.

Still, to understand how racism works today, we must recognize that generations of African Americans were disadvantaged by slavery, wage theft, "Jim Crow" laws, and by the systematic denial of access to numerous wealth-building opportunities reserved for others. This has left many African Americans without hope, discouraged, disheartened, and feeling unloved. While it is true that some individuals and families have thrived, significant numbers of African Americans are born into economic and social disparity. The poverty experienced by many of these communities has its roots in racist policies that continue to impede the ability of people to find affordable housing, meaningful work, adequate education, and social mobility. The generational effects of slavery, segregation, and the systemic use of violence—including the lynching of more than 4,000 black men, women, and children across 800 different counties throughout the United States between 1877 and 1950 are realities that must be fully recognized and addressed in any process that hopes to combat racism.

To press forward without fear means "to walk humbly with God" in rebuilding our relationships, healing our communities, and working to shape our policies and institutions toward the good of all, as missionary disciples. Evangelization, which is the work of the Church, "means not only preaching but witnessing; not only conversion but renewal; not only entry into the community but the building up of the community." Racism is a moral problem that requires a moral remedy—a transformation of the human heart—that impels us to act. The power of this type of transformation will be a strong catalyst in eliminating those injustices that impinge on human dignity. As Christians, we know this to be true, for with "God all things are possible" (Mt 19:26). It is the Lord who, by his grace, forgives and restores us to these relationships and heals the wounds between us. After all, the aim of salvation history is reconciliation and entering the heavenly Jerusalem, a communion of all peoples and all nations.

To press forward without fear also means cooperating with God's grace by taking direct and deliberate steps for change. It means opening doorways where once only walls stood. As bishops, we commit ourselves to the following actions with the hope that others, especially those in our spiritual care, will do likewise in their own lives and communities.

Examining our sinfulness—individually, as the Christian community, and as a society—is a humbling experience. Only from a place of humility can we look honestly at past failures, ask for forgiveness, and move toward healing and reconciliation. This requires us to acknowledge sinful deeds and thoughts, and to ask for forgiveness. The truth is that the sons and daughters of the Catholic Church have been complicit in the evil of racism. In his Papal Bull *Dum Diversas* (1452), Nicholas V granted apostolic permission for the kings of Spain and Portugal to buy and sell Africans, setting the stage for the slave trade. Even though subsequent popes strongly renounced and rejected the international slave trade, much to our shame, many American religious lead-

> ers, including Catholic bishops, failed to formally oppose slavery; some even owned slaves.
>
> We also realize the ways that racism has permeated the life of the Church and persists. To a degree even today....Not long ago, in many Catholic parishes, people of color were relegated to segregated seating, and required to receive the Holy Eucharist after white parishioners. All too often, leaders of the Church have remained silent about the horrific violence and other racial injustices perpetuated against African Americans and others.
>
> Therefore we, the Catholic bishops in the United States, acknowledge the many times when the Church has failed to live as Christ taught—to love our brothers and sisters. Acts of racism have been committed by leaders and members of the Catholic Church—by bishops, clergy, religious, and laity—and her institutions. We express deep sorrow and regret for them. We also acknowledge those instances when we have not done enough or stood by silently when grave acts of injustice were committed. We ask for forgiveness from all who have been harmed by these sins committed in the past or in the present.

Dorothy Mensah-Aggrey, in the chapter "Curriculum, Content, and Racism: The Need for a Paradigm Shift," cites a 1993 interview with Father Cyprian Davis, OSB, the distinguished African American church historian, on the African American Catholic experience. He said that "the Church in this country reflects the problems of the country, which has yet to solve the question of race; that has been America's tragic flaw." The author continues, "The question of race, really has been the universal Church's flaw, not just America. Herein lies the paradox of the Church's mission of evangelization and discipleship, and a sad, but true contribution to the intersection of religion and racism in general."

Near the end of her essay she asks, "Does your institution's curricula reflect the changing needs and views of a modern, diverse society?" This is a challenging question for the future of the Catholic Church in the United States. Are Catholic elementary schools, secondary schools, colleges, universities, seminaries, parish schools of religion, sacramental preparation classes, youth ministry, adult education, and faith formation programs, and Sunday sermons developed with an awareness of what Father Davis called America's tragic flaw and what I call the flaw at the foundation of American history that continues to have an impact on the Catholic Church? The scholarship, wisdom, zeal, and pastoral insight in the following pages are an excellent contribution to the curricula of Catholic education and formation activities seeking to address the changing needs and views of modern and diverse societies in the hope of bridging the racial divide.

INTRODUCTION

Concern for the dignity and for the social well-being of humankind are not new ideas in the church. They have been the *principal concern of the church from her birth.* For human beings, both our dignity and our well-being have been God's main concern since the beginning. Thus, biblical faith, in general, and the teaching of the prophets, in particular, insist that fidelity to the covenant joins obedience to God (his laws) with reverence and concern for the neighbor and the care of creation (cf. Isa 24).

Therefore, the church believes that a reflection of the meaning of human life and its authentic development and growth in life, history, and culture found expression already in Scriptures and in the writings of the church fathers and are now taught by the church's magisterium as the church's social teachings. Indeed, our faith reflection on what it means to be authentically human in history and culture goes back to the scriptures and the church fathers. In the Scriptures, and later in the writings of the fathers, the human being, created in the "image and likeness of God" and bearing the spirit of God within himself or herself, is fundamentally a personal and relational being.

A human being has a personhood or a personality, which is the supreme social principle of the church's social teaching; and the free development of the human person—respect for his/her dignity and its promotion—are the central measure of social order. For, created in the image of God (cf. Gen 1:27), every man, woman, and child possess dignity in their personhood.

Subsequent biblical teaching about the human family as constituted by brothers and sisters, products of or born out of the same womb (*adelphoi* and *adelphē*), makes members of the human family—brothers and sisters—equal in nature and dignity (cf. Eph 1:5; Rom 8:29).[1] No person has more intrinsic dignity than the other. By implication, human activity that results in any "deficit in basic human dignity"—such as impoverishment, enslavement, torture, or the privation of freedom—violates the dignity of the human person and the fundamental integrity of God's plan for creation and humanity.

Personal progress that realizes human flourishing, well-being, or dignity, must apply to everyone. Every person is an end in themselves, never merely an instrument, valued only for utility's sake, such as production or consumption. True development of human potential only fulfills the norms and demands of human dignity[2] when personal capacities are given space and scope to flourish.[3] This universal dimension is not abstract. In concrete and practical terms, it means that a person is not something, but someone.[4]

With this God-given dignity, the vocation of every man and woman is to attain that integral human development[5] that is destined to be fulfilled in authentic love: the love of our sisters and brothers in truth.[6] Freedom is a fundamental expression of this dignity, including those free rights to work, housing, and to possess land (*trabajo, techo, tierra*),[7] to worship, to exercise conscience and civil liberties, to exercise choice (e.g., voting), and to bear responsibility for action and to form associations or communities for common purpose. Pope Francis points to the holy core of human dignity, when he writes, "Humanity is the 'sacred temple' in which 'merchants' are prevented from speculating," and which "may not be reduced to serving money."[8]

But, this explication of the church's "concern for the dignity and the social well-being of humankind" cannot be a mere affirmation, it must engender a mission, an action, a way of life for the church; for as Pope Benedict XVI observed in the opening mass of the Second African Synod, "fare proposte senza passare all' azione è un' ideologia" (to merely make proposals without passing to action is an ideology). Accordingly, reflecting subsequently on the theme of the Second African Synod to the Roman Curia, Pope Benedict XVI observed, "The task of Bishops was to transform theology into pastoral care, namely into a very concrete pastoral ministry in which the great perspectives found in sacred Scripture and Tradition find application in the activity of Bishops and priests in specific times and places."[9] This is when the rubber must hit the road! So, must the church's teaching about the personhood and the dignity of the human person find expression in her catechesis, in the homilies of pastors, in pastoral programs and action, and in the lives of her faithful to make her concern for the dignity and for the social well-being of humankind real.

The murder of George Floyd by a police officer in Minneapolis in May 2020 sparked worldwide protests, not simply about the suffering of civilians at the hands of police officers, but the despicable and inhuman treatment of minorities, especially African Americans (Blacks) by white police officers in the United States, and, as it emerged from the spread of protest marches, also in the United Kingdom and parts of Europe (France, Germany, etc.). The Black Lives Matter movement captured a racist phenomenon that had become identifiable as part of a police culture and that festered in the privacy of homes and workplaces, where Blacks and minorities were excluded. It could not and cannot be dealt with only by legislation nor even by the threat of imprisonment. It has become a subculture of people in parts of the United States and elsewhere, and structures, institutions, and legislations have been created to perpetuate and nourish subtly a racist culture of nonbelongingness, manifested in forms of segregation, discrimination, denial of rights and opportunities, and victims of mudslinging.

The presence of racism is a serious perversion of God's creation of the human person in his image and likeness. The church's belief and teaching in the unity of the human family is incompatible with racism—where the integrity of God's plan of creation, fulfilled in Christ, the firstborn of many brothers, is not believed to apply to all. Lately, the introduction of sociopolitical categories—such as modern liberal left wing and conservative and right wing—into the church and her practice of religion has been a pretext to avoid the sharp and challenging demands of the gospel; but the proclamation of the gospel in and out of season is still the mission of the church, and the dignity and the social well-being of people remain her concern from birth!

This coming together of African theologians to consider this mission and concern of the church was occasioned by the incident of George Floyd's murder; they variously consider the realization in the different places and contexts of their ministry and profession the mission and concern of the church. Thus, some authors deepen the understanding of this mission and concern; others recount instances and situations that make this concern and mission urgent. Some are critical about their awareness and their implementation in local churches while others study possible solutions to the racial issues underlying the church's concern and mission.

The views expressed and the positions adopted in the following chapters are those of the authors. It is our hope that they help us all in the church to overcome a phenomenon that dims her light as a beacon of salvation and diminishes her glory in the world!

1

IS CATHOLICISM RACIST?

A South African Perspective

Anthony Egan, SJ

In this chapter, we look contextually at the question, "Is the Catholic Church Racist?" from the historical experience of racism within the church in South Africa. Yet, far from seeing this as an isolated case (a product of "loss of nerve" on the part of the church in colonial South Africa until well into the 1950s), I am going to suggest that a form of racism (sometimes subtle, sometimes less so) has been and to an extent is still a fundamental tendency within Catholicism, and by extension, almost all the great streams of Christianity.

Sociologically, Christianity—and Catholicism, in particular—is a system of power based on knowledge: the church (system of power) imparts doctrine (knowledge) for human salvation in its broadest sense. This point is essential to my South African case studies and my general thesis and is grounded in adapting the theories of two twentieth-century social theorists, both atheists/agnostics from Catholic backgrounds, to this question.

TWO (VERY LAPSED) CATHOLIC INTERLOCUTORS

My two (very lapsed) Catholic interlocutors for this discussion are Antonio Gramsci (1891–1937), a founding member of the Italian Communist Party (PCI), and Michel Foucault (1926–1984), the French postmodern philosopher and historian. Breaking ranks with Lenin's classical Marxist understanding of hegemony as the working class's role of leadership in a socialist revolution,[1] Gramsci interpreted hegemony differently: rather than being an expression of revolutionary power, it was often the subtle, ideological power of ideas of a ruling class over the ruled. He acknowledged in this his indebtedness to the early modern Italian political theorist Niccolo Machiavelli, notably the idea of "relations of force" that for Gramsci had a threefold, political-military-social dimension.[2] But power as domination was crude and could be resisted. Dominating mindsets was subtle and less easy to resist. In effect, the ideology—be it religion or capitalism—exerts a form of control that is ultimately taken for granted by everyone through a "manufactured consent"[3] without the need for force to maintain it in most circumstances. Western culture—and by implication, Christian culture—he notes, has exerted hegemony over world culture,[4] though he is by no means as sure as Hegel (and modern Hegelians like early Fukuyama) would be that such hegemony is permanent. When such a crisis of control or authority occurs, this constitutes a crisis of hegemony.[5]

A necessarily short observation on the relevance of Gramsci to reading Catholicism is apposite here. Gramsci himself noted the power the Catholic Church had over ordinary people, by making its message accessible and all-pervasive, narrowing the gaps between "intellectual" and "popular" religion. Power is both institutional and cultural, centralized and diffuse; at times coercive, at times exhortatory (even inspirational). In the language of political science, it is a subtle combination of hard, soft, and smart power.

Foucault's theory of power-knowledge, later refined during his time at the College de France into the term *governmentality*, draws on similar ideas to Gramsci (cf. Machiavelli), though rooted more deeply in Nietzsche's philosophy of power.[6] Foucault was unhappy with the idea of centralized power. Indeed, he rejected a "fundamental source of power," arguing,

> It is in this sphere of force relations that we must try to analyse the mechanisms of power....We need to go one step further, do without the persona of the Prince, and decipher power mechanisms on the basis of a strategy that is immanent in force relationships.[7]

For Foucault, this is the means to see how humanity is turned into a subject through power relations, expressed through knowledge systems such as science, medicine, categories of dividing practices (sane/insane), or self-subjectification (e.g., sexuality). Power is rooted in knowledge; power produces and reproduces knowledge, for the sake of maintaining power. He insists that

> the word power is apt to lead to a number of misunderstandings-misunderstandings with respect to its nature, its form, and its unity. By power, I do not mean "Power" as a group of institutions and mechanisms that ensure the subservience of the citizens of a given state. By power, I do not mean, either, a mode of subjugation which, in contrast to violence, has the form of the rule. Finally, I do not have in mind a general system of domination exerted by one group over another, a system whose effects, through successive derivations, pervade the entire social body. The analysis, made in terms of power, must not assume that the sovereignty of the state, the form of the law, or the over-all unity of a domination are given at the outset; rather, these are only the terminal forms power takes.[8]

Power, for Foucault, is not centralized, but diffuse:

> The omnipresence of power: not because it has the privilege of consolidating everything under its invincible unity, but because it is produced from one moment to the next, at every point, or rather in every relation from one point to another. Power is everywhere; not because it embraces everything, but because it comes from everywhere.[9]

With power, within the exercise of power, there is resistance and the possibility to resist. This account suggests the diversification of power within Catholicism, for the tendency toward diversity in Catholicism itself epitomized in the variations and "schools" of theology and spirituality, despite and perhaps even because of the (historically recent) tendency to centralization of the church around the figure of the Bishop of Rome. This is most evident in the complex formulation of collegiality at Vatican II: collegiality with and never without *Peter*. It is also manifest in the glocalization[10] of Catholic theologies—particularities of context engaging with universal theological language and symbols, often with difficulty.

These theories of hegemony and power-knowledge, of control from above and the localization of resistance are important when considering the Catholic Church and racism in South Africa. Using our interlocutors' terms, for much of the time in our case study of South Africa, the hegemonic power of the church was still centered on Rome, on a notion of a universal authoritative body of ideas that were considered divine truth, but ideas that were themselves mediated and articulated through a lens of Greco-Roman and European language. For most Catholics, certainly those missionaries who brought the faith to southern Africa, the truth and how it was expressed was so interconnected as to be almost the same.[11] The problem with such a view—crudely, even if subliminally stated: Catholicism is European—is that it feeds into a subtle, and sometimes not so subtle, notion of cultural supremacy that supports and rationalizes colonial authority and even race supremacy, even if it also creates an internal unease within a religion that expresses universal truth claims like our equality before God.

RACISM AND HEGEMONY

One of the features of any colonial project is the notion of colonizer entitlement. While the reasons for colonial expansion are varied—economic benefits, access to resources and captive markets,[12] desire for territorial expansion, sometimes to settle "surplus" populations from the metropolis,[13] and the strategic control over territory to block the expansion of a rival metropolitan power—the formal rationale for it, particularly by countries that pride themselves on being "enlightened" and "liberal," may often include the claim that they are "civilizing" those societies they occupy. Behind this perspective lies a further assumption: that some peoples or communities are "inferior" and need to be "raised" to the standards of the colonizing power.

Often in history, the "civilized" were identified with Europe and the "inferior" with non-European peoples. This was further rationalized by a rising current of "scientific racism"[14] in the nineteenth century. It had started in the 1600s and continued until the mid-twentieth century. Misusing established science, sometimes inventing its own pseudo-sciences, this movement constructed an ideology of difference that divided humanity into distinct races, all at different levels of "development," a development that coincided with skin color, culture, and the degree to which a people differed from the European "standard"—often, conveniently, peoples whom Europe needed to colonize. Though the church never formally blessed these ideas, the influence of them on the colonial setting in which missionaries found themselves was pervasive.

THE COLONIAL CHURCH: COMPROMISE AND CONFORMITY

Let us turn now to the historical case study that informs our examination of racism within the church: South Africa.[15]

The Catholic Church was a prohibited institution in the territory that would become South Africa from first Dutch settlement in 1652 until de facto toleration in 1818. I do not think this fact should be underestimated, for out of it came a diversity of "morbid symptoms," if I may wax Gramscian. Suppression and a subsequent history of uneasy toleration made the Catholic Church wary of a state it deemed doubly hostile—both Protestant *and* anti-Catholic—resulting in an even greater conformism, first to the norms of a colonial and later white supremacist state. Adopting a subconscious strategy of assimilation into that dominant culture was further compounded by the largely unselfconscious epistemology that identified and privileged (indeed considered the fullness of truth) Catholic Christianity with European culture.

Apart from a brief period at the end of the eighteenth century, where Catholic chaplains were allowed to minister to Dutch troops stationed in the Cape Colony, all public expressions of Catholic faith were banned. No churches could be built; even Catholic clergy passing through Cape Town were forbidden to celebrate sacraments on Dutch ground.[16] From 1806 to 1837, the British government at the Cape were increasingly tolerant, but the first bishop and permanent clergy only arrived in Cape Town in 1838. With its history of being repressed and marginalized in South Africa, it might be assumed that the Catholic Church—once it got established—would have been more critical of colonial power than its Protestant counterparts, even indeed more sympathetic to African resistance to colonialism.

This was not the case. There were several reasons for this. First, the experience of suppression had a deep and lasting impact on the Catholic Church in South Africa. Even in the early nineteenth century, as prohibitions were lifted, the Church understood that the territory it was entering retained strong anti-Catholic sentiments. Though, after initial prohibition, the freedom to function was granted in the Boer republics of the Transvaal and Orange Free State, the residue of anti-Catholicism remained throughout the territory of modern South Africa well into the twentieth century. That, and the vulnerability of an overwhelmingly foreign-born clergy to deportation, was even a constraining factor in speaking against apartheid in the minds of bishops (and Vatican officials) until well into the 1960s.

Second, for much of the first fifty years of its existence in South Africa, the Catholic Church's ministry emphasized that Catholic colonists were spread very thinly in cities, towns, and villages across a vast area of land that had limited means of communication. The tiny number of priests in the country had to cross difficult terrain to reach pockets of Catholics. They traveled by ox wagon, on horseback, and later along the network of railways, stopping off for a day or two in a place to administer sacraments and encourage their flock, before heading out again. Such a "traveling priest" would cover a circuit of thousands of kilometers each year.

In some places, colonists built small chapels or churches; in some cases, an older priest might settle there and establish a permanent parish. Many other villages served by traveling priests would simply borrow a venue (e.g., a dining room in a hotel, a school hall, even in one Free State town the local Masonic Hall) for worship when their priest arrived. The priest would stay with a parishioner or sometimes with a sympathetic citizen. On several occasions, the host would be a non-Christian. There are accounts of a priest staying with a village doctor, a Jew—who would have sympathized with his Catholic patients and guest because a similar phenomenon of traveling rabbis existed.

In many places, in towns with Catholic parishes and in areas where there was this an ad hoc arrangement) Catholic worship was in theory "open" to all races, though often observing a spatial segregation within the assembly; but one should also remember that until the turn of the twentieth century African urbanization was limited. As segregationist ideology hardened from the late nineteenth century onward—reaching its apex/nadir after 1948—Black Catholics were less likely to feel welcome in the "white" urban and suburban parishes. Given the church's unease in what it perceived to be an anti-Catholic culture and a sometimes-unwritten agreement to conform to the norms of the society, in some places satellite worship centers would be created in the African "locations" on the fringes of white towns. These became the nuclei of today's extensive township parishes.

Since whites entering townships for any reason—apart from the police and later the army in the 1980s—entailed obtaining permits, few ventured there to worship. An interesting exception in the 1970s and 1980s was a small group of white Catholic charismatics in Johannesburg,[17] who apparently ignored restrictions and visited Black counterparts for "praise and worship" meetings. White clergy assigned to township parishes were confronted with the choice: either commute or live there with permits, thus conforming to apartheid law or living there illegally.

Finally, one must admit that the church itself often imbibed, consciously or unconsciously, the dominant racial ideology or at very least made a pragmatic decision to conform to segregationist laws. This cannot be explained simply by the influence of its initial focus on colonial Catholics. Clergy from Europe brought with them not only the universal values of Catholicism that they would apply without adaptation to Africa. They were also influenced by the intellectual currents of a Europe that was colonizing the world: the stark dichotomies of civilization (almost exclusively European civilization) versus barbarism (the non-European/non-white Other), in other words, Western enlightenment versus superstition. At its worst, this included, as noted earlier, what we know today as pseudoscientific race theories that questioned whether Black people were even human.[18]

Paradoxically, the best philosophies of the eighteenth and nineteenth centuries—liberty, equality, fraternity, democracy, and some forms of social democracy—were the last ideas to be adopted by the Catholic Church.[19] In the century following the French Revolution and Napoleonic Era, the rise of liberal democracy and the workers' movements were largely anathema to the church, who saw them as anticlerical—as many, in fact, were!—promoting separation of church and state—that they most certainly did!—and a threat to faith itself.[20]

Only later, as the twentieth century began, did Catholicism start to make peace, often grudgingly, with these progressive forces, constructing through Catholic Social Teaching a series of dialogues with liberal democracy and social democracy. These ideas, pioneered by a handful of clergy, such as the Mariannhill missionary Bernard Huss[21] and later embraced by leaders like Archbishop Denis Hurley, OMI, of Durban,[22] forced a church still dominated politically and economically by a white lay minority and a foreign-born missionary majority finally to confront apartheid after 1948. The acceptance of these ideas at every level of a still white-dominated church was a difficult process.[23] Arguably the process continues.

A (LESS-THAN-SALUTARY) PIECE OF HISTORY

In 2008, the book *The Other Side of the Story: The Silent Experience of the Black Clergy in the Catholic Church in South Africa (1898–1976)* was published by historian George Sombe Mukuka.[24] Based on his master's and doctoral research at the University of KwaZulu Natal,[25] it recounts the often difficult experiences of the first Black Catholic priests in South Africa.

Mukuka's central thesis is that European missionary control of the Catholic Church in the nineteenth century was informed by notions of European cultural, educational, and political supremacy that demanded the acceptance and compliance of local African cultures and especially the nascent African clergy. Those who bucked the system—who challenged this hegemony—got hurt. Mukuka recounts the ongoing struggle by Black African priests for full participation in, and ultimately identification with, the Catholic Church in which they served. It started in the then Natal area around present-day Mariannhill with four young men who traveled to Rome to train as diocesan priests. Returning with doctorates, they found themselves treated very much as perpetual assistant priests, subject to discrimination by the state and, as Mukuka points out, the church. Drawing on very limited documentary evidence—often representing the "other side" of their conflicts, namely the positions of the Catholic "establishment"—and on interviews, many of which are grassroots recollections of what might be called "folk memory," the author tells of their conflicts with religious authorities and their ultimate marginalization.

Father Edward Kece Mnganga (1872–1945), ordained in 1898, was placed as an assistant to Mariannhill priest A. T. (David) Bryant, an eminent ethnographer, historian, and Zulu linguist. Initially doing very well—popular in the parish and developing a successful mission school—Mnganga began to feel that Bryant was undermining his work. Whenever he was away, for example, Mnganga argued that Bryant would expel his most promising students. Confrontation ensued and Bryant and Mnganga apparently came to blows. Bryant then accused Mnganga of threatening to kill him, and had him declared insane and shipped off to a mental asylum in Pietermaritzburg, where Mnganga remained for seventeen years.

For Father Alois Majonga Mncadi (1877–1933), who was ordained in 1903, the issue with his superiors was that he was unwilling to live alone. He wanted family members to live with him and—to make matters worse—he bought a farm for himself that his bishop ruled was against canon law prohibitions on priests' trading. Similar problems arose between Fathers Andreas Mdontswa Ngidi (1881–1951) and Julius uMkomazi Mbhele (1879–1956). Ngidi was also accused of being a radical African nationalist, while he complained bitterly that his superiors stole his writings and tried to obstruct his pastoral work when it entailed what we would today call development work among the Zulu people. Mbhele, too, clashed with his superiors over pastoral work, his refusal to sell his farm, and was suspended for a while after allegations that a divorced woman was living on his farm.

In the 1920s, the farm-owning priests brought their complaints with their bishops to Archbishop Bernard Gijlswyk, the apostolic delegate of the Holy See to South Africa, arguing that they were not in violation of canon law, since they employed farm managers to run their farms. They also denied the claim that they were disobedient to their bishops and unwilling to be assigned to other parishes. The dispute was never resolved. Despite suspensions and controversies—

including accusations (and counteraccusations to their white clergy accusers) of sexual misconduct and drunkenness—they remained priests until their deaths.

Ngidi found an outlet for his development work interests in the Catholic African Union (CAU), a self-help movement started by the "liberal" Mariannhill priest Bernard Hüss,[26] as an alternative to the Industrial and Commercial Workers Union (ICU), a Black trade union perceived wrongly by many in the church as dominated by the Communist Party.[27] He and Mbhele were also highly regarded for their work in Zulu linguistics and Bible translation. But, in a church still dominated by foreign missionaries and rooted in European Catholic culture, they were lonely figures.

Apart from these few "turbulent" pioneers, very few Black men were recruited to the priesthood. A trickle of men was recruited by the mid-twentieth century into religious orders—but often as brothers. Among many male clerical religious congregations at this time, the vocation of the brother was seen as a kind of spiritual "second prize" for men who were deemed not quite fit for the priestly state. This reflected the mentality we have seen played out above: the African priest as culturally "other," possibly unsuited for the Catholic clerical life—a mentality that was then, as now, contrary to the theology of vocation.

These stories clearly illustrate both the hegemony of the official Catholic position in South Africa—the language of a colonial church rooted in European structures of power and the power-knowledge of what constituted "orthodoxy" and the potential, suggested by Foucault and Gramsci alike, of a counter-hegemonic discourse of resistance.

Lest we imagine that these stories reflect an earlier era, before the church woke up to the evils of segregation and apartheid and became the church in struggle that it is rightly remembered for today, the following narratives highlight an ongoing tension in South African Catholicism. Well into the twentieth century, Black clergy still struggled to fit into the Catholic Church. The first African bishop in South Africa, Bonaventure Dlamini, served the diocese of Umzimkulu from 1954 to 1968; he was part of the first "active" period of Catholic resistance to apartheid and had less confrontation in his life than the first four priests mentioned above, but no fewer problems. Once the diocese he would lead was carved out of Mariannhill, most of the missionaries withdrew. Finances were tight and frequently mismanaged—in fairness, Dlamini had not been trained to run diocesan finances. Staffing was difficult and some of his appointments were questioned as nepotism, particularly by white laity deeply hostile to their Black bishop.

But things started to change. By the 1960s the training of local African clergy was largely done within South Africa at a few seminaries—though the seminaries were still segregated until the mid-1970s.[28] Seminarians and some Black priests in the 1960s drew strength from the Black Consciousness Movement, formed Black solidarity groups and started to challenge the hierarchy openly and vocally about the disparities between Black and white clergy. More than that, many argued for a more inculturated church in line with the new ideas that had emerged particularly after Vatican II (1962–1965). Many still felt subordinated—in both dioceses and religious orders—to white clergy. Even as seminary formation came to include courses in anthropology, religious inculturation, Black theology, and engagement with racism, the underlying atmosphere of formation remained Eurocentric.

Furthermore, by the mid-1950s the Catholic Church put aside the fears it had about possible state reactions (like deportation of clergy) and took an increasingly vocal stance against racism and apartheid. Despite opposition from many white laity—and some priests—the Southern African Catholic Bishops Conference (SACBC), led by the young Archbishop Denis Hurley, OMI, of Durban, became, in 1957, the first Christian church in the country to declare apartheid in effect a heresy *theologically*.[29] As the 1960s, the era of Vatican II at which Hurley himself played a significant part, moved through the 1970s and 1980s, and as the majority rebelled against minority rule, the Catholic Church took on an increasingly important role. Apart from condemning apartheid, it provided formation for activists through the Young Christian Students (YCS), Young Christian Workers (YCW), and other youth movements. Armed with such tools as Cardijn's See-Judge-Act methodology, these youth—mostly but not exclusively Black—took on leadership roles in social movements, political parties, and trade unions that eventually forced the government to negotiate a transition to nonracial democracy in 1994.[30] The church acted in tandem with other Christian communities, Muslims, Hindus, Jews, and persons of no faith.[31] In this period, too, the church engaged with and came to appreciate the political ideas of Black Consciousness, Africanism, and Non-Racialism.[32]

In South Africa, the church initiated numerous projects in this regard, the most notable being the Lumko Institute in the Transkei (later moving to Germiston, near Johannesburg). Initially, Lumko started to train foreign-born or white South African clergy in African languages. This expanded into developing African church music and new forms of liturgical celebration, notably the use of traditional dance. A new generation of Black South African theologians—inspired by counterparts elsewhere on the continent—started to develop a homegrown African Catholic theology. This project was delayed, however, by the renewed church engagement in the struggle against apartheid. Many rightly saw that, before one could have an African Catholic theology, there needed to be liberation from colonialism's pervasive legacy—apartheid. But in the postapartheid era, this new theological discourse did not significantly arise.

While it is true to say that the Catholic Church in South Africa underwent a practical conversion from what might be called a partly conscious, largely subconscious racism, stemming from its relative privilege in the colonial order, to actively fighting a racist system, the conversion has been slower on a cultural level. Today, in the postapartheid era, where local clergy are almost entirely Black and the vast majority of missionaries come from other parts of Africa, the church still battles with the question of the extent of inculturation, institutional culture, and shifting demographics in parishes and church organizations. At its roots, beneath surface inculturation—attempts to create a local African/Black theology, vernacular liturgies, African hymns, art and occasional borrowing of traditional symbols—the core of Catholicism in the country remains culturally European. Indeed, in the last few decades there has been a "resurgent Romanism" and clericalism among many clergy. And the great project that was Lumko has effectively been closed. As Mukuka concluded in 2008: many things have changed, much remains to change.

THEOLOGICAL REFLECTION

The complexity of Catholic missions in South Africa reflects the moral ambiguities and political ambivalence of wider Christian mission enterprises in South Africa. Unlike other countries, Christian missionary work was not initially part of the Dutch colonial enterprise from 1652 onward. At first, the Dutch seemed singularly uninterested in converting local peoples or slaves they imported to the Cape Colony from Asia and other parts of Africa. It was quite acceptable to them that slaves, Blacks, and Khoisan peoples—subjugated peoples all—remained unevangelized. They were, after all, subject peoples under the domination of white, Christian (and Calvinist) authorities who, at some level, saw their authority as divinely ordained. For the Dutch, the word *Christian* was synonymous with domination and Europeanness. In this they were in a perverse way consistent: as Calvinists, Christianity implied for them equality in Christ, something that the colonial enterprise could not countenance. When the Protestant missions began, missionaries had an ambivalent role: Christianity's universalism implied equality in Christ, while proclaiming the cultural superiority of Europeanness. With a few notable exceptions, these Protestant missionaries did not advocate social equality, and some even rebelled from Dutch rule in the name of their new faith.[33] Even for those who embraced the "European" religion of Christianity, they largely refused to connect the dots between the spiritual and social realm, even if some indigenous communities actively did so.

Although it came relatively late into the mission field of South Africa, well after even the establishment of a white colonial Catholicism, the Catholic missions to indigenous South Africans, as has been noted, settled quite easily into this dominant missionary paradigm. The clue to why it did so, why it exercised the kind of adjustment to the colonial order is, on closer reflection, quite obvious. Apart from any uneasiness at being a Catholic minnow in a sea of often hostile Protestantism, the very theology of Catholicism made this accommodation to racism possible.

J. Kameron Carter has observed that there is something in early Christianity that makes it racist.[34] He notes that early Christianity, including what would become "Roman" Catholicism, sought to sever itself from its Jewish roots in two stages. First, he suggests, Jews were defined as a race group. Western Christians (i.e., Christians in the wider Roman Empire) came to see them as an "oriental" mirror (a borrowing from Edward Said's theory of orientalism). Jews were then declared inferior to *Western* Christians and the West, in general, with the resulting identification of Christianity with European culture.

This was further consolidated by the framing of Christian thought within Greco-Roman—Platonic, Aristotelian, and Stoic—philosophical systems and by the identification of Christianity with European history and culture, to the extent that Christianity was for over a millennium defined against Jewishness in what amounted ultimately to anti-Semitism (culminating in pogroms in the East, ghettoization of Jews in the West, and finally, the Shoah under Nazism). To be Christian was to be European, even if by and after the Enlightenment the converse was no longer necessarily true. Until the twentieth century, this was equally true in territories conquered by European colonizing powers (e.g., Africa, the Philippines, and Latin America) or where local powers retained control (e.g., China).

In latter places, the non-European powers withstood Catholicism's influence, in some cases like China, because the church considered it impossible (despite some visionary attempts, blocked by Rome, to inculturate Catholicism) to adapt its European/Eurocentric thought systems that underpinned Christianity to indigenous philosophies and knowledge systems.[35] In colonialized territories, the church built upon the political-military subjugation of indigenous polities and thought systems, replacing them with European Christianity of a Catholic type. The same was true of Protestant churches in "Protestant" colonies.

Even where Catholic missionaries defended aspects of local culture, for example, the Jesuit Reductions of Paraguay, it was a defense rooted less in attempting to inculturate Christianity than in an attempt ultimately to protect peoples seen as on the way to "Westernized" Christianity. The bottom line in this is that to be Christian was to be "Western"; and to be Catholic was to be "Roman." Following Carter's interpretation, this is construed as racist. But how racist? One might argue in mitigation that such thinking was above all rooted in an evangelical desire to save souls—to "make disciples of all nations" (Matt 28:19)—and culturally insensitive assumptions that even the best missionaries in Africa, like Daniel Comboni,[36] had. As a historian, I am the first to admit that there is a danger of historical "presentism," where the past is judged by moral criteria of the present. It is easier to suggest that the Combonis, Griffiths, Husses—and even progressives like Hurley—were products of their time. Such a claim, though utterly true, seems theologically inadequate, even relativist. Better to own and recognize the faults and failings of the past, with a view that we can learn from them.

CONCLUSION

The official discourse of the Catholic Church was—and is—framed within a dominant European cultural and intellectual framework that most who lead the church took (and take) for granted. Sometimes the subtle and unsubtle merged into hurtful practices at variance with the universal and inclusive vision of Christianity. Even today, within the limits of orthodox Catholic thinking, Eurocentric assumptions still privilege European over non-European culture. If the church is to move beyond such subconscious "racism," Catholics and other Christians need to be *conscious* of these assumptions and the tensions they create in a pluralistic society and world. Beyond that, we need to consider seriously a much deeper inculturation of the faith that goes beyond the tip of the religious iceberg. The Catholic Church's struggle with racism, in general, and apartheid, in particular, was at a certain level "a struggle within." It is also a struggle that continues.

2

THE LIES THAT BIND US

Rethinking Race, Racism, Black, and Blackness

Evelyn Birabwa M. Namakula

Born and raised in Eastern Africa (Kenya, Rwanda, Tanzania, the DR Congo, and Uganda), I have a sense of belonging to each of these countries. I have not only lived in each one of them, I trace my roots to them. I have also lived in other countries (e.g., Australia, Canada, Italy, and the United States). I consider these countries as my second homes. However, I am often reminded that I do not belong with such questions: Where are you from? For how long have you been here? When did you last visit home? And because of the color of my skin, Black, I encounter inclusion and curiosity from some people, exclusion, suspicion, and humiliation from others. In these countries, sometimes I fear for my life and that of my family. Blackness has been demonized, synonymized with criminals, gangs, killers, drugs, and often being on the bad side of the law.[1] Black people being roughed up by the police and shot are a real threat in these nations. To mitigate such threats, "the Talk"—the rite of passage in Black families in the United States of America—is given as early as at age ten. My nephews and nieces were taught what to do or say, and what not to do or say when they are pulled over by the police. Black parents know that their children's survival depend on "the Talk." While their white friends could do several things without consequences, a slipup or forgetting the right responses to the police could take a Black person's life: his or her right to breathe. The thinking is that Blacks do not belong in the United States and other racialized states.

Aware that racism toward other races exists,[2] this chapter aims to debunk the lies that pitch Blacks and Blackness against white and whiteness. These are the binaries through which racism is prominently propagated. The first section examines the concepts of race and racism as foundations to understanding the lies around anti-Blackness. The second section examines the lies around Black and Blackness, created to augment anti-Black racism and white supremacy. Those lies have shaped the sense of who Blacks are, how the world perceives Blacks and Blackness, and who whites are and how they behave toward Blacks and vice versa. The third section highlights the repercussion of racialized lies. The final section suggest an emancipation pedagogy rooted in the gospel: "You will know the truth, and the truth will make you free" (John 8:32).

CONCEPTUALIZING RACE AND RACISM

Revisiting race and racism theories and practices may seem pedantic and outmoded, but they remain "primal representations," lenses through which Blacks (and other people) are perceived, treated, and mistreated. Throughout history, race theories have been crafted and transformed to reinforce white supremacy and privileges, on one hand, and Black inferiority and exploitation, on the other hand. Race and racism are significant to national and global social systems, ideologies, politics, economics, structures, institutions, and policies.[3] Racism remains entrenched in colonial capitalist structures, systems, institutions, languages, the media, and everyday practices. Structures and institutions, such as the slave trade, colonialism, wars, and the looting of natural resources, are anchored and propagated through race and racism. Although race is a social construct, whose sense and meaning enjoy little consensus, assumptions and judgements have been made based on race theories accredited as scientific. For example, Ann Morning analyzed school textbooks, interviewed college students and professors across disciplines, and concluded that the common understanding of race as a social construct is often illusive.[4]

In the nineteenth century, colonizers with the backing of acclaimed racial scientific discoveries[5] deployed phrenology and anatomy to justify colonialism and slavery. For example, Samuel Morton's 1839 book *Crania Americana* claimed that skull configurations determined mental capabilities of races, with the brain shapes of Blacks and Native Americans deemed to represent low IQ, and beastly sexual orientations.[6]

Morphometric works, however, claimed that racial features were heritable, shared, linked to behaviors, and cultural predispositions of individuals from a racial group. For example, Max Weber (1864–1920) used race to refer to a common identity derived from heredity and endogamous conjugal relations in social groups.[7] Although racial differences could be minor, they become problematic once they are believed as scientifically proven, politicized, institutionalized, and used to determine access to social services, property rights, and inequity.[8] Racial differences, on the one hand, result in racism—discrimination, prejudice, exclusion, and contempt, racial similarities; on the other hand, they lead to affiliation, affection, and appreciation.

However, increasingly empirical and critical race scholarship debunk the validity of the acclaimed scientifically proven race theories. Race, like other social forces (e.g., heteropatriarchy, sexism, and classism) is a phenomenon that is constructed and reconstructed to justify the supremacy of the group in power with consequences of inequality, exploitation and marginalization of the "other." [9] Miles and Brown note that "there is no scientific justification" for using "phenotypical features" to represent racial hierarchies.[10] Race is nothing more than a distorted ideology that represents "human beings and their relations," that, for centuries, has "undermined consciousness among the victims of racism...'racial' solidarity and an anti-racist praxis" among racists.[11] According to Du Bois, race and racism are white racial myths to augment Europe's imperialist expansion, capitalism, colonialism, white supremacy, white normativity, racial domination, and discrimination.[12]

Antiracial critics have also problematized the falseness of racial hierarchies. For example, Anthony Appiah and Naomi Zack argue that the term *race* does not refer to any world reality.[13] Naomi notes that "essences, geography, phenotype, genotypes, and genealogy which are the only known candidates (elements) for physical scientific bases of race" do not justify social racial taxonomies.[14]

Contradictions inherent to racial theories illustrate how racism is a capitalist vehicle to deny the dignity of Black people and to reinforce inequality, colonialism, slavery, and resource exploitation. According to Hanna Arendt,

> It is highly probable that the thinking in terms of race would have disappeared in due time together with other irresponsible opinions of the nineteenth century, if the "scramble for Africa" and the new era of imperialism had not exposed Western humanity to new and shocking experiences. Imperialism would have necessitated the invention of racism as the only possible "explanation" and excuse for its deeds, even if no race-thinking had ever existed in the civilized world.[15]

Racism increases in concomitance with the entrenchment of capitalism. Patrick Bond captures how slavery, the scramble, and partition of Africa, portray racism as a capitalist construct to legitimize slavery and resource looting:

> Trade by force dating back centuries; slavery that uprooted and dispossessed around 12 million Africans; land grabs; vicious taxation schemes; precious metals spirited away; the appropriation of antiquities to the British Museum and other trophy rooms; the nineteenth-century emergence of racist ideologies to justify colonialism; the 1884–85 carve up of Africa, in a Berlin negotiating room, into dysfunctional territories; the construction of settler-colonial and extractive-colonial systems—of which apartheid, the German occupation of Namibia, the Portuguese colonies and King Leopold's Belgian Congo were perhaps only the most blatant....Cold War battlegrounds—proxies for US/USSR conflicts—filled with millions of corpses; other wars catalysed by mineral searches and offshoot violence such as witnessed in blood diamonds and coltan (colombo-tantelite, a crucial component of cell phones and computer chips); poacher-stripped swathes of East, Central, and Southern Africa now devoid of rhinos and elephants...societies used as guinea pigs in the latest corporate pharmaceutical tests...and the list could continue.[16]

Since slavery and colonialism, the concentration of wealth in the Global North has thrived on racism. Whites are always at the core of global society and Blacks at the periphery. Whites believe and fight for their supremacy and privileges, while Blacks have been made to believe that Blackness is inferior, and whiteness is superior. These beliefs became universal truths. Whiteness and white interests receive global recognition, while Blackness and Black interests are relegated, as Blackness is humiliated and denied humanness and dignity. Thus, Blacks and whites are bound by primordial and conventional lies that reinforce racism. However, due to the limited size of this chapter, the following section examines only the lies around Blackness.

THE LIES AROUND BLACK AND BLACKNESS

We live in a world dominated by white, Western, capitalist, and racialized ideologies, discourses, and narratives. To reinforce white power and privileges, lies against Black and Blackness are rampant, some of which are acclaimed as scientific discoveries. White power has implied claiming knowledge and everything valuable and meaningful to whiteness and whatever is deplorable to Blackness. As Foucault argues, power is synonymous with knowledge forms of "hegemony, social, economic, and cultural" ideologies, narratives, and discourses.[17] The 1837 painter and theorist Jacques Nicolas Paillot de Montabert wrote,

> White is the symbol of Divinity or God;
> Black is the symbol of the evil spirit or the demon.
> White is the symbol of light...
> Black is the symbol of darkness and darkness expresses all evils.
> White is the emblem of harmony;
> Black is the emblem of chaos.
> White signifies supreme beauty;
> Black ugliness.
> White signifies perfection;

Black signifies vice.
White is the symbol of innocence;
Black, that of guilt, sin, and moral degradation.
White, a positive color, Black indicates misfortune.
The battle between good and evil is symbolically expressed
By the opposition of white and black.[18]

De Montabert's words epitomize the image of Blacks in the world.

The Latin word for Black is *negro*, which implies a being with "a strange shape, roasted by the rays of the celestial fire, endowed with an excessive petulance, captive to the empire of joy, and abandoned by intelligence."[19] According to Hegel, "The Negro...exhibits the natural man in his completely wild and untamed state. We must lay aside all thoughts of reverence and morality—all that we call feeling—if we would rightly comprehend him. There is nothing harmonious with humanity to be found in this type of character."[20] Blacks are perceived as brutes. Writing about the atrocities of Leopold II in the Congo Free State, Joseph Conrad noted how Kurtz, a corrupt ivory trader, ordered the extermination of brutes and how the sailor Charles Marlow perceived Blacks as ugly.[21] Later, Marlow compares Blacks, who served as firemen on the ship, to "a dog in a parody of breeches and a feather hat walking on his hind legs."[22] The perceptions of Hegel, Marlow, and Kurtz represent how whites (and other races) have invented and portrayed Blacks.

Blacks are considered perpetually inferior, "Peter Pan children who can never grow up, a child race," who must be controlled by the master.[23] Albert Schweitzer opined that the negro "is a child, and with children nothing can be done without authority."[24] British colonizers called every male "boy" (house boy, office boy), and the French used the pronoun *tu*, which was used to address children, for every African regardless of age. Christian Smut, who was a soldier and prime minister during apartheid in South Africa, noted to a British audience that the Black person was a perpetual child, inferior, and only fit to be a slave.[25]

Black is also a name. A racial category. An identity. Those named Black bear the brunt of the name they never created, and are forced to own it, as "a mechanism for objectification and degradation...a link, a relationship to subjection."[26] Blackness dictates a destiny and a generalized condition where those christened "Black" experience the "name's power of falsification."[27] To be Black is to be untrustworthy and suspected of being a thief, a killer, a rapist, a drug trafficker, and more. This categorization has played a key role in the killing and incarceration of Blacks in North America, Europe, and elsewhere in the world. Being Black also implies being less intelligent, lacking originality, and with nothing to teach but only to learn from the white counterpart. A Black person is "stuck at the foot of a wall with no doors...knocks, begs, and knocks again, waiting for someone to open a door that does not exist."[28]

Slavery cemented processes and structures that reinforced contemporary relations and systemic racism toward Blacks. According to Mbembe, "The Black slave, in his (or her) dark splendor, was the first racial subject: the product of the two impulses, the most visible symbol of the possibility of violence without limits and of vulnerability without a safety net."[29] Black men and women were perceived as

> merchandise, man-of-money...fated to become an essential mechanism in a process of accumulation that spanned the globe. Through the triple mechanism of capture, removal and objectification, the slave was forcibly locked within a system that prevented him (and her) from freely making of his (and her) life...something with its own consistency that could stand on its own.[30]

Black bodies, minds, and labor were owned by slave owners.

After slavery, the imperialists created Africa and Blacks according to their interests, and justified colonialism as a *mission civilisatrice*. Victor Hugo boasted that "whites made Blacks into men" and made "Africa into a world."[31] Under the umbrella of civilizing the pagans, African religions were denied existence, yet we know that God transcends race or ethnology. White missionaries introduced a white God, a white savior, a white mother of Jesus, white saints, and white prophets. The Congolese singer Verckys Kiamuangana Mateta's song "Nakomitunaka" (I ask myself) laments the origin of the Black skin, given that Jesus, Adam, Eve, angels and saints are all white, but Satan/demons are Black. Even biblical stories have been used to justify racism and colonization. Subduing the world (cf. Gen

1:28) was instrumentalized to express the colonization of Africa. The so-called curse of Ham (cf. Gen 9:22–29) has been used in reference to Blacks' predestination to slavery. In the sixteenth and seventeenth centuries, slave owners appealed to the curse of Ham to justify racialized slavery as a predestined condition for Blacks. Other biblical passages also encouraged slaves to obey their masters as God's representatives (cf. Eph 6:5 and Col 3:2).

The plunder, destructions, and dehumanization that characterized slavery and colonialism were coated as philanthropy to civilize and evangelize the Black savage and bring light to the dark continent.[32] To dominate, Black was perceived as a color of invisibility and "obscurity [that] lives the night...whose life is turned into night...the tissue out of which its flesh it made."[33] A Black person is invisible, which justifies *thingification* of shadows, grotesque, and howling mobs who adore the white master abroad and in colonial Africa.

The list of such lies could go on and on. However, as Mbembe argues, slavery, colonialism, and other forms of anti-Blackness are "primitive form(s) for racial despotism" and "the ruthless drive for dominance."[34] Nevertheless, such lies have numerous derivations:

1. The negro, Black, or Blackness is a white invention, a judgmental categorization of those who became the wretched of the earth. Faced with the discourse of white domination or supremacy, Blackness remains inferior, abhorred, and not allotted with universal attributes of being human. Blacks are perpetually enchained, enslaved, colonized, and their resources plundered.
2. The lies have advanced Black racial inferiority and reinforced white supremacy, economic, institutional, and systemic privileges.
3. Throughout the world, no race is deprived of dignity like the Black race.
4. The indignity of racialization has forced Blacks and movements like the Black lives Matter to fight against anti-Black racism, although racialized systems, structures, and institutions have not changed, highlighting the need to debunk racial lies, some of which became global "truth," given that a Black person is hardly respected globally.

5. Some Blacks have believed and internalized those lies as truth that determine their being and whatever they do in the world.
6. The lies around Black and Blackness remain a scar in the consciousness of humanity with repercussions that have damaged Blacks. The next section discusses some of those repercussions.

REPERCUSSIONS OF THE LIES OF RACE AND RACISM

The lies of race and racism have had consequences for Blacks. Throughout the world, no people and no continent has been invented,[35] except the Blacks and the African continent. Invention has implied being universal skunks. Cited by Frantz Fanon, Juan de Merida, the negro, said,

> What a disgrace to be black in this world!
> Are black men not men?
> Does this mean their soul is uglier, viler, more useless?
> And for that they have earned scornful names
> I rise burdened with the shame of my colour
> And I declare my courage to the world
> Is it so vile to be black? [36]

Blacks have developed an inferiority complex. In fact, according to Fanon "inferiority complex" is deep among Blacks.[37] Some Blacks consider whites superior and prioritize them over fellow Blacks. Many have lost pride in their Black identity, personhood, cultures, and civilization. They pride themselves in imperialist traditions and acclaimed independence flags. For many Blacks in Africa and abroad, to be dignified is to be like a white man or woman and imitate white culture.

Some Blacks also hate their skin color and hair texture. Endeavors to alter Blackness have become lucrative businesses worldwide as Blacks use glutathione treatments, bleaching creams, and soaps to brighten/whiten skin tones and chemicals to alter hair texture, or wear wigs. It is projected that by 2024, the global profit from bleaching products will be approximately $31.2 billion.[38] In 2014, Reuters reported that people in Cameroon, South Africa, and Nigeria alone spend about $1.1 billion on hair care products and about $6 billion on dry hair.[39] Blacks are not only feeding capitalism, they also expose themselves to dangerous chemicals attributed to causing cancer.[40] Scientific warnings against health hazards due to exposure to chemicals in skin bleaching products (e.g., mercury, hydroquinone, and steroids) and hair straighteners abound.[41] Movements and philosophies such as Leopold Sedar Senghor's Negritude and the 1964 Black Is Beautiful Movement in Harlem aimed at empowering Blacks inside out has not yet convinced them to love Blackness. The engrained belief is that only a white skin, straight long hair, red lips, and a slim body is the epitome of beauty.

Black self-hatred goes in tandem with abhorrence for African cultures, history, epistemology, religion, and values, because colonial masters considered them primitive, fetishistic, backward, unsuitable, or nonexistent. The closer one comes to whiteness—for example, speaks colonial languages, wears European clothes, eats Western foods, bear a white name (commonly known as Christian or first names), or enjoys white sports—the more one feels a sense of fulfillment and freedom. The entire African continent and Blacks in the diaspora alike are brainwashed to imitate the believed-superior white cultures and values. The perception is that only whites have values that Blacks must emulate. In the words of Fanon, they are striving to whiten their nations and institutions.[42] Africans in Sub-Saharan Africa (SSA) pride in being Francophone or Anglophone because that affiliation brings them closer to whiteness. Failure to pride and use local languages implies loss of culture, indigenous epistemology, history, and capacity for innovation. As Ngugi notes, "The choice of language and the use to which language is part is central to a people's definition of themselves in relation to their natural and social environment, indeed in relation to the entire universe."[43] Ngugi further refers to cultural destruction as "the biggest weapon wielded and...daily unleashed by imperialism" against those who resist and retain beliefs in themselves, their capabilities, their African names, languages, and unity.[44]

Blacks were indoctrinated to hate their religions as polytheism, fetishism, and paganism. In the search for the "true God" Blacks embraced Christianity, a white-founded religion, yet we know that

Africans were religious before the introduction of Christianity. Mbiti notes that before the introduction of Christianity or Islam, Blacks were "notoriously religious."[45] Religion permitted behaviors and practices without a separation between the "sacred and the secular, between the religious and non-religious, between the spiritual and the material area of life."[46] However, Christianity in Africa remains like a dress that people wear when they are in church and remove once they are outside. Rwanda is a vivid example of Christianity's shallowness in Africa. In 1994, Catholic Hutus and Tutsis sung the Easter Sunday alleluia, but once they left the church, they massacred each other.

Besides, Blacks mistrust each other and perceive whites as superior beings. I remember how my bag was checked at shopping malls while whites were never checked. Why? Whites are least suspected of crimes such as shoplifting and are perceived as people with superior intelligence. I have participated in meetings and conferences between whites and Blacks in SSA and realized how even African heads of state bow to whatever whites say. In peacebuilding and business meetings, white mediators and investors are preferred over Blacks. African universities train engineers but even road construction is entrusted to whites or Chinese engineers. Why? A Black person is expendable in SSA and abroad. The killing of one white person makes global news while that of millions of Blacks hardly makes global news headlines.

Africa has been perceived as the poorest continent and Blacks have interiorized the belief of begging from the West. Annually, the global development index reports rank almost all African nations among the poorest. However, we know that other nations have become economic powers from looting Africa's (human and natural) resources. It is estimated that about twenty million able-bodied men and women were captured and taken as slaves to the Americas and to Europe, and that millions perished along the way and others suffered under the yoke of colonialism. For example, when Leopold II colonized the Kongo kingdom, one in four Belgians lived on relief, suffering from "poverty and even malnutrition."[47] From looting Congo, Belgium became an economic superpower. Between 1887 and1953, Belgium's capital outflow from Congo was around "4,300 million pounds, exclusive of profits retained within the Congo," and "reached massive proportions" in the five years that preceded independence.[48]

In 1906, Leopold II was shipping about six hundred ounces of gold monthly to Brussels.[49] Congo financed "all the expenditure of the Belgian government" including the diplomatic missions and armed forces.[50] In the process, Leopold's rule killed about ten million.[51] In 1945, Africa contributed 446 million pounds to Britain's economy, which, in 1955, increased to 1,446.[52] France earned about $5.6 million from selling bananas, coffee, and bauxite from Guinea, exported all surplus natural resources, levied taxes for military purposes, and took Africans to fight in European wars.[53] France's former president François Mitterrand admitted that without Africa, France would "have no history in the twenty-first century," while Jacques Chirac admitted that "we have to be honest and acknowledge that a big part of the money in our banks comes precisely from the exploitation of the African content. Without Africa, France will slide down in the rent of a third world power."[54]

Many are the situations and factors illustrating how Blacks have internalized anti-Black racial lies and the importance of Black emancipation that we examine in the following section, termed as the pedagogy of liberation.

TOWARD A PEDAGOGY OF LIBERATION

There would be no lies if there was no truth. It is only the truth that sets people free (cf. John 8:31–32). How does one come to the truth and get liberated? Liberating the oppressed begins with the oppressed recognizing their oppression and developing an emancipation pedagogy for themselves and their oppressor. According to Paulo Freire,

> It is only the oppressed who, by freeing themselves, can free their oppressor. The latter, as an oppressive class, can free neither others nor themselves. It is therefore essential that the oppressed wage the struggle to resolve the contradiction in which they are caught by the appearance of a new man (people): neither oppressor nor oppressed, but man in the process of liberation. If the goal of the oppressed is to become fully human, they will not achieve their goal by merely reversing the terms of the contradiction, by simply

> changing poles....Resolution of the oppressor-oppressed contradiction indeed implies the disappearance of the oppressors as a dominant class.[55]

The pedagogy requires "starting over a new history...which takes account not only of the occasional prodigious theses maintained by Europe (and the world at large) but also its crimes, the most heinous of which have been committed" toward Blacks, other races, and the planet.[56] Fanon urges Blacks to think and search for solutions "night and day, all the time" of people of good will, looking at the oppressors with compassion in order to breathe into them the humanity that capitalism has usurped from them and from the rest of the world.[57] Instead of copying Western values, it is crucial that Blacks search from their traditional wisdom, to create a new world order rooted in such values as human dignity and planetary integrity. For example, Ubuntu includes universal values of compassion, dignity, interconnectedness of people and nature, common humanity, and responsibility of everyone toward others. Such values are crucial to liberating Blacks, other races, and the planet.[58] Steve Biko, a famous Black Consciousness Movement leader, wrote, "We believe that in the long run, the special contribution to the world by Africa will be in the field of human relationships. The great powers of the world may have done wonders in giving the world an industrial and military look, but the great gift still has to come from Africa—giving the world a more human face."[59] In a world where European racialized values have failed to create peaceful and secure societies for all, African values have much to offer.

Racialized crimes must be acknowledged and condemned as violence,[60] brutalism,[61] and a violation of fundamental human rights. Historical and present perpetrators of racial crimes must be brought to justice. Instead, human rights violations, killings, and exploitation linked to slavery, colonialism, resource looting, wars, and hate crimes against Blacks have prevailed with impunity. Throughout Europe and North America, statues of brutal colonizers were erected to immortalize them as national heroes, thus glorifying colonialism and its atrocities. For example, in the United States history of police killing, lynching, and Jim Crow laws, the sentencing of Derek Chauvin is one of the very few cases where a white man has been condemned for killing a Black person. Equally, former colonizers and slave traders have never been brought to justice, and no restitution has ever been given to descendants of African slaves abroad and in Africa. When Western nations provide conditional foreign aid to Africa, they consider themselves philanthropic. From the standpoint of racial restitution, foreign aid should be perceived as returning part of the wealth that has been looted from the continent. Moreover, all forms of racial violence and atrocities committed toward Blacks require prosecution from international criminal courts. Blacks must unanimously demand international condemnation and restitution. But what is a suitable compensation and condemnation for the magnitude of atrocities being committed against Blacks? What punishment is suitable for enchaining people like beasts of burden, lynching, the deceptive immunization of Black women to make them infertile and reduce Black populations,[62] the contamination of water and land by corporations, and subjecting communities to insecurity and displacement to exploit natural resources?

In addition, Blacks need to de-learn the lies that they have believed as truth and rediscover their true selves in a world where racial ideologies, politics, economics, structures, and institutions are deliberately and intelligently crafted to dehumanize, weaken, and eliminate them. De-learning requires acknowledging the impact of colonialism, slavery, and other atrocities committed toward Blacks in the name of racial inferiority and white superiority. Those who understand the impact of colonization on the psyche such as Frantz Fanon, Aimé Césaire, and Ngugi wa Thiong'o advocate for decolonizing the mind. Considering how racism has victimized, traumatized, and conditioned Blacks to hate themselves and to hate each other, along with Black cultures and values, decolonization needs to start by rediscovering and proudly reclaiming Black personhood without shame or fear. Like other races, we know that we are handsome and beautiful. Ugly as well. Not perfect. Like the sound of the drum, Blacks weep, feel pain, laugh, and want to be treated well. As George Floyd cried out on May 25, 2020, "I can't breathe!" when Derek Chauvin pinned him down, racism has suffocated and murdered Blacks and Blackness for centuries. Blacks have suffered the indignity of being the skunks of the world. Blacks must reclaim their breath, de-learn the lies they have been told and accepted, and restore Black dignity and identity from the scourges of dehumanization, thingification, commodification, objectification, and subjugation.

It is also important to understand that racism is a socially constructed capitalist strategy to dehumanize, humiliate, and make Blacks feel that, as formerly enslaved and colonized, they are less human, expendable, and without bio-symbiosis and planetary habitability. This strategy is not a historical residue. The killing and incarceration of millions of people of African descent in North America, Europe, and other parts of the world and the incessant proxy wars in Africa attest to these facts. Blacks need to develop a critical perception and consciousness of the world, listen, unlearn what has been lodged into the global psyche, and devise ethical and emancipatory methodologies of caring and compassion in order to "repair" people and the planet. This process requires Blacks to "see themselves" clearly and reject the lies that whiteness and the West are the ideal for Blacks and Africa.

Liberation is for Blacks as it is necessary for whites too. The oppressor and the oppressed, the colonizer and the colonized, the slave and slave master, the racist and racialized are both dehumanized. Racism and hatred for Blacks illustrate inner enslavement, fragility, and the need of liberating whites as well. Racism "distorts human beings and social relations, brutalizes and dehumanizes its objects, and in so doing also brutalizes and dehumanizes those who articulate it."[63] Paulo Freire writes, "As the oppressors dehumanize others and violate their rights, they themselves also become dehumanized."[64] White or European atrocities and violence toward Blacks because of their skin color can only be committed by psychopaths. The drive for white supremacy illustrates how societies are diseased in that they have turned accidentals of skin colors into destinies. Whites and the whole world need to realize that white supremacy and Black inferiority are lies, pathologies, and ideological ignorance that have diminished Blacks humanity for far too long. In psychology, both superiority and inferiority are pathologies. A person who believes themselves to be superior to others suffers from superiority complex, which conceals inner fragility and inferiority.[65] Psychologists such as Maslow note that self-actualized people empower others while those who are morally and psychologically weak bully and terrorize others, believing that they have power and privileges when others are dehumanized. White supremacy exposes "white" fragility, where they find self-worth in skin color and in degrading those who are not white. DiAngelo notes that "white fragility" is exposed where they become angry, defensive, or hostile when confronted with the fact that they are complicit in systemic, structural, and institutional racism.[66] Whether white people believe it or not, they derive material and psychological benefits from racialized organization of society, feel entitled and deserving of societal privileges, comforts, riches, and advantages that they have ensued from oppressing, dehumanizing, enslaving, commodifying, scapegoating, incarcerating, looting, and killing the "Other" because of being Black or indigenous (e.g., in North America and Australia).

CONCLUSION

This chapter began with my life experiences and stories as a statement of my position, a Black woman. I write as a committed anti-racist, seeking justice and appealing to the human condition shared by all humans to end Black racial oppression, because it has dehumanized, brutalized, destroyed, and killed people. The chapter has highlighted four factors around racialized lies: (1) racism as violence, brutalism, violation of fundamental human rights and, therefore, a crime against humanity must be condemned and punished; (2) racism as a fundamental part of the liberal capitalist world order augments the exploitation of those considered to be "less human" and their natural resources to sustain white privileges; (3) Black emancipation must be endogenous, from within the consciousness of the Black people in solidarity with those on the side of humanization and planetary integrity; and (4) the lies used to racialize and dehumanize Blacks point to inner enslavement and white fragility, necessitating white liberation.

The chapter has also highlighted how white supremacy epitomized by capitalist colonialism, slavery, and their residues have and continue to kill (physically and psychologically), destroy, and traumatize Blacks. Like George Floyd, Blacks being killed are wives, husbands, children, parents, nephews, and nieces of people who love and sometimes depend on them. Systemic, structural, and institutional racism has repressed and denied the humanity, dignity, human rights, and potentials of Blacks (and other non-whites) to exist and to breathe, to sustain white privileges and superiority.

Every corner of the globe has been "poisoned" by white supremacism. In this world, race, ethnicity, and tribe are the lenses through which Blacks, Blackness, white, and whiteness are perceived and treated in sociopolitical and socioeconomic relations. Those lenses have conditioned Blacks to perceive, present, and treat themselves and each other different from those who are white. They exalt whiteness at the expense of Blackness. However, race, racism, ethnicity, and tribalism have affected Blacks so deeply and in so many ways. Scenarios such as the slave trade, colonization, lynching, and the continued killing of African Americans, inequalities, poverty, dehumanization, and wars have been performed in the name of race. Racial discrimination is deeply engraved to the extent that instruments such as the Universal Declaration of Human Rights and the International Convention on the Elimination of All Forms of Racial Discrimination have not curbed it. Therefore, we "must step away from the pious ritual" (e.g., turning the other cheek) and mediocrity and confront racism as violence, as a crime, and as a violation of dignity and human rights.[67] Racism should be problematized and condemned. It is also crucial to raise consciousness among oppressed—the racialized Blacks—to stop being sheepish under the yoke of racism and whites to stop condescending because they are insulated from racism, feel "entitled" and "deserving" of the advantages and privileges that ensue from racial inequalities, injustices, genocides, and resource plunder.[68]

There's little doubt that events such as the convicting of the white police officer Derek Chauvin, who killed George Floyd (May 25, 2020), and the rise of Black Lives Matter (BLM) movement illustrate that humanity is going through change in conceptualizing race and racism, and the relationship between Blacks and whites. These changes require us "not to think (act and behave) as we always did, keeping faith by trying to hold the terrain together through an act of compulsive will, but to learn to *think* (act and behave*) differently*."[69] As Aimé Césaire argues, "The problem is not to make a utopian and sterile attempt to repeat the past, but to go beyond. It is not a dead society that we want to revive....It is a new society that we must create...a society rich with all the productive power of modern times, warm with all the fraternity of olden days."[70] Césaire lost hope in the Western world and believed in the oppressed spearheading a new society. Similarly, Fanon warns Blacks not to mimic Europe, old humanism ideologies, and their claim of universalism, "and reach for the light. The new day which is dawning must find us determined, enlightened and resolute."[71] In Fanon's words, the new day invites Black and white, colonized and colonizer, to "move away from the inhumane voices of their respective ancestors....Superiority? Inferiority?...so that a genuine communication (and transformation) can be born."[72]

Like other Africanists, the chapter contributes to the discussion and knowledge necessary for Blacks and whites to develop a critical perspective and consciousness of themselves, and to devise liberation strategies for peaceful coexistence, concomitant with the twenty-first-century levels of human, scientific, and technological advancement. Blacks need to perceive themselves clearly and reject knowledge systems and discourse that maintain whiteness and the West as the mirror through which Blacks must see themselves and that they must emulate. In other words, rediscovering, de-learning, and relearning the truth is a sine qua non to Black emancipation and agency toward transforming and healing people and the planet from the wounds of colonial and neocolonial capitalist liberal world order, driven by conquest, plunder, genocides, drilling, extraction, militarization, violence, wars, and racial polarization.

Equally, whites need to liberate themselves from superiority complexes and unethical behaviors that for centuries have facilitated the elimination and enslavement of Blacks, denied their values and contribution to global civilization, and looted their resources. The atrocities whites have committed against Blacks must be recognized and restitution provided. To build healthy communities, churches, and societies, whites must reflect and transform their behaviors and practices toward Black and other races. We live on a warming planet of more than 7 billion humans that cannot continue sustaining white supremacy, exploitation, and greed. The situation calls for reflection, humility, sorrow, shame, and repentance, for the atrocities committed toward Blacks and the planet in the name of race. Being human should be the identity that binds us and not racism that divides us.

3

RACES, NATIONS, AND TRIBES

Evolutions of Meaning

Festo Mkenda, SJ

The images of a white police officer in Minneapolis in the United States of America kneeling on the neck of a Black man until the latter died revealed the ugly underbelly of recent human history. The most impactful image from the incident reminded one of pictures of European trophy hunters in nineteenth- and early twentieth-century Africa, who, invariably, posed over carcasses of their leonine victims as if to demonstrate ultimate triumph. Mr. Derick Chauvin, the officer who committed the crime on May 25, 2020, was later found guilty of, among others, the more serious crime of "unintentional second-degree murder while committing a felony." During court proceedings, the defense offered explanations as to why Mr. Chauvin could have been driven to behave the way he did, including his victim's physical appearances and the presence of supposedly threatening onlookers, several of whom were Black. Covered live on television channels, the three-week trial that preceded the judgment was as graphically horrifying as it was informative. The public could also see clearly what the jurors saw and thus make sense of their unanimous guilty verdict. The way in which Mr. Chauvin caused the death of Mr. George Floyd (1973–2020) was so exceptionally cruel that it had no correspondence to the crime the latter was alleged to have committed. As many wondered what the unexplained motive for the murder could be, racism easily filled in the blanks.

The global outrage that greeted the recent invasion of Ukraine by Russia could hardly be missed. Unlike the ongoing conflicts in Ethiopia and Myanmar that are generally viewed as "civil wars" in the sense of internal quarrelling among citizens of the same country, the Ukraine-Russia conflict is an attack of one sovereign nation by another sovereign nation. This understanding flows from recent history, which compartmentalizes humanity within national units that are presided over by states. The nation-state, as opposed to the race, the ethnic group, or the tribe, has become the accepted locus for both inward and outward political action and nationalism is the appropriate spirit possessed of those who behave and act in the interest of their own specific nation or nation-state. Thus, Ukrainians fighting in defense of their country are laudable nationalists. On the contrary, Russians who declare themselves against the invasion are scolded at home as wanting in the proper spirit of nationalism and praised abroad for having the courage to do the unexpected.

Shortly after a difficult 2007/8 experience of postelection violence in Kenya, a book appeared with the provocative title: *It's Our Turn to Eat.*[1] The violence was both expressed and understood in ethnic or tribal terms. Implied in Michela Wrong's title was the outrage of people from various communities in Kenya who had come to be disenchanted with the political reign of individuals from the Kikuyu and Kalenjin ethnicities over the shared Kenyan nation since independence in 1964. It was believed that, with such reign came opportunities to eat, not just for the few in elected positions, but also for entire ethnic populations behind them. The ideology that renders credence to this logic is usually referred to as tribalism. In a country of up to seventy ethnic communities (also referred to as tribes), and after forty-three years with only the Kikuyu and the Kalenjin enjoying the eating, was it not time to allow others also to eat?

Following below is an observation of five terms that have been used in the English language in different times during the modern period to define clusters of humanity. These terms are *race, nation, people, tribe* and, to a lesser extent, *ethnicity. Race, nation,* and *tribe* will be covered in detail because of their implication for Africa and other postcolonial societies. Kenyan politician and author Koigi wa Wamwere's coinage of the phrase *negative ethnicity* notwithstanding,[2] it is *race, nation,* and *tribe* that have given us the categories of identity to which racism, nationalism, and tribalism appeal. Whereas characteristic features of the named categories are predominantly cultural and largely nonexclusivist (for example, a language can be learned), appeal to the mentioned *isms* seeks to create natural protections around them, making them completely exclusivist (for example, skin color or shape of nose cannot be easily altered). It is this latter appeal to nature that, over time, has given rise to so many social and political aberrations—some as institutionalized policies (like apartheid in South Africa) and others as sinister beliefs that influence group and individual action on streets and in workplaces (like fear of Black people). To facilitate analysis over time, my point of departure will be a biblical verse in which the words *race, nation, tribe,* and *people* are often used.

LAYERS OF MEANING

The historical period sometimes called the Age of Discovery coincides with the early modern period, extending roughly from the fifteenth to the eighteenth century. During this period, Africa—as also the Americas and, to a different degree, Asia—was gradually locked into an orbit that had Europe as its defining center. The changes implied in this phenomenon affected every sphere of life, from religion, science, and education to economics, politics, and the family. As a result, humanity came to perceive itself differently. The very drive to explore, encounter, and conquer others was fueled by a new self-perception in some European societies where power defined nationhood and granted rights to dispossess, dominate, and reorder other societies far beyond the European vicinity. New identities emerged and language was adjusted accordingly to reserve these changes.

From a purely linguistic viewpoint, a significant portion of the verse from Revelation 7:9 offers a window through which to view the evolution of the meanings ascribed to the terms *race, nation,* and *tribe* in the English language during the modern period. Here, two assumptions are necessary: first, that the Greek original text of this biblical verse has remained stable,[3] and second, that it is English translations that have varied over time, either because of a better understanding of the original text or—and most likely—because of the changing context in and for which translations were made. As classicist Richard Lattimore (1906–1984) insists, "context is all" and "no translator can escape being colored by his own time," just as no one can "translate in a vacuum."[4] Over the centuries, new English translations have been produced to address constantly varying audiences.

At stake are the four Greek words ἔθνους, φυλῶν, λαῶν, and γλωσσῶν (respectively: *ethnos, phulē, laōs,* and *glōssa*),[5] which English translators have understood differently over the centuries. While our focus must remain in the modern period, we may want to begin with an earlier English translation of the verse to appreciate better the idea of evolving meanings. The first complete English Bible before the modern period—indeed the only one that merits attention because of its influence and popularity—is the Wycliffe Bible produced in 1380 and so named because of its producer, John Wycliffe (1330–1384). It belongs to what is known as *Middle English,* roughly from the eleventh to the fifteenth century. In this important translation, the verse in question appears as follows:

> Aftir these thingis Y sai a greet puple, whom no man myyte noumbre, of alle *folkis,* and *lynagis,* and *puplis,* and *langagis,* stondinge bifore the trone, in the siyt of the lomb; and thei weren clothid with white stoolis, and palmes weren in the hondis of hem.[6] (Italics added)

If we put the four words in modern spelling, the quartet of identity groups includes *folks, lineages, peoples,* and *languages* (in that order).

The next important translation would only be produced in 1526, thus at the early part of the modern period. This is the Tyndale New Testament,[7] so called because of its translator William Tyndale (1494–1536). This is understood to be the earliest direct translation from Greek to English. Unlike the translators of the Wycliffe Bible, Tyndale had to address a world that had expanded almost exponentially in a matter of a few decades. His predecessors could have even assumed that their readers knew most of the *folks, lineages, peoples,* and *languages* mentioned in the verse; Tyndale could not make that assumption. In his translation, the verse appears as follows:

> After this I behelde and lo a gret multitude (which noman culde nombre) off all *nacions* and *people* and *tonge* stode

> before the seate and before the lambe clothed with longe whyte garmentes and palmes in there hondes.... (Italics added)

Tyndale prefers to use *tongue* rather than *language*, then introduces us to the word *nacions*. Derived etymologically from the Latin, *natio*, which means "birth," the most ubiquitous sense of *nacion* during Tyndale's time would have been the *native population of a particular town or city*,[8] or, literally, the "natives" of a locality, considered together. While this change in the translation is significant, it is important to note that *nacion* had not yet undergone the full evolution that would shroud it with its contemporary meaning. Tyndale also reduces the four identity groups in the Greek original into three in English. This could either be an intentional avoidance of redundancy or an unintended omission. The latter case is the likeliest, because Tyndale uses the fourth word *kynreddes* in Revelation 5:9 and 14:6.

In any case, whether an oversight or not, Tyndale's abbreviation was corrected in all the translations that appeared after his own: some with his direct involvement and many others building upon his influential work. The most important of these was the so-called Geneva Bible,[9] which first appeared in print in 1560. While remaining close to Tyndale's translation, it supplied the fourth missing identity group in English using the word *kinreds* (*sic*), which Tyndale had used elsewhere in a different spelling. Now the verse read "...of all *nacions* and *kinreds*, and *people*, and *tongues*..." (italics added). A characteristic feature of this specific Bible is, we are told, that it "was a translation from the original languages in straightforward contemporary language, rather than in ritualistic manner full of jargon."[10] In other words, the language used by the translators is that spoken in towns and villages of the sixteenth-century English-speaking world. While it was not the only one, the Geneva Bible dominated the rest of the sixteenth century as the most popular English translation of the Bible.

By the seventeenth century, Europe was well advanced toward the peak of its dominance over other parts of the world. This was also the context of several translations. The beginning of that century saw a major revolution in the history of English Bible translations. The King James Version (KJV), sponsored by King James (1566–1625, r. in Scotland throughout his life, and in England and Ireland

1603–1625) was first printed in 1611. Sanctioned by royal authority, the KJV gradually replaced the Geneva Bible as the most important English translation, a fame it retained to the nineteenth century with enormous linguistic and, more generally, cultural implications. Writing for the *Guardian* in 2010 as the quartercentenary of the KJV was approaching, Robert McCrum described the Bible as "a number one bestseller of unprecedented literary significance."[11] Emphasizing the same point, emeritus professor of English James Hedges makes the observation that "Oxford atheist Richard Dawkins, who in *The God Delusion* denies the God of the Bible but insists we should remain acquainted with KJV phraseology and imagery in order to understand our cultural past, cites more than 100 expressions to underscore its pervasive presence, from 'signs of the times,' to 'grapes of wrath,' to 'no peace for the wicked.'"[12] Yet, save for updated spelling, the words for the quartet of identity groups already in existence in the Geneva Bible were retained in the KJV, now reading as "...of all *nations*, and *kindreds*, and *people*, and *tongues*..." (italics added).

However (and this is an important however), notwithstanding its royal imprimatur, the KJV did not impress all. Several other translations in English appeared in the eighteenth century, some with notable diversions from the KJV. In 1729, for example, Daniel Mace's (d. ca. 1753) New Testament[13] rendered the verse as follows:

> After this I beheld, and there was a great multitude, which no man could number, of every *nation*, *tribe*, *people*, and *language*, who stood before the throne, and before the lamb cloathed in white robes, having palms in their hands.... (Italics added)

Here, Mace, most likely seeking to expand—or simply match—the scope of his readers' imagination, substitutes *kindreds* with *tribe*, and *tongues* with *language*. Of these two substitutions, *tribe* marks a more substantial shift since *language* had been used at least once before and future translators oscillate considerably between *language* and *tongue*. Although the word *tribe* existed in the English language before Mace's translation, it appears to have had acquired a new meaning in his context.

The Oxford English Dictionary communicates this transition in meaning well. It highlights up to seven senses in which the word *tribe* has been used over time, although only the first three are relevant to the current discussion. To begin with the oldest first, the second sense given in the dictionary is that of *tribe* as "[one] of the traditional three divisions or patrician orders of ancient Rome in early times." Later on, the same title was applied to "the 30 political divisions of the Roman people instituted by Servius Tullius [r. c. 578–535 BC], and in B.C. 241 increased to 35."[14] Even though examples provided for this usage in English go only as far back as 1533, this is the oldest sense from whose Latin form *tribus* (with the root *tri* implying three) we have the etymological ancestor of this identity category.[15] Referring largely to nonbiological political divisions that an emperor could decree almost arbitrarily in the interest of census and collection of taxes, this second sense in the dictionary is hardly controversial in its application. Presumably, this sense was known to Tyndale and to the first translators of the KJV in the early modern period. However, to them, "kindred" (in its varying spellings) must have translated the Greek φυλῶν better than did tribe.

The first sense in the dictionary is *tribe* as "a group of persons forming a community and claiming descent from a common ancestor," with the best example being "the twelve divisions of the people of Israel." Examples cited in the dictionary for this usage go back to 1250, so it can be assumed that it was also known to our translators in the early modern period. In fact, in all the translations we have observed from the Wycliffe Bible in Middle English to Mace's New Testament in 1729, the word *tribe* is employed in this sense. All—without exception—use the word *tribe* thirteen times in the five verses prior to the one under discussion (cf. Rev 7:4–8) to refer to the twelve groupings of the descendants of Israel. Yet, before Mace, it did not appear to them to be a good translation of the Greek φυλῶν in Revelation 7:9.

The third sense of *tribe* is most likely the one Mace had in mind when he introduced the word to the quartet of identity groups in his 1729 translation. According to the dictionary, *tribe* referred to "a race of people; now applied [especially] to a primary aggregate of people in a primitive or barbarous condition, under a headman or chief" (we suspend the discussion of the word *race* for later). In this third sense, examples in usage begin at the end of the sixteenth century. From seventeenth and eighteenth centuries, examples include phrases and sentences like the following: "...one, whose hand (Like the base Indean) threw a Pearle away Richer then all his Tribe" (1604); "Him shall all the tribes of earth obey..." (ca. 1745); "Territory...occupied by numerous and warlike tribes of Indians" (1823); "Engaged in trading expeditions...among the tribes of the Missouri" (1836); "The tribes themselves, and all subdivisions of them, are conceived by the men who compose them as descended from a single male ancestor" (1875); and, "In some cases the Tribe can hardly be otherwise described than as a group of men subject to some one chieftain" (1875).[16] Even just from these examples, it becomes obvious that this new sense of *tribe* was largely based on an awareness of the existence of large communities of others (like Indians) who were organized in a manner that was different from that of those describing them (under some chieftain, for example).

Of the two changes that Mace made, only *tribe* had an enduring impact. After Mace, almost all switched to the use of *tribe*. For example, in 1752, the Douay-Rheims Translation stayed with Mace on *tribe(s)* but reverted to *tongues* for the last identity category, hence: "...of all *nations* and *tribes* and *peoples* and *tongues*...."[17] By the end of the century, even those who, led by William Newcome (1729–1800), sought to improve on the KJV had adopted *tribes* as the appropriate translation.

To the present, exceptions to the word *tribe* have been few, even though they stand out wherever they have occurred. A radical one was that of William Gilpin's (1724–1804) translation, first printed in 1790, which reduced all four identity categories into one, rendering the verse into "an innumerable multitude of people gathered from all nations standing before the throne."[18] There are also occasional cases where translators have reverted to using *kindred*, for example, in the 1839 *The New Testament in the Common Version* of Noah Webster (1743–1843)[19] and in the 1971 *New Testament* published by the Church of Jesus Christ of Latter Day Saints.[20]

While nearly all others have been confident in their continued use of the quartet *nation, tribe, people* and *language* or *tongue*, in recent times there have been attempts to restructure the verse in which the words appear in a manner that communicates ambiguity. For example, in 1901, the American Standard Version had "...out of every nation and of all tribes and peoples and tongues...," a structure suggestive of nation as a category that stands separately from tribes, peoples, and tongues. A similar implication is also achieved in the 1952 Revised Standard Version, which has "...out of every nation, and from all tribes and peoples and tongues...." The 1989 New Revised Standard Version and the 2021 English Standard Version communicate the same sense through the format "...from every nation, from all tribes and peoples and languages...." The 1982 New King James Version frowned upon this trend as it remained with its time-tested format, "...of all nations, tribes, peoples, and tongues...," except that now it also switches to *tribes* instead of *kindreds* and changes *peoples* into plural. Despite the KJV exception, the recent effort to render the nation separate from the other identity groups is too consistent to be considered a mere accident in translation.

Another current major change avoids, like the KJV, the special treatment given to *nation*, but introduces the word *race* into the quartet of identity groups. The Jerusalem Bible (TJB), first published in English in 1966, aimed at keeping the language "always as a living language of the twentieth century."[21] To achieve this goal, it delicately restructured the portion of the verse that we have been discussing and offered to the reader the following sentence:

> After that I saw a huge number, impossible to count, of people from every *nation*, *race*, *tribe* and *language*; they were standing in front of the throne and in front of the Lamb, dressed in white robes and holding palms in their hands. (Italics added)

The Contemporary English Version (CEV) of 1995 followed suit, but rearranged the identity groups in different sentences, now reading, "...I saw a large crowd with more people than could be counted. They were from every *race*, *tribe*, *nation*, and *language*...." Both TJB and CEV remove *people* from the quartet and replace it with *race*, although they still give *people* a role somewhere else in the verse. However, although they agree on the usefulness of the word *race* in their contexts, they do not seem to agree on what it means. If each translation maintains the order in which the identity groups appear in the Greek original, then what TJB translates as *nation* appears as *race* in CEV, what TJB translates as *race* appears as *tribe* in CEV, and what TJB translates as *tribe* appears as *nation* in CEV.

In the end, it probably does not even matter what *race*, *nation*, or *tribe* really means. We ascribe our own meanings to these words, or we can even use different words if we want to. In their online Easy

English Bible, the Christian charity MissionAssist has opted for "…so many people that nobody could count them. They came from every country, from every family group and from every language."[22] Who could say they are wrong? Well, a host of scholars could, as we shall see presently.

RACE, NATION, AND TRIBE IN RECENT TIMES

To focus more on race, nation, and tribe, we need to dismiss *people* and *language* (or *tongue*) with just a few observations. The two have been used quite consistently throughout the modern period, suggesting a more general acceptance.

The word *people*(s), as used in the verse we just discussed, has an appearance of imprecise inclusivity that renders it generally unclear and therefore harmless. It is hard to imagine a culturally unified cluster of human beings that could not claim to constitute a people if they wanted to, regardless of the strength of their unity. When the twenty-eighth president of the United States of America, Thomas Woodrow Wilson (1856–1924, in office 1913–1921) advocated for the right of self-determination for peoples to avoid conflicts similar to World War I (1914–1918), he had no idea what kinds of peoples would present themselves to claim that right. As he then viewed it, "no peace can last, or ought to last, which does not recognize and accept the principle that governments derive all their just powers from the consent of the governed, and that no right anywhere exists to hand peoples about from sovereignty to sovereignty as if they were property."[23] In Europe, the smallest cultural units that had resented the unity imposed on them by a common state above similar other units organized themselves and claimed their separate right to self-determination. The result was the fragmentation of parts of Europe into the smallest units possible, a phenomenon that gave birth to the term balkanization. Acting in exactly the opposite way, Africans, who had suffered the humiliating imposition of foreign colonial states above them, combined in their various cultural units to claim peoplehood together within existing colonial boundaries and to demand the same rights to self-determination. The unpredictable fecundity of the principle of self-determination attracted negative and positive popularity in post–World War I diplomacy. Described by Wilson's critics as "patchwork Wilsonianism,"[24] the principle was deplored by diplomats as inapplicable, but that did not prevent unsuspected autonomy seekers from deploying it effectively.

Language is also inclusive in an interesting way. The capacity to communicate through some form of invented speech is one of the most universal elements that all cultural units have, albeit in innumerable varieties. A statement like "a multitude from all languages" leaves out no one, not even those whom we have never heard speak. In a way, even the deaf using sign language can constitute their own group. There is another reason that makes this identity category appealing. If language is a boundary around a particular cultural unit, then it is a very porous boundary. Language can easily be learned by others from outside that restricted cultural unit. Within a generation or two, people of foreign descent can speak the local language with native fluency, sometimes even better than those who claim to have inherited it from ancestors five generations down the biological line. Today, many of those who have won international awards because of their exceptional command of the English language have zero claim to English ancestry and they might even take offense to be considered English. If we were verifying language groups present at the roll call of Revelation 7:9, the kinds that turn up for the English-speaking group might surprise many.

For many more, surprising in a different way would be the entrance of the word *race* into the quartet of identity groups so late in the history of English Bible translations. A nonexpert would be excused for wondering why one would opt for such a loaded word in the second half of the twentieth century, for, even though translators may know what they imply in their choice of words, they may not claim to have control over the way readers will understand those same words.

In a way, even Tyndale could have used the word *race* as early as 1526 because it existed in his repertoire of vocabularies, but it would have referred to all humans together as a single group and thus failed to communicate the variety intended in the biblical verse. To say that "all human beings were present" is not the same thing as to say that "human beings of all colors were present." But, during Tyndale's time, the word *race* had very little to do with people's skin colors, if anything at all.

With time, the word *race* did acquire new layers of meaning. Probably from the Medieval Latin *ratio*, which meant a species, *race* made a transition through French into English, where it already bore myriad senses in the early modern period. These ranged from "a group of persons, animals or plants connected by common descent or origin" to "a particular class of wine," and many other things in between. Literally, *race* could simply mean a kind of thing, be it animate or inanimate. In one of the oldest senses, *race* meant any one of the great divisions of living creatures, in which case it was applied to human beings when globally considered as "the human race" or "the race of men or mankind." Hence: "From among the humane race [though shalt] Roote out their generation" (ca. 1580), or "His hate may grow to the whole race of Mankinde" (1607). As a group of persons connected by common descent, *race* could further mean a generation or descendants of a particular ancestor, among other things. For example: "Thy remembrance ever doth abide from race to race" (1549–62); "In several orders of knighthood, the candidates must prove a nobility of four races of descents" (1727–41); and "We were two daughters of one race" (1833).[25] The KJV and all earlier translations found absolutely no use for these meanings of *race*.

Other examples with special prominence in the seventeenth and eighteenth centuries suggest that, at least in that period, a race was not clearly distinct from "a tribe, nation, or people, regarded as of common stock." This observation becomes clear in examples like "Llewelyn ap Gruffudd the last Prince of Wales of the British race" (before 1600); "No government to be conferr'd upon strangers in blood; but such onely to have the place, to whose race it did belong" (1653); "A mighty people come! A race of heroes!" (1726–46).[26] Probably it is this sense that translators in the twentieth century have employed the word *race* in the Bible, especially in the verse that we discussed. However, as already cautioned, there cannot be any guarantee that their readers have understood it in the same way.

As we get into the nineteenth century, *race* becomes increasingly refined to mean divisions of human beings into groups that are larger than the tribe or the nation, but distinct enough not to include the whole of humanity. The dictionary describes this sense as "a group of several tribes or peoples forming a distinct ethnical stock." Two observations are in order here. The first is the entrance of the category of "ethnicity" that will be useful as we proceed below. The second is that, in this sense, *tribes* and *peoples* appear as subsets of *race*. All examples of usage given for this sense of race are drawn from the nineteenth century: "No two races of Men can be more strongly contrasted than were the ancient Egyptian and the Syro-Arabian races" (1842); "They were all different tribes and peoples of the one great Hellen race" (1868); "Courage...was a heritage of the whole German race" (1883). Refined just slightly, this usage of *race* could also mean "one of the great divisions of mankind, having certain physical peculiarities in common." Hence: "The second great variety in human species seems to be that of the Tartar race" (1774, just before the nineteenth century); "Considerable differences occur in the general stature of the several races of mankind" (1839); and "Blumenbach proposed to establish five races: 1st, the Caucasian; 2nd, the Mongolian; 3rd, the Ethiopian; 4th, the American; 5th, the Malay" (1861).[27] This last sense, with its examples in usage, brings us to the ubiquitous meaning of *race* as employed from the late modern to contemporary period. It is also from this sense that the ideology of *racism* arises.

On the surface, many of the activities that accompanied the encounters and conquests of the early modern period suggest an earlier utility for the category of race. The fact that the slave status was so completely identified with Blackness might even give a hint to the racial origins of slavery and the slave trade that became characteristic of this period. Yet, to do so would be to put history upside down. The ideology of racism did not give rise to slavery or to the slave trade. Rather, slavery in the modern period, together with the slave trade that serviced it, gradually contributed to the emergence of the ideology of racism according to which humanity was supposed to be reimagined and reorganized. While this development was gradual, its flowering came about in the late eighteenth century at the earliest. As is usually the case, the meaning of *race* was adjusted to serve a particular need that was felt from that time onward.

One of the ironies of history is that normalized racism flowered when colonial societies in the Americas, including the United States and Haiti, were becoming independent and Christian campaigners were challenging the very institution of slavery on moral grounds. This moral outrage against institutionalized slavery, at once belated and justified, never extended to racial prejudices engendered under slavery itself. Nor did it prevent the practically racist arguments for imperial expansion and colonization of Africa in late nineteenth century or the massacre of Jews in mid-twentieth century. A possible explanation for this cohabitation of moral thinking and racial prejudice is that privileged societies that felt threatened by emerging possibilities for others needed to construct and maintain new boundaries to protect their usually unearned and now endangered privileges.[28] The material for that construction already existed in the repertoire of social and cultural prejudices gathered during centuries of racialized slavery as well as in the economic limitations imposed on those on the receiving end of those prejudices. However, as historian of science and medicine Nancy Stepan so eloquently argues, for the edifice of normalized racism to rise, there was need for the intellectual input that came from modern biological and human sciences.[29] These first emerged in late eighteenth century and were later nourished by ideas borrowed from Charles Darwin's (1809–1882) theory of evolution of species through a process of natural selection. Unlike other animals that needed muscles and agility to survive the brutal process, argued British anthropologist and biologist Alfred R. Wallace (1823–1913) in 1864, human beings needed brains, of which the so-called Germanic races had in excess

> the better and higher specimens of our race would therefore increase and spread, the lower and more brutal would give way and successively die out, and that rapid advancement of mental organisation would occur, which has raised the very lowest races of man so far above the brutes, (although differing so little from some of them in physical structure), and, in conjunction with scarcely perceptible modifications of form, has developed the wonderful intellect of the Germanic races.[30]

With racism as the offspring of racial prejudice and science, "the moral claim of the Black and other so-called 'inferior' races, slave and free, to equality of treatment was taken to be a matter not of ethical theory but of anatomy," says Stepan.[31] Even the best minds of the period could not easily think outside the compartment of racialized morality, ethics, and aesthetics. Although from an earlier part of the period under discussion, and even though its author is acknowledged to have grown out of his earlier positions on race,[32] the over-cited statement by German philosopher Immanuel Kant (1724–1804) remains one of the most concise applications of this kind of racialized value system. Considering an opinion reportedly expressed by "a Negro carpenter" regarding relations between husbands and wives, Kant says, "There might be something here worth considering, except for the fact that this scoundrel was completely Black from head to foot, a distinct proof that what he said was stupid."[33] In this moral system, the test for worthiness had finally been made simple: "If all races were found to be anatomically and psychologically alike, then the rights and privileges enjoyed by the European would be guaranteed for all peoples." To conclude with Stepan, "The appeal to nature in deciding what was in reality a moral issue was fatal, but one made by the anti-abolitionists and eventually the abolitionists alike. Nature was now the arbiter of morality."[34]

In the parameters of this chapter, one would wish to declare race and racism exhausted. However, the malignancy of normalized racial prejudice affected all the other identity categories. Nineteenth- and twentieth-century debates about nations and tribes proceeded directly from the resignification of race during that period. As French philosopher Étienne Balibar states, "Thinking about racism led us to nationalism, and nationalism to uncertainty about the historical realities and categorizations of the nation."[35]

Although translations of the Scripture verse we discussed manifest great consistency in the use of the word *nation*, recent literature shows little agreement on its meaning. Specifically, scholars dispute the appropriateness of applying the term to political entities in Africa and in other similar postcolonial situations. The appellation *African nation* is considered a misnomer when the entity in question is not the Zulu, the Oromo, or the Hausa, but South Africa, Ethiopia, or Nigeria. At the same time, "the nation form"—to borrow Balibar's favored expression[36]—is seen as the only recognized way of organizing human society and, therefore, the only socio- and geopolitical subdivision of the world worth working for in Africa as elsewhere. There is a certain presumed respectability in the expression *community of nations* that is never accorded to, for example, *community of tribes*. Similarly, we are somewhat expected to esteem *nationalism* like that which dismembered the Balkans but shun *tribalism*, as is often attributed to African realities.

Twentieth-century opinions on nations can be clustered into two periods. The first begins at the turn of the twentieth century and continues to include the self-determination discourse after World

War I and the establishment of the League of Nations, to which we referred above. In this period, there was less talk about the origin of nations and more about their nature at that time. Emphasizing the role of ideas and institutions in the formation of nations, this earlier school marks a civic-ideological trajectory to nationhood. Most Africans who claimed nationhood to gain access to the rights reserved to the so-called community of nations or family of nations followed this trajectory. The second period lasted between 1980s and 1990s when there was increased scholarly interest in the origins of nations rather than in their contemporary nature. The contested, disproved, and sometimes endorsed view was that of the nation as a product of a quasi-natural process of cultural evolution from a preexisting *ethnie*, basically meaning an ethnic group—the category I promised to return to. Representative examples are usually the English, the French, and the Germans. Here, ethnicity is used in a manner that links descent affiliation to culture, thus connecting perceived physical beauty, moral nobility, and material achievement.[37] An extreme rendering of this link is probably National Socialist Kreisleiter of Innsbruck Hans Hanak's 1938 declaration that "culture is in the blood," citing as proof what he understood to be Jewish inability to absorb German culture, hence the impossibility of accommodating Jews in the German nation.[38]

The link between blood and culture points to a delicate and often unspecified balance between what is given naturally and impossible to reinvent, acquire, copy, or modify (unless by genetic modification), and what is cultural, obviously a changeable human invention. Looking at this balancing process, anthropologist Ana Maria Alonso observes that "what is called race in much of the literature is the variant of ethnicity that privileges somatic indexes of status distinctions such as skin color, hair quality, shape of features, or height," whereas "what is called ethnicity is the variant that privileges style-of-life indexes of status distinctions such as dress, language, religion, food, music, or occupation." However, Alonso concludes that "somatic and style-of-life are used simultaneously as signifiers of hierarchized categorical identities; hence, there is no sharp distinction between these two variants of ethnicity."[39] Biological nature is thus deployed to barricade cultures with impenetrable walls.[40] This ambiguous nature-culture union is carried over to the nation once it has been associated with ethnicity.

Because of the importance borne by ethnicity and evolutionary processes in nature in this second way of thinking about nations, we have what we might call an ethno-biological trajectory to nationhood. The increase of arguments in this school between the 1980s and 1990s could as well have been a reaction to the fact that earlier predictions of the imminent collapse of nation-building projects in postindependence Africa had by then come to naught. The logic, then, could have been that, even if they remained unified in what were called national borders, the political entities in Africa could not be nations in any way. Ironically, under colonialism, Africans were referred to as "natives," which should have qualified them for the nation title, but the meaning had since evolved to mean something else.

One of the strongest proponents of the ethno-biological trajectory to nationhood is British historian and sociologist Anthony D. Smith (1939–2016). Smith insists that "ethnicity and ethnic communities form the models and groundwork for the construction of nations" and that "to forge a nation today, it is vital to create and crystallize ethnic components, the lack of which is likely to constitute a serious impediment to 'nation-building.'" In fact, to verify the national claims of a particular identity group, Smith says, "it becomes important to enquire into the 'state of the cultural identity' of a given community on the eve of its exposure to the new revolutionary forces, in order to locate the bases of its subsequent evolution into a fully-fledged 'nation.'"[41]

This line of thought excludes Africans and several others like them almost permanently, not only from nationhood, but also from the rights and privileges reserved to members of the so-called community of nations. The problem with them is that their evolutionary process was presumably stopped in its tracks at a tribal stage, imagined (as we saw above) as a primary aggregate of people in a primitive or barbarous condition, under a headman or chief. Such aggregates of humanity could not demand rights similar to those reserved to civilized nations. This, for example, is the thinking that informed reactions to Ethiopia's request, in 1935, that the League of Nations intervene on its behalf when it was aggressed by Italy, a fellow member of the league. The league dithered over how to respond, with some of its members wondering whether the protections implied in the leagues' treaties could be justly extended to "an amalgam of uncivilized tribes" in Africa such as Ethiopia supposedly was.[42] The allies would later intervene, but only when British possessions in the Sudan had been sufficiently threatened by continued Italian presence in Ethiopia. Writing with reference to Haiti, historian Julia Gaffield explains this logic rather pithily: "Throughout the [nineteenth] century, the foundation for membership in the family of nations was an implicit and then explicit 'standard of civilization,'" she says, "which was continually ever-changing and continually reacting to economic, social, cultural, and political changes in deeply complex ways."[43]

CONCLUSION

While we presume that the biblical verse that we used above to be completely free from all the biased layers of meaning heaped upon the quartet of identity groups in English translation, it still matters which group we are actually placed in, be it race, nation, or tribe. It also turns out that meanings can be regularly adjusted to include those deemed qualified and to exclude some undesirables. Our identity category could determine what rights we can enjoy or what indignities we must suffer in silence. The power to identify others, whether as of one race or another, or from a tribe or a nation, goes hand in hand with the presumed right to control them and the obligation to intervene in their affairs in one way or another. The full length of this logic is similar to our ability to identify a winged, two-legged creature as "a chicken," which then gives us the right to control the bird and even to eat it, unless it is already owned by someone else of our kind.

Who, then, decides who belongs to what identity category? This is a difficult question about power, not a simple pastime for scholars. Power to control others largely depends on the capacity to monopolize the identification process. A keen South African student of philosophy who grew up under apartheid once said, "Whoever controls the process of identification wields power to even determine existence."[44] This is true, for example, in so many cases where indigenous communities are forcefully displaced from their ancestral lands to pave the way for what others determine to be desirable civilization and modernity. This is also true when a person's physical appearance is presumed to constitute enough ground for categorizing the person as a threat and for taking action to eliminate that threat.

4

A CHURCH AFFECTED BY RACISM

Aimé Kameni Wembou

CHURCH DOCTRINE

Today, the Christian faith is pleased that the principle of the equal dignity of all humanity already has a solid foundation on the scientific and philosophical level, as well as on the moral level and for religions, in general. The doctrine of the Church is firmly founded on the revelation received from God. Furthermore, all citizens are equal before the law, without distinction of sex, race, language, religion, political opinion, personal and social condition.[1]

According to biblical revelation, God created human beings—male and female—in his own image and likeness (cf. Gen 1:26–27; 5:1–2; 9:6). It is the fundamental basis of human dignity and its inalienable rights that do not come from a government, nor from us, nor from international agreements, but from God himself the Creator who insists on the unity of the human family: all men are sons and daughters of Adam and Eve.[2] In the New Testament, the Son of God assumes human nature. With Christ and in Christ, all are called to enter, through faith, into the definitive covenant with God (cf. Rom 1:16–17). This covenant was made and sealed by the sacrifice of Christ, who obtains the redemption of a sinful humanity. Christ created unity among all peoples, "he has made both groups [Jews and Gentiles] into one and has broken down the dividing wall, that is, the hostility between us" (Eph 2:14). So that today "there is no longer Greek and Jew, circumcised and uncircumcised, barbarian, Scythian, slave and free; but Christ is all and in all" (Col 3:11; cf. Gal 3: 28).

Bringing together this doctrine, the Second Vatican Council teaches,

> Since all men possess a rational soul and are created in God's likeness, since they have the same nature and origin, have been redeemed by Christ and enjoy the same divine calling and destiny, the basic equality of all must receive increasingly greater recognition....True, all men are not alike from the point of view of varying physical power and the diversity of intellectual and moral resources. Nevertheless, with respect to the fundamental rights of the person, every type of discrimination, whether social or cultural, whether based on sex, race, color, social condition, language or religion, is to be overcome and eradicated as contrary to God's intent.[3]

In his address to the United Nations Special Committee on Apartheid, Pope John Paul II stated,

> Man's creation by God "in his own image" (Gen 1:27) confers upon every human person an eminent dignity; it also postulates the fundamental equality of all human beings. For the Church, this equality, which is rooted in man's being, acquires the dimension of an altogether special brotherhood through the Incarnation of the Son of God.... In the Redemption effected by Jesus Christ the Church sees a further basis of the rights and duties of the human person. Hence every form of discrimination based on race, whether occasional or systematically practised, and whether it is aimed at individuals or whole racial groups, is absolutely unacceptable.[4]

In fact, creation, as established by God, is characterized by diversity.[5] Creation is not a monolithic reality; diversity is a key feature. In the story of creation, as the Book of Genesis recounts, diversity is a reality that is found everywhere. In the context of God's creation, diversity is a source of enrichment that acquires its true meaning and value through unity. In fact, the creation of the universe and of humanity is, in essence, a concrete manifestation of diversity in unity and of unity in diversity.[6] It is a gift from God that must be preserved to ensure the integrity and sustainability of creation. This fundamental affirmation of Christian theology is found in all current religions.

RACISM TODAY

Racism is the awareness of the biologically determined superiority of one's race or ethnic group over others. It is believing that one's ethnicity is superior to others. It is the belief that races have specific cultural characteristics defined by hereditary factors, and that these give some races superiority over others.

In common parlance, the term *racism* is used to refer to the discrimination of specific groups. Each of its forms is characterized by a process of racialization that is distinguished by the historical and political context, the type of categorization, the structure, and the intrinsic dynamics. This process follows consolidated canons of categorization and stereotyping, whereby groups are defined and labeled based on their physical (skin color, skull shape) or cultural characteristics, national or regional origin, lifestyle, or religious beliefs. Starting from the premise that these characteristics are given by nature and therefore immutable, stereotypical properties are attributed to people, as determinants of their essence. They are clichés that demean members of a particular group and make their penalization and discrimination appear justified. Racism manifests itself in individual attitudes and actions on a personal level. Institutional racism discriminates against people in important settings, such as schools, health care, and the police. Structural racism reflects the way a society, through explicit and implicit norms, as well as structures, organizes itself historically, politically, and economically. These hierarchies in society produce inequalities and hinder or prevent access to social, cultural, political, and economic resources. It is important to emphasize that these different levels are interrelated and interdependent.

While racism is manifested by an attitude or an ideological or mental disposition, racial discrimination entails an action that effectively penalizes a person who is the victim of racism. Such actions may consist of comments, physical violence, or other forms of unequal treatment or discrimination. Indeed, if situations of segregation based on racial theories are rare, the phenomena of exclusion or aggression against minority groups are numerous. The appeal launched by those who fight to advance the cause of ethnic and racial justice is also addressed to the church that is called to continue to defend the rights of the oppressed minorities within it and to bring them concrete solidarity. We are all called to reflect on what it means for a church to "overcome racism," and to recognize that the time is now for "transformative justice."

THE SIN OF RACISM

Racism is a sin because it separates us from God and other human beings and prevents us from seeing the reality of people's suffering that allows racist attitudes and practices and institutional racism to continue. Racism is a sin because it is necessarily accompanied by silence and indifference or a failure to act. No one saw or heard anything. Racism is a sin because it is a manifest denial of the Christian faith, and it is incompatible with the gospel. Racism is a sin because it is a flagrant violation of human rights. All human beings are living icons of God, fundamentally worthy of such respect and dignity. Whenever human beings do not treat others or creation with due respect, they are insulting God, the Creator.[7]

Racism is a sin not only because, by asserting that human beings are not equal before God, it contradicts biblical teachings, and particularly that of Galatians 3:28. Racism is sinful also because it is a denial of fundamental justice and human dignity. Above all, racism is a sin because it destroys what is at the very root of humanity—the image of God which is in every person. Racism is a desecration of the *similitude* of God that is in each of us; therefore, it rejects the Creator God and denies creation and its goodness. We are only truly human when the divine flame of God's image shines within us to dispel evil. The fight against racism is an affirmation of truth and of life in its fullness.

THE CHURCH AND RACISM

As Pope Francis has stated, "We cannot tolerate or turn a blind eye to racism and exclusion in any form and yet claim to defend the sacredness of every human life."[8] It is true today that racial prejudice or racist behavior continues to cloud relations between people, human groups, and nations. Public opinion is showing itself to be more sensitive to it. And moral conscience alone cannot deal with it. Thus, we must make a commitment to refuse to ignore that any form of racism, including in the life of the church, is contrary to the word and the will of God.[9]

To be the church today requires becoming ecclesial communities that live fully the diversity of the members who compose them and of their cultures, to clearly reflect the creation and the image of God in humanity.[10] To be the church today means to commit resolutely to abolishing one's own racial and ethnic divisions.

The church has the sublime vocation to realize, in herself first of all, the unity of the human race beyond ethnic, cultural, national, social, and other differences, in order to show precisely the transience of these differences, abolished by the cross of Christ.[11] To be the church today means to be healing communities transformed by the life, the gifts, and the spirit of all the members who constitute it and, at the same time, to ensure that vision of life in which all aspects are bound together by love and solidarity.[12] The church must overcome racism through the gospel of Christ who invites every person to forgiveness, to permanent conversion, and to love, and helps people to change their life and their mentality to fully live their prophetic vocation.

Today, the church's plan of action should focus particularly on the aspect of her cleansing from the sin of racism and its consequences. Other steps will follow, such as improved preaching and evangelism, and further steps to address structural racism and reform society and the church.[13] We must bring about a change of hearts and develop new habits in hearts that will transform our communities with the wisdom and mercy of Jesus.

THE DUTY OF TRUTH

Increasingly, people and peoples want the truth to be told, past and present wrongs to be acknowledged, impunity to be challenged, healing relationships to be established, and processes of reconciliation within the church itself to be initiated. In the context of ethnic/

racial justice, neither churches, governments, civil society, the victims, nor the offenders can repair or restore what has been lost or broken. Centuries of racism and racial discrimination cannot be erased with the stroke of a pen—whether historically, collectively, or individually. The life, culture, language, way of life, liturgy, and spirituality of the victims can no longer be what they used to be.[14] Transformative justice is about the past in the present. Its purpose is to overcome racism and to achieve healing, reconciliation, and the restoration of personal relationships, with a particular focus on justice for members of the church who are victims of racial and ethnic oppression.[15] Respect and acceptance of others with their qualities and faults is fundamental to building a lasting relationship based on love, solidarity, and friendship.

Clearly, racism is one of the greatest obstacles to promoting the spirit and practice of respect for the dignity of every human person created in the image of God. The church has tried in many ways and on various occasions to raise the awareness of the world to this problem, especially when it becomes painfully topical.[16] The Apostolic See, even in the seventeenth century, insisted that a distinction be maintained between the work of evangelization and colonial imperialism.

As a historical institution, the church advances toward the fullness of its essence—the community of the children of God. The perspective that moves us forward—as a church and a world of just and inclusive communities free from racism—calls us to become completely transformed children, a church, a people, and a new creation. "Do not be conformed to this world, but be transformed by the renewing of your minds, so that you may discern what is the will of God—what is good and acceptable and perfect" (Rom 12:2). A vision that calls for the establishment of truly just and inclusive communities, transformative justice necessarily involves *metanoia*. This means that we must modify and reorient our conceptions, our way of thinking and our way of life.[17] Transformative justice calls us to overcome this ambiguity of human existence; to believe and act as saints; to probe each day and in depth our capacity for good, generosity, and love; to open ourselves to the newness of not conforming to the standards of the world but, on the contrary, to take deliberate, consistent, and constant action against racism.[18] It is daring to have a renewed passion for racial justice, it is also having the capacity to take risks, it is to establish between us more egalitarian relations. This implies changes in conceptions, practices, actions, and structures, operated by the church and in the church itself. A reorientation of the mentality is necessary so that radical changes can occur. Transformative justice involves a paradigm shift that will transform structures, culture, and core values.[19] It is the whole community that should make the decisions on how to transform the reality of the church and the communities so that they become truly multiracial and multiethnic and that relationships based on justice are reestablished, with the addition of the will to take into account fully what this implies for creation.

In our present or past existence, the cancer of racism calls for healing and restoration of wholeness as it harms not only the victims but also the entire church community. Transforming an entire community also means transforming the individuals who form it. This requires everyone to be determined to set out on a road that is likely to be long and arduous. From the experiences of those who have embarked on a healing journey for the sin of racism, we have learned that anger, pain, and suffering are inevitable, especially when communities are confronted with the truth and must find a way of accepting this knowledge. Yet the truth brings healing to both victims and offenders. The truth brings healing both to the community and to its institutional life and its members.

RESPONSES TO RACISM

For the sons and daughters of the church who experience racism, the sense of loss, pain, suffering, and a broken spirit are so heavy to bear that the only response that can inspire compassion is affliction. Gregory Baum points out,

> While it is true that we cannot erase the past, reconciliation involves a change of register in our faith in order to chart a course towards a future filled with life. Those who have caused suffering to others, those who have directly or indirectly participated in acts of oppression must recognize that it is evil that is the source of their power and

their privileges, they must repent and be ready to make restitution.[20]

Those who have experienced racism need to talk about it. We must avoid staying silent and suffering in silence, so as not to sink. Bigotry and hate speech must also be destroyed.[21] The church must teach children from an early age the idea of compassion, fairness, and human rights, so that they grow up to build a more just and united world. The more a child is in contact with people from different communities, the more that child is open to diversity. Each parent must teach their child how to fight against discriminatory behavior by referring to historical events, such as the story of Rosa Parks in the United States, the apartheid regime in South Africa, and the impact of colonization.

CONCLUSION

In a society where racism is still present, the word of God obliges us to intervene. It forbids us to turn our heads away pretending not to see. With the grace of God, we must work to overcome pride and break down any prejudice that may arise in our lives, families, and churches. We must think about how to apply the word of God in a society with a wide range of colors and a multiplicity of cultures, all for the glory of the Lord. We live in a culture where we are constantly immersed in discussions about race and racism. We need to organize welcome conferences and forums, sponsor debates, encourage dialogue, write articles, and deliver speeches on how to resolve racial tensions within our society. Let's look at the starting point offered by the word of God for the social problems we face. The Lord decided to create us equal; no human being is worth more than another.

It is lack of faith in this gospel truth that has led to unspeakable horrors in human history. All these evils caused by racism are all derivatives of satanic deception. It must be understood that all men and women are made in the same way and refer to the immutable image of the living God.[22] We must avoid being afraid of the other that we do not know. A culture of *encounter* generates friendship and brotherhood. The culture of openness to *difference* (the different) is an important sign of cultural growth and not a barrier.

The church is a community of disciples who should constantly come together and reconstitute themselves around the problems posed by suffering.[23] The church must never distance itself from the poor and the powerless and each of us must pray that the Lord grant us to live always in love, forgiveness, and peace.

5

RACE, ETHNICITY, AND IDENTITY

A Theological Account

Emmanuel Katongole

The eminent Ghanaian theologian, the late Kwame Bediako, was right to note that the issue of identity is at the heart of Christian theological reflection.[1] Who am I as a Christian? What is Christian identity? What does it mean to be a Christian, and how does this relate to one's identity as a member of a race, a tribe, or an ethnicity? Does being a Christian make any difference to my being Black, white, American, European, Igbo, Chagga, and so on. If so, what is the difference? If these and similar questions of identity are central to the process through which Christian reflection is carried forth, this reflection becomes more urgent in our time in the face of two recent events. The two events I have in mind are the murder of George Floyd in the United States in May 2020 and the 1994 genocide against the Tutsi in Rwanda. Some might already wonder why I refer to the latter—that happened more than twenty-seven years ago—as a "recent" event. It is a "recent" event because its memories are still fresh, and the questions it raises are ongoing and urgent. Moreover, Ferguson, Missouri and 1994 Rwanda have much more in common than we might think. Both are watershed events. Christian theological reflection on identity cannot, in the face of these events, proceed in the same way, but must search for fresh ways of conceptualizing and living out what it means to be a Christian in a world so deeply marked by racial, ethnic, national, and tribal identities and loyalties. In this connection, these two events not only define the urgency, but also the context as well as metaphors and questions that drive our reflection on Christian identity. The two events also suggest that a Christian reflection on identity begins and is sustained in lament.

A CRY OF LAMENT: "I CANNOT BREATHE!"

A video clip that went viral throughout the world shows a white police officer kneeling on the back and neck of a handcuffed Black man, George Floyd, for nine minutes and twenty-nine seconds, as Floyd desperately pleads, "I cannot breathe!" Derek Chauvin, the white police officer, has since been convicted of the murder of George Floyd. Floyd's "I cannot breathe" is the cry of a dying man—a Black man at the hands of a white police officer. Whatever one may say about this event, there is no denying that the issue of *race* is at the heart of Floyd's tragic death.

"I cannot breathe" is also the cry of lament of the crowds that spontaneously gathered in protest following Floyd's murder in the Twin Cities and across the rest of the United States, later spreading around the world. Some carried signs stating, "I cannot breathe," as they protested police brutality against Black persons, and the structural and systemic racism within the United States. The protests were a spontaneous lament of "how long?"—a public expression of anger and of "enough" and an affirmation that Black lives matter. The Black Lives Matter movement is the most visible institutional expression of this public lament and protest.[2]

Something about the "I cannot breathe" protests that erupted in Ferguson and in other places across the United States and around the world is particularly provocative, from a theological perspective. The crowds were not only huge; they consisted of white and Black and brown, young and old, and male and female. They reminded me of the multitude in Revelation 7:9. Accordingly, in the protesting crowds, I caught a glimpse of the church, as God's "new we"—drawn from every nation, tribe, people, and language—and bearing signs that read, "I cannot breathe." It was a glimpse of a church that laments and protests the ways in which the identities of race, ethnicity, and nationalism have so defined and so constricted—so framed—Christian faith, that the church is quite often unable to breathe any new insight into the discussion about identity. I saw a glimpse of the church that has for so long defined herself along racial, tribal, ethnic, and national labels that she has lost her own identity; that she is not able to breathe and live out her own unique vision of baptism that sets her on a journey toward "a new we"—toward a new identity as God's children.

This is what connects Ferguson, Missouri to Rwanda 1994—to a genocide in one of the most Christianized nations in Africa where over 85 percent of Rwandans self-identified as Christian. In the spring of 1994, in this Christian nation, during the Easter season, Hutu Christians killed Tutsis, often in the same churches where they worshiped together. How could this be possible? Soon after the genocide, Cardinal Etchegaray, the papal envoy to Rwanda, posed this question to the Christian leaders: "Is the blood of tribalism deeper than the waters of baptism?"

Christian reflection on identity begins with this haunting question—whether *the blood of tribalism and racism run deeper than the waters of baptism*. For racism in America and tribalism in Africa are two sides of the same coin. It may take us too far afield to get into the history of race as a social identity, and to discuss the shared philosophical and ideological assumptions behind the notions of race, tribe, and ethnicity.[3] Suffice it to say that both the categories of race and tribe reflect ways in which European Enlightenment and modernity continue to "imagine" a natural essence or shared culture as the basis and justification for belonging and political organization. The effect is that we have come not only to define ourselves as white, Black, American, African, Chagga, Ganda—that is, along racial and tribal lines—but to think these designations as our "natural" or primary identities. Moreover, once racial or tribal imagination has become the dominant ways in which we imagine ourselves and others imagine us, then Christian faith does not seem to have any power to alter these so-called natural identities. It is in this sense that "race" and "tribe" and "ethnicity" choke the life out of Christian imagination. This is where a Christian reflection on identity must begin: with a recognition—indeed a cry of lament—that the church cannot breathe. She is unable to breathe not simply because of widespread racial, ethnic, or tribal discrimination even within the church itself, but most importantly, because of the ways Christians have come to assume race, tribe, and ethnicity as a natural and inevitable lens through which we see others, the world, and ourselves.

LIES THAT BIND

The first task of Christian theological reflection on identity is to name the lies that seem to make race and tribe "natural" identities. Two such lies are predominant: the lie of "natural" identity and the lie of "spiritual" identity.

The Lie of "Natural" Identity

We tend to believe that there is a certain "essence," a shared culture, or a shared set of characteristics among the members of a certain identity. For example, an essence that all "white" or "Black" people share—and that is what makes them, naturally and without effort connected to others with whom they share their identity. However, as Anthony Appiah and others have persuasively argued, essentialism, the belief that our identity is grounded in some stable essence—be it biology, culture, or history—that all members of a particular identity share is both a myth and lie. First, Appiah notes the simple fact that we are each the bearer of multiple identities. We always find ourselves caught up in many entanglements and identities, such that it is a "lie" to reduce these to one identity that is *really* me! Moreover, given the circulation of cultures, there can be no such thing as a pure Igbo, Black, white, Western, or African culture, no such thing as a fully autochthonous *echt*-African culture or identity. "We are already contaminated by each other."[4]

Equally important is Appiah's observation that identities are historical, political actualities, and are thus fluid and always in an ongoing process of interpretation and reinterpretation.[5] Being an "African" or "Black," for example, is not a static identity that reflects a certain biology or essence, but like all identities, this identity is fluid and dynamic, and is thus capable of being constantly shaped and reformed in the context of present realities and future ideals and aspirations. This insight lies behind the conclusion that race, just as ethnicity, are historical constructs. This, however, is not to say that these realities are not real. As he would later note in *The Lies That Bind*, "There is no dispensing with identities, but we need to understand them better if we are to reconfigure them."[6]

From a theological viewpoint, understanding identities in this way is understanding how historical identities fit with God's plan and mission in the world, and how these historical identities might be reconfigured to better reflect God's own identity and God's mission. Unfortunately, by and large, Christian theology, and African Christian theology, in particular, has not yet fully grasped the fluid and dynamic nature of identity. Much of Christian theology and popular sentiment is built on what Appiah describes as the myth and lie—on the feeling that racial, tribal, and ethnic identity is a "natural" identity; that "tribe," "race," or "ethnicity" simply name the way one was born. "I did not choose to be born that way, do not blame me, there is nothing I can do about it," are expressions one will often hear. Or as the Ghanaian theologian Pobee once noted,

> Before I became a Christian by baptism and confirmation, I was ensouled with Africanness, which was taken in with my mother's milk. Africanness is more than color of the skin. It is culture and worldview taken for granted, which cannot be erased.[7]

Even though Pobee was talking about African identity, his sentiment is shared by many who feel that being "white," "Black," Chagga, Kikuyu, Igbo (or whatever one's tribe), is one's "natural" identity—the way one was made by God—and Christianity simply builds upon this natural identity. Pobee's essay in which he first develops this observation is tellingly entitled, "I Am First an African and Second a Christian."[8] The critical issue, here, is that within this understanding of race or tribe as a natural and stable essence is the assumption that the Christian identity simply builds on but does not alter racial or tribal identity. And so, the best that Christian faith can do is to motivate the Christian to work for racial reconciliation or racial justice, which often means nothing more than encouraging Blacks, whites, and browns not to hate or kill each other, but to learn to get along and live together, while leaving each in their own identity. This is, of course, not an adequate understanding. For Christian identity does not simply build on our so-called natural identities, it transforms them and redirects them toward their true end or telos—which is the creation of a new people in the world that reflects God's own life and identity.

The Lie of "Spiritual" Identity

Another predominant (mis)understanding understands Christian identity in purely "spiritual" terms, and thus as an essence or reality that operates on a totally different plane from other historical identities. According to this view, in baptism, when one accepts Christ as Savior, one is born again as a new person, with a new identity. This new spiritual identity transcends all social identities whether based on race, nation, tribe, or ethnicity. It is, in fact, this new identity that gives the Christian the "freedom" to be whatever he or she wishes to be in the world. As the late John S. Mbiti, a foundational figure in African theology famously states, identity in Christ

> makes nonsense of all other identities in that it claims the whole person and the whole cosmos as the property of Christ. Then, deriving from this Christocentric identity, the person is free to become whatever else he wishes, to be identified as an African, nationalist, neutralist, trade unionist or even beggar. That is the height to which Christianity in Africa must soar.[9]

According to this view, which is a form of Gnosticism (the belief that Christian faith is a form of knowledge that gives one power, for instance, to be intimate with God and to live with God eternally), it becomes possible for the Christian to say, "I do not see any color, because we are all brothers and sisters in Christ!" Practically, however, it means that as a spiritual person, Christian identity does not question or affect the social, material processes that shape the politics and economics of everyday life, and often marginalize the lives of millions of one's brothers and sisters in Christ. On the contrary, holding onto his spiritual identity, the Christian can be a white supremacist and even a member of the Ku Klux Klan. This is perhaps why many otherwise good Christians do not see a major contradiction between their Christian faith and such practices as racism, over consumption, and ecological degradation.

Christian identity is not a "spiritual" identity; it is not an inner sentiment or ghostly, supernatural thing. Christian faith is not, in the first place, a matter of beliefs. It is as much about practice and about community. The goal of Christian faith is to change us, and Christian identity names that change—in the way that Christians live, the way they shop, to whom they marry, the way they eat, and with whom they eat. Christian identity is not only about the question of "Who am I?" but also of "Who are my people?" In other words, Christian identity is not a thing—it is not a badge or a uniform that one puts on and off! It is a journey into a new community, and a new sense of belonging into a new we!

CHRISTIAN IDENTITY AS A JOURNEY

The notion of journey is central to Christian faith and life. God himself is on a journey: a journey that begins with the creation of the world, and moves toward the redemption of all creation, and thus the full realization of a "new creation." This is what we encounter in Scripture, which recounts this journey of God with creation, and which comes to a definite climax in the Christ event. Paul describes this journey as a journey of reconciliation: "God was reconciling the world to himself" (2 Cor 5:19), and this is what has been realized in Christ. That way, Paul can affirm, "In Christ, there is a new creation: everything old has passed away; see, everything has become new" (2 Cor 5:17). However, even as that is the case, Paul notes, the journey continues, for we now find ourselves in the in-between of the already and not fully yet of God's new creation, where creation groans, as if in an act of childbirth...eagerly waiting for the full redemption of our bodies (cf. Rom 8:22–24). The Christian is part of this journey, initiated in baptism, where she not only assumes a new way of looking at things ("we regard no one from a human point of view," writes Paul; "even though we once knew Christ from a human point of view, we know him no longer in that way" [2 Cor 5:16]), she's made part of a people that bears witness to and anticipates the full realization of the "new creation." This is what makes Christian identity not an essence or a finished product, but a journey—an ongoing and ever-expanding experience of belonging to the community of God's new creation.

This observation confirms that Christian identity is, like other identities, not a stable or fixed essence. Like all identities, Christian identity is open to an ongoing process of interpretation and reinterpretation. This also means that the call to become a Christian always finds one somewhere: as a member of a specific race, tribe, nation, gender; however, that "somewhere" is not "destiny"—it is the starting point of a new journey that reshapes and redirects one's sense of belonging. In this connection, as one of the pioneers of African theology, the Congolese Vincent Mulago noted that Christian faith reorders and redirects one's so-called natural identity. "In the Incarnation, the Son of God enters into a context to purify it, using elements within that context to reveal himself. He does not utterly demolish the context, but works with the elements there and fills them with a new reality."[10] Thus, according to Mulago, while cultural elements are not obliterated, they are "transformed," and through this transformation, "African identities are redeemed, to be made part of the overarching Christian identity."[11]

What Mulago's observation concretely means in terms of identity is that whatever one's cultural identity happens to be now—white, Black, Chaga, Luia, Ganda—this identity becomes a "stepping stone" to a journey, whose goal is belonging (Mulago uses the theological term "incorporation into") God's new people in the world.

A similar vision of Christian identity as a journey of stepping out of one's cultural identity is behind Miroslav Volf's influential book, *Exclusion and Embrace: A Theological Exploration of Identity, Otherness and Reconciliation*. "Departure," Volf writes, is part and parcel of Christian identity: "At the very core of Christian identity lies an all-encompassing change of loyalty, from a given culture with its gods to the God of all cultures."[12] The story of Abraham provides support for this imperative. On the very foundation of Christian faith stands the towering figure of Abraham, who Genesis informs us "went forth" (12:1–4) even before the text tells us that he "believed" (15:6). If Abraham is to be a blessing, he "cannot stay; he must depart, cutting the ties that so profoundly define him."[13] He leaves not even knowing where he is going. Volf elaborates: "The courage to break his cultural and familial ties and abandon the gods of his ancestors (Joshua 24:2) out of allegiance to a God of all families and all cultures was the original Abrahamic revolution. Departure from his native soil, no less than the trust that God will give him an heir, made Abraham the ancestor of us all (see Hebrews 11:8)."[14] Christian faith, Volf rightly concludes, invites us into a similar Abrahamic revolution. "To be a child of Abraham and Sarah and to respond to the call of their God means to make an exodus, to start a voyage, become a stranger."[15]

BELONGING AND EATING TOGETHER

One might wonder, what is the "toward what"—the telos of this voyage that makes one a "stranger" to one's cultural identity? While Volf neither explicitly nor sufficiently answers this question, the telos of the journey is a new sense of belonging—a new sense of community—that is realized through practices of "coming together" and of "eating together" with those who are different from us. This is what the missiologist Andrew Walls describes as the "Ephesian Moment."[16] In the Letter to the Ephesians, Paul celebrates the coming together of Jews and Gentiles for the first time around the meal table! Traditionally, Jews and Greeks were seen as distinct communities, and the distinctiveness of each was marked by the meal table. Jews ate with Jews, and Gentiles ate with Gentiles. How was this division to be reconciled with shared membership in one church? The compromise reached at the Council of Jerusalem (Acts 15) produced two distinct Christian lifestyles corresponding to these ethnic and cultural divisions: the one for Jewish Christians; the other for Hellenistic or Gentile Christians.

Paul was not comfortable with this compromise. Emphatically, there was to be only *one* Christian community. God's purpose in Christ, Paul writes, was to create, out of many, "one new humanity" (Eph 2:15) so that Jewish and Gentile Christians now share "one Spirit" (2:18), "one hope" (Eph 4:4), "one Lord, one faith, one baptism, [as they are all children of] one God and Father of all" (4:5–6). This is what had happened in Ephesus, the coming together for the first time of Jewish and Gentile Christians. It is this coming together of two communities historically separated—the breaking down of the wall of separation brought about by Christ's death (cf. Eph 2:13–18)—that Paul celebrates in the Letter to the Ephesians. Jewish and Gentile Christians are "no longer strangers and aliens," but fellow "citizens" and "members of the household of God" (2:19).[17] Thus, if Paul recognizes the cultural and political realities of being Jewish and Gentile, this fact, in itself, was not theologically interesting—and this is not what Paul celebrates. What he celebrates is the fact of their "coming together," of their being "made alive together" (2:5), of being "raised up" together, and of being "seated" together (2:6). Jewish and Gentile Christians "belong together" as "bricks"—used in the construction of a single building—the "temple where the One God would live" (cf. 2:19–22). They do not constitute two separate communities, but one community, of which they are both members, constituting as it were different parts of a single body of which "Christ is the head, the mind, the brain, under whose control the whole body works and is held together" (cf. 4:15–16).[18]

Several aspects of Walls's description of the original Ephesian moment are relevant for a discussion of Christian identity in our time. First, in the Letter to the Ephesians, Paul realizes that on their own, Jewish and Gentile Christians remain but "fragments" of God's purpose. Together, and only together, can the fragments come to experience and reflect what Paul describes as "the measure of the full stature of Christ" (4:13). The implications are obvious. On our own—as American, Asian, African, white, Black, Hutu, Tutsi—we remain but "fragments." It is only by coming together that these different fragments are "incorporated" into—made part of—Christ's body and are thus able to reveal the height of Christ's full stature.[19]

Second, the coming together of Jewish and Gentile Christians at Ephesus and elsewhere created something new—a new social reality, and in terms of the available cultural designations, a confusing social reality. What Paul celebrates as "the measure of the full stature of Christ" is this new and odd communion of believers that is neither Jewish nor Gentile (cf. Gal 3:28). A similar phenomenon was underway at Antioch, where the term *Christian* was first used. In a unique Ephesian moment, Jews and Gentiles came together and created a new "we" that required a new name. No one had needed such a term when Christians existed independently as only Jew and Gentile.

Third, the act of eating together was both the test and expression of the coming together. "Two cultures historically separated by the meal table were now able to come together at table to share the knowledge of Christ."[20] Thus, the meal table—the institution that had once symbolized the ethnic and cultural division—now became the hallmark of Christian living. What the act of eating together confirms is that the coming together is not simply a "spiritual" fellowship. It is a real, concrete, and "bodily" fellowship that is realized in and through working out together and sharing the material, and thus, economic realities of everyday life. In fact, it is only through such collaborative efforts to meet the needs of the body—food, shelter, labor, health—in a word, of "eating" that we become truly Christian. For indeed as the Rwandan proverb goes, *akamwa karya ntimumve, kavuza induru ntimumve*—roughly translated, "Unless you hear the mouth eating, you cannot hear the mouth crying." This is also the reality of new friendships arising out of and through the experience of "working together" that is confirmed by the story of Father Andre Sibomana, a Rwandan priest, who narrowly survived the genocide in Rwanda. In the aftermath of the genocide, he mobilized his Christians for the reconstruction of schools, public places, as well as houses for genocide survivors. The Christians were both Hutu and Tutsi. At the beginning of the building project, the Hutus and Tutsis each kept to themselves and did not speak to one another. However, the communal work helped to build bridges. At the inauguration of the first two hundred houses on August 21, 2005, Hutu and Tutsi drank banana beer from the same jug.[21]

WHO ARE MY PEOPLE?

What the foregoing discussion confirms is that the telos of the journey of Christian identity is to *nurture* and *sustain* such Ephesian moments of coming together and eating together across racial, national, and ethnic divides. The goal of this journey is not simply to affirm, and thus simply build on our so-called natural or cultural identities, but to draw us out—to be part of a new reality that more accurately reflects God's own identity as the "father of all." It is for this reason that I have argued in another place that the mission of the church is not to make Americans, Africans, or Europeans more Christian. It is to make American Christians less American, European Christians less European, and African Christians less African. It is to make white Christians less white, Black Christians less Black, Igbo Christians less Igbo, and Hutu Christians less Hutu so as to discover friendships that lead to the formation of a new people in the world.[22] This is what makes Christian identity a potent political notion in that there is something subversive and disruptive about the journey of Christian identity. It creates a sense of "confusion"—an interruption of our so-called natural or cultural identities, as it presses toward a "new we"—a community that is neither Black nor white, neither African nor American, neither Hutu nor Tutsi.

The foregoing discussion also confirms that racism, tribalism, or ethnicity cannot be overcome by argument and theory! Bringing people to understand how irrational their racism or tribalism is cannot create the beloved community of the "new we." Even legal frameworks, necessary as these are, cannot, on their own, bring an end to racism. America is a good example of this. In fact, as the historian Charles Marsh notes, "While the civil rights movement defeated segregation and forever changed American society, the nation has experienced precious little of repentance, reconciliation and costly discipleship."[23] The case of George Floyd in Ferguson, Missouri, is a testimony to this. What offers hope in the face of racism and tribalism is "encounter"—concrete possibilities that allow people from across different divides to "come together" and to learn to "eat together" in ways that build friendships and affirm a shared sense of belonging. As Pope Francis notes in *Fratelli Tutti*, "The process of building fraternity, be it local or universal, can only be undertaken by spirits that are free and open to authentic encounters."[24] What perhaps one has to realize is that such authentic encounters are not a onetime event, but require sustained practices and opportunities of working together and of building solidarity and nurturing social friendships. It is through such practices that we begin the long and difficult journey of unlearning the lies and fears that would rather keep us apart under the pretext of affirming every one's cultural identity! But this is also the reason why even as significant as the spontaneous protests of solidarity in the wake of George Floyd's murder are—protests that brought together Black, white, brown—they are not enough. They are, however, a necessary starting place, pointing to the work ahead if such coming together across racially divided communities are to become not an occasional event, but a characteristic of daily life in America. For that to be the case, the desire for "eating together" across racial divides needs to be cultivated. Cultivating that desire not only takes time but also requires conscious and determined efforts to form and sustain friendships across racial lines that might be seen as a threat to a society that is built on a racial or tribal imagination. It is for this reason that antimiscegenation laws—laws that prohibited interracial marriage and interracial sexual relations—were popular in the United States once slavery was outlawed. For perhaps nothing threatened to expose the lie of race as a "natural" and stable essence as clearly as friendship, affection, and sexual intimacy across racial lines, as well as the possibility of biracial offspring! Anti-miscegenation laws were seen as necessary to prevent such exposure and perpetuate "race" as an ideological foundation for American society. However, even though most of these laws were repealed in the wake of the Civil Rights Acts of 1964 and 1968, there have been no determined efforts by society, in general, or the church, in particular, to promote friendship across racial lines. The result is that the cultural, ideological, economic, and social, and to a large extent, theological scaffolding that structured a racialized society and thus upheld white privilege and perpetuated the marginalization of Black/brown populations have remained in place.

That is why, from a theological perspective, there might be no better starting point in the journey of racial healing and reconciliation than from an explicit pastoral policy of encouraging interracial (intertribal) friendships and marriages. For it is from such friendships that we might begin to chip away at the entrenched idolatries of "race" and "tribe." Were Christian churches to adopt and implement such an explicit pastoral policy and practice, they might discover that they have something theologically interesting to say about identity, in general, and racial, tribal, and ethnic identity, in particular. As a result, Christian churches and congregations might be viewed as a political and economic threat, but at least this will help them not only to recover their relevance, but to "breathe," and thus drink from their own rich theological wells. In this connection, I find the story of the "confused" Hutu boy during the Rwanda genocide to be telling, in terms of the work that is needed to chip away at the ideological foundations of race and tribe as natural—and thus fixed essences. The Hutu boy fled to the bush with the Tutsis during the genocide. After two or three weeks of hiding, the Tutsis pointed out to him that he was Hutu and so he could be spared. He left the marshes and returned to the village and was not attacked. Neither did he participate in the killing. The mixed-up boy had spent so much time with the Tutsis in his early childhood that he was confused. He did not know how to draw the "proper" line between the two ethnic groups. The *interahamwe* militias did not force him to kill because his mind was confused or, in their words, "clearly overwhelmed."[25]

I point to this story of the confused Hutu boy because it is an illustration of the kind of formation that the church should be about nurturing and encouraging through concrete possibilities of everyday interactions and of eating and working together across racial, tribal, and ethnic divides. It is these daily opportunities of interaction that constitute what Pope Francis describes as a "culture of encounter" (*Fratelli Tutti*) that breaks down the walls of racial, tribal, or ethnic division and fosters solidarity and social friendships across the divides. Fostering a "culture of encounter" is the key reason behind Bishop Paride Taban's Holy Trinity Peace Village at Kuron in South Sudan. Amid tribal and religious violence, Paride set up the Peace Village as a cooperative where Muslims, Christians, traditionalists, Nuer, Dinka, and other tribes live together, raise families, and work together in programs of social and community development. This is how tribalism is overcome, Paride says—in a "small way," he adds.[26]

What both stories—of the Hutu boy and of Taban's Holy Trinity Peace Village—point to is the significance of the "margins" in reimagining Christian identity. For, as Pope Francis reminds us—in a way similar to Elizondo's Galilean principle (see below)—"God chose the peripheries as the place to reveal, in Jesus, His saving action in history." Moreover, it is "here that the Church was born, in the margins of the Cross, where so many of the crucified are found."[27] For Pope Francis, this theological observation makes the margins a central aspect of God's revelation, and the church's missional and pastoral vocation is an invitation to the "margins"—not simply to respond to the needs of a suffering world (thus, the church as a "field hospital"), but to "invent" new social historical dynamics.[28] For hidden in the margins "are ways of looking at the world that can give us all a fresh start."[29] It is in this connection that Pope Francis points to and hails social movements at the margins that bring people together and help them become protagonists of a new social history.[30] Pope Francis calls these movements "social poets" of a new history, mobilizing and addressing people's everyday needs of "land, lodging, and labor."[31] These are the concrete material realities of what we have been describing as "eating together"—the kind Paride Taban is realizing at Kuron Holy Trinity Peace Village.

Finally, what the stories of the Hutu boy and Taban's Peace Village confirm is that it is in this "small way"—daily interactions of working with and eating with the other—that in the end change us in ways that interrupt, confuse, and expand the notion of "who are my people." However, to the extent that one might end up "confused," just like the Hutu boy, this simply indicates that the journey of Christian identity is not simply to confirm or unproblematically build on one's racial, tribal, or ethnic identity. The journey thrusts the Christian into a crisis—an ongoing identity crisis—in which the questions, "Who am I? and "Who are my people?" are never settled. As my former colleague at Notre Dame, the late Fr. Virgilio Elizondo reminded us, the Christian journey presses toward a *mestizo* or "mixed" sense of identity.[32] To highlight this dimension of the journey of Christian identity, and draw out the implications for the nature and mission of the church more explicitly, it might be worthwhile to attend, even if briefly, to Elizondo's work.

THE FUTURE IS MESTIZO

The core of our existence, Elizondo writes, "is to be other"; is to embrace a "new identity"; is to live "in-between" cultures—neither this nor that but fully both, always straining ("journeying") toward the fuller reality of a new humanity that Jesus himself represents.[33] For Elizondo, this understanding of Christian identity reflects Christ's own identity and is described by Elizondo as the "Galilean Principle." In the incarnation, Jesus is both divine and human. He is not either/or; he is both! He is also a Galilean, or from a place known as "Galilee of the Gentiles" (cf. Isa 9:1–2). Occupied by many nations, its land and its people marked by centuries of continuous rebuilding, Galilee was a frontier region of Israel surrounded by foreign nations, a land of multiple borders! Being surrounded and even partially populated by various ethnicities, Galilee would inevitably have been a city of cultural encounters, tensions, and exchanges. This Galilean Principle, Elizondo notes, is central to understanding God's work in history: out of the rejects and ridiculed of society a new society of universal welcome and love emerges. From the margins, Jesus initiates not a new center but rather a new movement of the Spirit that enables people to cross boundaries and form a new human family based on love of God and love of neighbor.[34]

Speaking of his own mestizo identity as a Mexican American, and what it had taught him about the Christian identity, Elizondo writes, "Mestizo are part of both while not being exclusively either.... I am always both kin (at home) and foreigner at the same time."[35] This "in-between" state is the pain and potential, the suffering and the joy, the confusion and the mystery, the darkness and the light of mestizo life: "As I claim this ambiguity and recognize it for what it truly is, I become the bearer of a new civilization that is inclusive of all the previous ones. No longer do I carry the burden of the shameful news, but rather become the bearer of the good news of the future that has already begun in us."[36]

Elizondo uses various expressions to describe the goal of the mestizo identity. Its telos is to create something new: a "new movement," a "new human family," and a "new civilization." Behind all these expressions is the same conviction as we noted in relation to Volf and Walls—namely, that Christian life does not leave us where we are, but creates a "new future" out of our old identities. This future, Elizondo notes, is not a self-enclosed community, but an ever-expanding journey of radical biological, cultural, and spiritual openness to others: "the mestizo 'in between' keeps expanding, as the *frontera* keeps expanding both north and south at the same time it keeps including more and more peoples, more ethnicities, and races."[37]

I draw extensively on Elizondo because his insights make clear the ever-expanding journey of Christian identity and its goal for a new human family that not only cuts across, but exists beyond, race, nation, tribe, language, and ethnicity. Elizondo's notion of an ever-expanding *frontera* also means that the church, as the sign and sacrament of this new family, cannot become its own "tribe" that lives and ministers out of her own stable *esse* or identity. Rather, it means that the church's own identity, her *frontera* or boundary, keeps expanding. From an ecclesiological viewpoint, therefore, Elizondo's vision of the church has much in common with Pope Francis's understanding of the church as a "field hospital." For behind the image of the field hospital is an understanding of the church not so much as an institution, but as an event[38] that, in the very process of healing wounds, opens up fresh visions of what it means to be human—created in God's image—and initiates new social possibilities that reflect God's identity and work in history. As Pope Francis notes, "God manifests himself in historical revelation.... Time initiates processes, and space crystallizes them. We must not focus on occupying the spaces where power is exercised, but rather on starting long-run historical processes. We must initiate processes rather than occupy spaces. God manifests himself in time and is present in the processes of history. This gives priority to actions that give birth to new historical dynamics."[39]

CONCLUSION

In relation to race, tribe, and ethnicity, the "new historical dynamics" that Pope Francis alludes to in the quotation above have to do with interactions, friendships, political and economic arrangements, and indeed, conceptions of identity and belonging that do not assume "race" "tribe" and "ethnicity" as natural, and therefore, inevitable building blocks for our life together. Moreover, what our discussion has confirmed is that there is no such thing as a fixed identity. All identities are fluid and in a constant process of reinterpretation. Likewise, Christian identity is itself not a fixed essence, but an invitation into an ongoing journey of crossing boundaries—into, an ever-expanding *frontera* of community and belonging. Such boundary crossing or "encounters" cannot but give rise to a crisis of identity—a restless journey in which the Christian constantly asks oneself the questions "Who am I?" and "Who are my people?" These, however, are not abstract nor merely theoretical questions, but the kind of questions that can be asked only by one who has found ways of "coming together" and of "eating together" with those who are so unlike her—and whom she has learned to call "my people." That is why, in the face of deeply entrenched politics and economics based of race, tribe, and ethnicity, the hope that Christianity can offer to the world is processes, events, and opportunities of "eating together" that trigger an identity crisis, and thus give birth to and sustain Ephesian moments of a *new we*!

6

RACISM AS A REALITY AND PROBLEM

The Solution

John O. Egbulefu

The fight against racism is primarily a moral combat between right and wrong, justice and oppression, freedom and bondage; and it will be won, not merely by human power or artifice, but with the help of the omnipotent, unconquerable, ever-victorious Spirit of God and Lord of Hosts, who is with us, as the God of freedom and our stronghold (cf. Ps 46:6–8).

Fighting for freedom is not a sprint, but rather a marathon, and when one likens *racism* to such a long event, one needs then to brace oneself to address the issues using the different competences: Catholic social teaching, theology, sociology, political sciences, and so on "*in such a way as to shape the earthly city in unity and peace, rendering it to some degree an anticipation and a prefiguration of the undivided city of God*."[1]

The following is a contribution in search of a solution to great problem of racism. It is a search for how to overpower, overthrow, and overcome racism among the peoples of the different races, and it consists of two parts: the reality of racism and a solution, both coming from my theological perspective.

RACISM AS A REALITY

When, as a young and combatant professor of systematic theology in Rome, I called on the then Holy Father, Pope John Paul II, to excommunicate racists who were staring us in the face and who, according to my perception, were heretics simply by their implying that God is imperfect and that they could improve on God's aesthetics, on the way God has designed and fashioned his creatures, and on his arrangement and government of the entire creation, one of the cardinals told me to calm down and that racism is incurable—*razzismo e inguaribile!* As a theologian, I obeyed and calmed down, but I did not agree with the cardinal's view that racism is incurable. I believed and still believe that for God anything that seems impossible for humans, like the cure of racism, is possible.

On June 8, 2005, shortly after the election of Pope Benedict XVI (April 19, 2005)—my fifty-fifth birthday—an assassin with a knife made an unsuccessful attempt on my life to silence me, to quench my voice, and stop me speaking out about racism. This attack on my life took place on Via Traspontina, a few meters from St. Peter's Square, but God refused that I should die on that day. And so, with divine assistance, I recovered from the deep wound inflicted on my right side by that assassin. I would have died in Rome long after the assassination of Rev. Martin Luther King Jr., but much earlier than the death of George Perry Floyd in the United States.

I recovered only to take up my vocation and mission, as my daily cross to follow the Lord Jesus as the truth: the truth in person, that liberates from death and restores to life, that brings light from darkness, knowledge from ignorance, freedom from bondage, and turns hatred to love, brings the margins to the center, glory from misery, holiness from sin, courage from fear, and strength to confront our enemies in one's life and environment.

Four years after my experience of that bloody attempt on my life, I wrote a paper titled, "Attempts to provide a vision and strategic plan to assist Africa emerge from the misery and marginalization in the overall movement of globalization."[2]

Believing in the dissolubility of "racism" and, therefore, in its solution, I am convinced that when Blacks, especially Black Africans, succeed in producing material goods that indispensably and irreplaceably serve the needs of humanity—not just a local group, but the global human family—they will gain respect and esteem, and be acknowledged and recognized as equal to the rest of peoples. Thus, they will be less and less discriminated against, till the discrimination that is associated with their lack of creativity and productivity—their lack, therefore, of contributing to technological advancement and to productive growth of humanity—dwindles and disappears. Hopefully, the contributions of Blacks to human and global enhancement and growth, and the respect and esteem that accrue from them, will promote a more peaceful coexistence among nations and races in this world, which is transitory, but which our human activity, with God's help, can shape into an image of the "undivided city of God" where there is no discrimination.

My inspiration for the title of my paper came from *Instrumentum Laboris* (8) that came out of the Second Assembly for Africa of the Synod of Bishops that was held in Rome October 4–28, 2009—four years after that failed attempt on my life. The Synod had the theme "The Church in Africa in the Service of Reconciliation, Justice and Peace," a theme that resonated with my view that racism is a stubborn obstacle to peace and progress in the church and in society, and is why I wrote the paper.

Instrumentum Laboris (8) had, in turn, been inspired by materials contained in the document released during the United Nations' World Conference against Racism, Racial Discrimination, Xenophobia and Related Intolerance held between August 31 and September 7, 2001, in Durban, South Africa. Its concluding document—the Durban Declaration and Plan of Action—was substantially a revision of the relevant reflections that were published by the former Pontifical Council for Culture in 1980 at the Vatican. The Durban document

- Expressed appreciation for the heroic struggle of the people of South Africa against the institutionalized system of apartheid.
- Recalled the Vienna Declaration and Programme of Action adopted by the World Conference on Human Rights in June 1993 that called for the speedy and comprehensive elimination of all forms of racism, racial discrimination, xenophobia, and related intolerance.
- Recalled the Commission on Human Rights resolution 1997/74 of April 18, 1997, the General Assembly resolution 52/111 of December 12, 1997, and the subsequent resolutions of those bodies concerning the convening of the World Conference against Racism,

Racial Discrimination, Xenophobia, and Related Intolerance.

- Recalled the two World Conferences to combat racism and racial discrimination held in Geneva in 1978 and 1983, respectively.
- Bemoaned the fact that, despite the efforts of the international community, the principal objectives of the three decades to combat racism and racial discrimination have not been attained and that countless human beings continue to be victims of racism, racial discrimination, xenophobia and related intolerance to the present day.

Recognizing, however, that the victims of racism, racial discrimination, xenophobia, and related intolerance are individuals or groups of individuals who are or have been negatively affected by and subjected to these scourges on the grounds of race, color, descent, or national or ethnic origin, this World Conference in Durban expressed its solidarity with the people of Africa in their continuing struggle against racism, racial discrimination, xenophobia, and related intolerance and showed recognition for the sacrifices they make, as well as their efforts in raising international public awareness of these inhumane tragedies. The creation of this awareness is the inspiration of this chapter.

RACISM AS A PROBLEM

Regarding its history, and specifically, its origin and development, racism originates from egoism and develops into nepotism, from nepotism to clannism, from clannism to tribalism, from tribalism to nationalism, and from nationalism to what it is as racism.

Racism, as a problem, consists in its deviation from and transgression of God's design and its related established order of diversity, but interdependence and the consequent communion of all members of the human family, as children of the same Father, who is God their creator. The church is a sacrament of this communion of God's children in their diversity.[3]

THE SOLUTION

The solution of such racism comes from education and living in relationships:

1. Educating the human mind and heart, *mens* and *cor*, toward a mentality and cordiality, a culture and civility, regulated by
   a) the law of dependence and solidarity of each and all together as creatures of the one Creator.
   b) the law of the brotherhood and kinship of all, as *adelphoi/adelphē*, coming from the same womb and sharing the same dignity, as children of the one God and Father.
   c) the law of mutual dependence among all creatures, all human beings, all species of the human family, and hence among human families, communities, societies, clans, tribes, nations, peoples, and races.
2. Educating the human individual to understand him- or herself not only as a *person*—an individual *personal being*—but also as a *relational being: a being in relationship* with God, the Creator, with other human beings, with one another as brothers and sisters, and with the earth, created nature, our common home.
3. Human life can be lived well only as a triadic relationship: the three constitutive poles of human existence—God, other persons, and the earth.
   a) God created all people for himself, the king of all creation, and he binds them to himself through the law of the irreversible dependence of creatures on their Creator; and in this bond, they find life and existence. In the special case of the human being, who bears the image and stamp of God, such a bond with God constitutes the religiosity that is innate in the human being, in every man and woman. The bond between the human person and God, which Scriptures describe as a *covenant bond,* consists in God's binding the human person to himself, as the Creator and Lord. Humanity's dependence on God is uni-

lateral and irreversible. For it is "in him we live and move and have our being" (Acts 17:28).

b) The relationship among human beings, as *relational beings,* can take several forms, such as
   - the relations among members of one and the same family, as *intrafamily* relations.
   - the relations between two or more families as *interfamily* relations or *intertribal, interclan* relations, and so on.
   - the relations with and within other human groupings that are *not families* as nations, corporations, unions, parties, and so on.

4. In the latter case, human beings can also live their *relationality* in the context of an ever-widening *intercommunitarian relationship,* in national, multinational, multilateral, or even global relationships. Human beings also live their *relationality* in the context of their ties with the earth, their *common home.* All these forms of human beings living their *relationality* affirm the *interdependence* and the *interrelationships* that exist between the living and the inanimate in God's creation. As Pope Benedict XVI states, "Nature, especially in our time, is so integrated into the dynamics of society and culture that by now it hardly constitutes an independent variable."[4] Everything is interconnected and interrelated; and within this scheme of things, everything acquires its dignity, its value, its importance, and its respect.
5. Within the setting of a *nation,* human beings live their *relationality* in several contexts and ways: within families, tribes, and clans. People also live their *relationality* in the context of churches and faith groups, business grouping, unions, political parties, clubs, and so on. In these contexts, the freedom and openness of human beings to live their *relationality* becomes their *right of association*: their *right of belonging* that is ultimately the proof and expression of their dignity and respect. Any interference with such an expression of right of association (right of belonging)—such as *racism* and *discrimination*—is

essentially a denial of the human individual's or group's being a *person(s)* and *relational being(s)*!

6. Altruism—recognizing the being of the other and making room for him or her in one's existence—sets the trajectory along which one can travel in the solution and dissolution of all forms of bigotry, self-centeredness and auto-referential mindsets and racism. Thus, egoism, as selfishness, needs to be replaced with selflessness, and inward-looking attitudes with a sense of universal brotherhood.
7. Racism, as the devaluation, degradation, discrimination, and isolation of fellow human beings by others, leads the victims into solitude, inferiority complexes, and loss of self-dignity, and is an act against the image of God that the human person is, and therefore, against the will of God. It is thus a grave sin!
8. For the many victims of interferences with and the denials of their *right of belonging* and *freedom of association* as expressions of the living out of their character and nature as *personal and relational beings*, the gospel of discipleship invites them to be *loving of enemies* and *forgiving of transgressors*. "We who are strong ought to put up with the failings of the weak, and not to please ourselves. Each of us must please our neighbor for the good purpose of building up the neighbor" (Rom 15:1–2).

7

INTROSPECTION, ACTION, AND CREDIBILITY

The Church and Africa

Fortunatus Nwachukwu

Racism is often practiced by the same people who condemn it. These people do not always match their words with concrete actions. They tend to focus more on the comportment of others and pay only minor attention, or none, to their own individual or group mentality and practice. That is why a balanced reflection on the plague of racism must involve sincere introspection by those involved in the conversation.

A MALIGNANT WEED

Racism is like a malignant weed that grows defiantly on all grounds, friendly and unfriendly, and sways in the wind as the superior invincible shrub. Such a weed often flourishes amid the good herbs and allows itself to be camouflaged by them. Like the weed, racism is stubborn and sometimes subtle. It resists eradication and rears its head repeatedly, assuming new expressions. In 1988, a document on racism of the Pontifical Justice and Peace Commission observed,

> Today racism has not disappeared. There are even troubling new manifestations of it here and there in various

> forms, be they spontaneous, officially tolerated or institutionalized.[1]

Sadly, since this observation was published decades ago, not much seems to have changed. There are still persons who take pride in being recognized as racist, although most people today would like to distance themselves from being identified as such. Those who openly portray themselves as racist or unashamedly manifest racist demeanors are often persons or groups of persons with a certain supremacist mentality. Ironically, many of those who spontaneously claim not to be racist, when presented with concrete questions or situations reveal the same supremacist mindset that characterizes the racist.

For example, I once read reactions of some young Italians to the assertion that at least one of the Roman emperors was Black, particularly Lucius Septimius Bassianus (April 4, 188–April 8, 217), also known as Caracalla, who ruled the Roman Empire in the years AD 211 to 217. Although most of the interlocutors would have presented themselves as nonracist, their reactions were nonetheless dismissive, insolent, or outrightly demeaning. They affirmed that no Black African could have ruled the Roman Empire. In fact, some openly declared, while others insinuated, that Africans were too inferior to have produced someone who would have ruled the great Empire. Incidentally, available historical data indicate that the Emperor Lucius Septimius Bassianus was born in the northern part of the African continent, which was then under the Roman Empire. He was of mixed parentage, but possessed physical features that today would characterize some Black Africans. Consequently, it is most likely that the judgment of the young men was the result of an acquired stereotype regarding Black Africans.

In most cases, the racist, like racism itself, mixes well and goes unrecognized or is purposely ignored. Some of those who remain indifferent in the face of racist comportment argue that Jesus said that the malignant weeds should not be uprooted lest "you would uproot the wheat along with them" (Matt 13:29). What is often forgotten is that Jesus also clearly indicated that "'at harvest time I will tell the reapers, Collect the weeds first and bind them in bundles to be burned, but gather the wheat into my barn" (Matt 13:30). Jesus does not encourage the malignant weed. He defines it as destined for eternal burning. There should never be a beatification or justification for a racist.

A DARNEL PLANTED BY AN ENEMY

Generally, someone is called racist if that person bears and manifests the mentality or attitude that considers and treats others as inferior because of innate biological characteristics pertinent to these others. Racial prejudice feeds on the arbitrary presumption of "awareness of the biologically determined superiority of one's own race or ethnic group with respect to others."[2] This usually involves an uncritical generalization that lumps people together based on their skin color, physical stature, or other biological peculiarities. The absurdity of such generalizations is not far-fetched. The same groups that consider themselves superior to others usually comprise members with the very characteristics based on those with which they discredit others.

It is difficult to find groups of human beings that are perfectly homogenous. Not even the Swedish naturalist Carl Linnaeus offered clear-cut lines of division in his skin-color-based classification of humankind, published in his 1735 book, *Systema Naturae sive Tria Naturae*.[3] His proposal, which was to become the point of reference for most racial classifications since the eighteenth century, divided human beings into four groups, namely, *Europaeus albesc(ens)*; *Americanus rubesc(ens)*; *Asiaticus fuscus*; *Africanus nigr(iculus)*. The adjectives he used are vague, broadly applicable and reflect mere approximations: whitish (*albescens*), reddish (*rubescens*), brownish (*fuscus*) and blackish (*nigriculus*). They suggest that Linnaeus did not mean to draw sharp distinctions between the groups he presented. His classifications have been likened to the abstract grid of parallels and meridians that underlies geographical maps, whereby, like the grid, they serve as a tool for ordering knowledge, rather than depicting some reality "out there."[4]

Consequently, the idea of race as a means of classifying human beings has emerged as a mental construct based on vested interests and without reliable scientific foundations. One thinks again of the proverbial darnel introduced among the good herbs by an enemy (cf. Matt 13:24–30). It is in this regard that racism is considered a relatively modern concept, developed in the context of European imperialism and the attendant capitalism; furthermore, it not only found breeding ground in the transatlantic slave trade but also became one of its principal driving forces.[5] A detailed survey of the topic of race as a mental construct, and of the possible merits and demerits of the arguments around such a theme, falls outside the scope of this chapter. Suffice it to mention a few elements of the issues at stake in the debate.

Staffan Müller-Wille's tour and appraisal of the historiography of race offers a privileged glimpse into the debates.[6] Müller-Wille considers the concept of race to be one of the most problematic legacies of the European Enlightenment. He identifies two historical moments that mark the modern notion. On the one hand, there is the invention of race by European naturalists and anthropologists, especially with Carl Linnaeus's (1735) *Systema naturae*. On the other hand, there follows what is considered the demise of racial typologies after the Second World War (WWII) in favor of population-based studies of human diversity, underlined especially by the UNESCO Statement on Race, issued in 1950. Unfortunately, however, racial typologies did not die as many had hoped they would. Müller-Wille demonstrates how, despite the wide rejection of race as a scientifically based thought category, it has remained until date a politically powerful and explosive concept.

Müller-Wille's presentation of the modern history of the notion of race recalls the contributions of some outstanding authors. For instance, Ivan Hannaford traces the concept of race back to the Enlightenment, where it originated from "the insouciant and deliberate manipulation of texts by scientists and historians abandoning earlier paradigms of descent, generation, and right order."[7] Nancy Stepan and Elazar Barkan, in their respective accounts of the history of racial anthropology, both speak of degenerating programs of research based on fundamentally mistaken assumptions.[8] Finally, Michael Banton, in his remarkably subtle treatment of race as a variable concept employed in the social sciences and a wide range of other disciplines, espouses a tripartite history of race: a first stage during which race had not found a systematic space in public affairs and discussions; a second, when the idea of race as a permanent typology became dominant; and a third stage, when the idea of race was overtaken by population genetics.[9] In his analysis of the available literature, Müller-Wille discovers a history of race that has mostly been based on a false idea. He concludes his article with a reference to Hannah Arendt[10] and Michel Foucault,[11] who retrace the concept of race to discourses on "history" rather than "nature."

Yet, there remains the dilemma of how an invented idea, not based on nature, would continue to rear its head although many people had declared its requiem after WWII with the 1950 UNESCO document. In fact, historical and sociological studies of this twenty-first century indicate that conceptions of race have continued to play a subtle but important role in post-WWII human sciences and have indeed gained a certain disturbing prominence in recent genomic studies of human diversity, as is typified in writings of Claudio Pogliano[12] and Jennifer Reardon.[13]

THE UNITED NATIONS

Whatever may be its origin, the idea of race and the pain it spreads through racial prejudice, profiling, and discrimination are very much alive. In this regard, the document of the Holy See on the church and racism declared that "racist ideologies and behaviour are long-standing: they are rooted in the reality of sin from the very beginning of humanity."[14]

This fact is not lost on the international community, as is evident in the amount of space the United Nations organization has devoted to the theme of race and racial discrimination. In fact, the first article (Art. 1.3) of the United Nations charter affirms that one of the purposes of the United Nations is

> to achieve international cooperation in solving international problems of an economic, social, cultural, or humanitarian character, and in promoting and encouraging respect for human rights and for fundamental freedoms for all *without distinction as to race*, sex, language, or religion.

In the same vein, the 1948 Universal Declaration of Human Rights proclaims that "all human beings are born free and equal in dignity and rights. They are endowed with reason and conscience and should act towards one another in a spirit of brotherhood" (Art. 1), and that "everyone is entitled to all the rights and freedoms set forth in this Declaration, *without distinction of any kind, such as race*, colour, sex, language, religion, political or other opinion, national or social origin, property, birth or other status" (Art. 2).

Of special importance is the fact that the first major international agreement on human rights adopted by the United Nations General Assembly after the approval of the Universal Declaration of Human Rights was the International Convention on the Elimination of All Forms of Racial Discrimination (ICERD). It was adopted in 1965, a year before the International Covenant on Economic, Social and Cultural Rights and the International Covenant on Civil and Political Rights (1966) and entered into force in 1969. The ICERD has 182 States Parties, including the Holy See, which signed the Convention on November 21, 1966, and ratified it on May 1, 1969.[15]

The ICERD defines "racial discrimination" as "any distinction, exclusion, restriction or preference *based on race, colour*, descent, or national or ethnic origin" (Art. 1.1) and provides that "States Parties condemn racial discrimination and undertake to pursue by all appropriate means and without delay a policy of eliminating racial discrimination in all its forms and promoting understanding among all races" (Art. 2.1).

Alongside the ICERD and its monitoring committee, there exist Special Procedures of the UN Human Rights Council that also deal with racial discrimination, for instance, the Special Rapporteur on contemporary forms of racism, racial discrimination, xenophobia, and related intolerance and the Working Group of Experts on People of African Descent.

The UN has also pursued and implemented various international and intergovernmental initiatives to fight racial discrimination. Among these, three major conferences stand out: first was the World Conference to Combat Racism and Racial Discrimination that was held in Geneva in 1978. It solemnly declared, "Any doctrine of racial superiority is scientifically false, morally condemnable, socially unjust and dangerous, and has no justification whatsoever."[16] The second was the World Conference on the same theme, held also in Geneva in 1983.

Then followed the World Conference against Racism, Racial Discrimination, Xenophobia and Related Intolerance, which was held in Durban, South Africa, in 2001. This conference produced the most authoritative and comprehensive program for combating racism, racial discrimination, xenophobia, and related intolerance: the Durban Declaration and Program of Action. In April 2009, the Durban Review Conference in Geneva evaluated progress towards the goals set by the 2001 Durban Conference and examined global progress made in overcoming racism and concluded that much remained to be achieved.[17]

On September 22, 2021, the UN General Assembly hosted a one-day event to mark the twentieth anniversary of the Durban Declaration and Program of Action, which proposed concrete measures to combat racism, racial discrimination, xenophobia, and intolerance. On that occasion, the Holy See, through its Secretary for Relations with States and International Organizations, Archbishop Paul Richard Gallagher, stated in a video message,

> Racism is rooted in the erroneous and evil claim that one human being has less dignity than another. This not only disregards the truth that all human beings are born free and equal in dignity and rights but also the foundational ethical summons to act toward one another in a spirit of brotherhood.[18]

The United Nations has also dedicated certain days or decades of observance including, for instance, the International Day for the Elimination of Racial Discrimination (March 21); the International Decade for People of African Descent commencing January 1, 2015, and ending on December 31, 2024, with the theme "People of African Descent: Recognition, Justice and Development."

In the wake of the murder of George Floyd, and upon the request of some member states, the Human Rights Council, during its 43rd Session in June 2020, held an "urgent debate on current racially inspired human rights violations, systemic racism, police brutality and violence against peaceful protests."[19] The debate gave birth to the Human Rights Council Resolution 43/1, which was adopted by consensus and, in turn, formed the basis for the report on racial justice and equality, released on June 28, 2021, by the High Commissioner for Human Rights.[20]

There is need to mention that, in its fight against racism, the UN enumerates different categories, comprising not only people of African descent, but also indigenous populations, Roma, Sinti, and other groups of persons considered vulnerable: travelers, minorities, migrants, refugees, people living in poverty, women and LGBTQI+.[21] This has a double consequence. On the one hand, it places the concept of race in its primordial context, that of discrimination and xenophobia, where race is only an indicator of difference and not of intrinsic human value of the persons concerned. This also is a welcome alert to those persons who condemn racism practiced by others while they themselves indulge in related and sometimes more annoying manifestations of prejudice and discrimination. On the other hand, placing racism with these other groups tends to deviate attention from what has been and remains the source of the most horrendous and despicable forms of discrimination in human history. This danger is aggravated when the list is made to include groups whose definition splits the habitual consensus that has characterized the condemnation of and fight against all forms of racial discrimination for years.

Such is the case when the Western inventors of the modern concept of race nonchalantly ignore it to focus on their newly created categories, particularly the gender-based ones. The same governmental and nongovernmental groups that fight for the mainstreaming of gender-related issues often shy away from or minimize cases of skin-color-based prejudices and discriminations. Some even dare to assert that prejudices and discriminations based on skin color have been overtaken! Yet, the fact remains that more people are discriminated against based on their skin color than for their gender. For example, hardly are people denied entry into countries because of their gender, nor is anyone subjected to the harrowing and sometimes insolent interrogations by passport control officers that are often directed at people because of the color of their skin. Worse still, some persons suffer compounded prejudices and discriminations when their skin color and gender are taken together. It may even be argued that, while at the time of the Enlightenment the West invented race and racial stereotypes, ignoring or undermining natural data to justify prejudices and discriminatory practices, the same West, in recent years, has been trying to foist on the international community newly invented gender categories and rights which arguably have dubious anchorage in natural data. The new inventions often serve to move attention away from irksome cases of racial prejudice and discrimination that are stubbornly recurrent not only in the West but also in other parts of the world. An example may be cited with the so-called rights associated with the insidious practice of eugenics in its diverse forms. In this regard, it has been observed,

> Today, we could say that a eugenic mentality often lurks behind artificial procreation techniques and the dark sides of pre-natal diagnostics, where the idea that there are human beings of inferior value because of disability, sex, or other traits often leads to the denial of their right to life. Such a mindset entrenches principles of discrimination squarely opposed to the Durban Declaration and cannot be ignored.[22]

BETWEEN BEAUTY AND FEAR

To employ racial categories as a means of sorting and ranking human beings is a morbid abuse of the term *race,* which was originally neutral or, indeed, one of the means of expressing the beauty of nature. Before Linnaeus and the Enlightenment introduced and popularized the deplorable use of racial categories for ranking human beings, the word *race* was already employed in English language alongside other terms such as *kind, type,* and *sort* to depict differences. One would find expressions like *a race of saints, a race of bishops,* or *a race of teachers,* without any demeaning connotation for the group in question. Race depicted distinction without indicating any value judgment or ranking of the persons or groups differentiated.

Differences belong to human nature. According to the Judaeo-Christian tradition, the distinction between individual human beings—and, in fact, between all living beings—is explicitly willed by God. The biblical narrative of the origin of the universe (cf. Gen 1:1–31) teaches that God created all living beings according to different species. The Hebrew expression *lemiynō* (*nah...ehem*), translated as "according to its/their kind or species," is recurrent in the creation account (cf. Gen 1:11, 12, 21, 25). The same word is also used to describe the creatures that God instructed Noah to take with him into the ark, to save them from the flood (cf. Gen 6:20). This should not surprise us. God, the Creator, is also the supreme Artist. No authentic artist likes to produce a monotonous piece made of one color, without shades. It is the harmonious correlation between the different species that manifests the beauty of creation.

In themselves, colors are neutral. They only acquire the significance that the artist or the society accords to them. For example, the black or dark color could be demonized or stigmatized by always painting the devil black in our artistic repertoire, or dressing up mourners in black, making it the color of death, or still by contraposing darkness to light and presenting it as the domain of bad spirits, dangerous beings, and phantoms. The same black or dark color, however, acquires a different significance when it is underlined as the mother-source and end of all colors. In fact, traditionally, the beauty of a photographic image was developed in a darkroom, while stars are better observed, and their beauty appreciated in the dark sky of the night. Human life, itself, is conceived and nourished at its beginning in the darkness of the mother's womb. Further still, the black color could be appreciated as the symbol of universality and humility, such that in many parts of the world, it is the preferred color of priests and religious persons. It is ironic that certain persons who recoil at the presence of persons of dark skin color would also spend hours under the sun to acquire a suntan.

Yes, colors are in themselves neutral. Distinctions and differences are an expression of the beauty of nature. The inability to appreciate and accept the beauty and enrichment portrayed by differences, and to manage situations related to their presence usually finds expression in racism, xenophobia, and other forms of discrimination and intolerance. When such inability emanates from a pathological or arrogant sense of supremacy over others who are different, we speak of racism. If it arises from a morbid fear of others because they are different, it is xenophobia. Both racism and xenophobia feed on preconceived biases and stereotypes that denigrate, deride, condemn, or exclude others, whether individuals or groups, who are perceived or classified as different because of their origin, skin color, ethnicity, tribe, clan, sectional affiliation, language, and the like. Sometimes, the diversity also may be from age, health, or social status.

THE VICIOUS VICTIM

This close association of racism with xenophobia and other forms of demeaning discriminatory comportment reveals the veracity of the affirmation made at the beginning of this essay, that the same people who decry the racism practiced by others are often themselves guilty of the same mindset and behaviors that gave rise to the things that are condemned. Sometimes, the victims of racism themselves extend the same or even more despicable treatment to their fellows whom they perceive as different. In some cases, the same victims encourage and disseminate among other members of their group the racial practices that they condemn. This is the phenomenon of the vicious victims that helps to camouflage racism as a pernicious virus that so permeates the cells of the entire system that it is difficult to extirpate. A few instances may help to drive this point home.

Many of my Arab friends readily denounce the racism practiced by Westerners, not only against Arabs but also against Black Africans and dark-skinned persons in general. They are often in solidarity with Black Africans and people of African descent in condemning the transatlantic slave trade that has been associated with the mainstreaming of racial categories, especially since the Enlightenment. Some of them take delight in underlining that the shameful trade was spearheaded by Western Christians, sometimes with the support of some exponents of the hierarchies of Christian churches. They then go on to extend the blame to the entire church, as having supported the slave trade and the inhuman practices associated with it. What is not mentioned is that before and during the transatlantic slave trade, there was also the marketing of Black Africans to the Arab world, both toward North Africa through the Trans-Saharan trade routes and toward the Arabic Peninsula in the northeast.

It is true that the Arabs did not begin slavery or the slave trade among Black Africans. However, it has been observed that "in the wake of the Arab wave of Islamic conquests, the Arab world was flooded with large numbers of captives of different ethnic groups including Syrians, Copts, Persians, Nubians, Berbers, Indians, Greeks and Turks."[23] Regarding the number of Black Africans taken from their homes to the Arab world, specialists have been divided. In the absence of documentation from medieval Africa, only estimates are available, and they vary according to the authors. For example, some authors speak of eight million Black African slaves moved from the continent between the eighth and nineteenth centuries along the Oriental and the Trans-Saharan routes to the Arabic Peninsula and North Africa respectively,[24] while others place the figures for the same period and through the same routes at seventeen million.[25]

Many Arabs, especially Muslims, try to deny the facts of the Arab trade in Black African slaves. Others endeavor to minimize the number of the victims involved and the harrowing inhuman treatment they encountered at the hands of their Arab masters. However, some have been more realistic. At the Second Afro-Arab summit held in 2010, Muammar Gaddafi uttered the following words of apology for Arab involvement in the African slave trade:

> I regret the behaviour of the Arabs....They brought African children to North Africa, they made them slaves, they sold them like animals, and they took them as slaves and traded them in a shameful way. I regret and I am ashamed when we remember these practices. I apologize for this.[26]

Slavery and trading in Black African slaves by Arabs have gone alongside the diffusion of a mentality of supremacy and racism among Arabs toward Black Africans. Unfortunately, the denial tendency has prevented many of them from making sincere efforts to heal the situation. This has led to the continued festering in many Arabs of a racist mentality toward Black Africans. For instance, around the year 2000, a young Black African diplomat on mission in Morocco was assigned an official car driver. When the Moroccan chauffeur arrived and saw the dark-skinned diplomat seated in the car, he simply walked away swearing that he would not be the chauffeur of a Black man. The embarrassed authorities had to make alternative arrangements rapidly.

VISITING ISRAEL

The Jews are known to have suffered the most horrendous form of racism in recent history. In the extermination attempt executed against them by the Nazis, racism as anti-Semitism reached its most hideous and repulsive expression. A great part of humanity has joined Jews around the world in condemning that Holocaust and the continued manifestations of anti-Semitic behaviors against them. One would expect that people who not only have been survivors of such inhumane acts but are constantly exposed to the threat of their renewal against them would be taught not to extend racially discriminatory treatments toward others. Yet, even among the Jews, we also find the phenomenon of vicious victims. I recall an incident.

In the summer of 1989, a young Black African Catholic priest was attending a Modern Hebrew language course at the Hebrew University, Mount Scopus, in Jerusalem. The audio clip played to his class in the language laboratory spoke of the comment of the then Roman Catholic primate of Poland regarding the reaction of Jews to the presence of a community of Carmelite nuns close to the extermination camp of Auschwitz. Later, after the laboratory session, conversations in the class came to dwell on cases of anti-Semitic behaviors of exponents of the Catholic Church in history. When the use of the audio clip and the same tone of conversation continued for a second day, the young African priest got up and told the teacher that he had had enough. This awakened the curiosity of the teacher and the rest of the students, who were mostly *ōlîm*, or young Jewish immigrants to the State of Israel.

The African priest then told the story of how he had been treated some days before by some Israeli young men where he went to play soccer. He had paid the necessary registration fees and stood by for his turn to join the game. There were turns of fifteen minutes each. The Israeli young men would not let him play but kept asking him to wait for the next turn. Some of them took two or three turns. He was the only dark-skinned person there and did not yet speak Hebrew. After waiting for one-and-half hours, he simply went and stood in the middle of the pitch and said he would not leave until he was allowed to play. A huge muscular man rolled to the center of the pitch and tried to nudge him with his broad chest. The African smiled calmly and said very loudly to the man, "They have asked you to come and force me out. I paid for this game. You are denying me my right. Tomorrow you all will turn around and cry about anti-Semitic discrimination." Then he started to leave. The man stood still and most of the young men ran after the African and started asking him to come back, but he would not. When the teacher and the class colleagues heard the story of the young priest, most of them spoke up to apologize to him.

THE CHURCH

The church, especially the Roman Catholic Church, has been, at least in our times, very clear in its condemnation of racism and racial behaviors. It has been at the forefront in proposing and fostering dialogue between peoples of different cultures, religions, ethnic origins, and social standings. For various decades, different dicasteries of the Holy See[27] have been charged with relations and dialogue with peoples of various cultures, beliefs, and thoughts, including the academic world and the domain of natural and social sciences. The contacts with these different groups and domains have continued to inform the evolution of the thought of the church, firmly based on the gospel and the church's magisterial tradition.

The 1988 document of the Pontifical Justice and Peace Commission, *The Church and Racism*,[28] was later updated and presented as the Holy See's contribution to the World Conference against Racism, Racial Discrimination, Xenophobia and Related Intolerance, held in Durban, South Africa, from August 31 to September 7, 2001. The publication, among other things, emphasized the "consistency of the teaching of the [church's] Magisterium concerning the phenomenon of racism" but noted also that such emphasis "by no means implies an effort to gloss over the weaknesses and even, at times, the complicity of certain Church leaders, as well as of other members of the Church, in this phenomenon."[29] In fact, the church has, on various occasions, acknowledged the failures of its members in living up to its teachings. The most outstanding instance of such acknowledgment in recent times was during the celebration of the Jubilee Year, when on March 12, 2000, Pope St. John Paul II offered special prayers in St. Peter's Basilica in Rome, with a confession of the faults of the church's sons and daughters, as well as petitions for pardon on their behalf. We recall here a part of the pope's prayer on that occasion:

> Lord God, our Father, you created the human being, man and woman, in your image and likeness, and you willed the diversity of peoples within the unity of the human family. At times, however, the equality of your sons and daughters has not been acknowledged, and Christians have been guilty of attitudes of rejection and exclusion, consenting to acts of discrimination on the basis of racial and eth-

> nic difference. Forgive us and grant us the grace to heal the wounds still present in your community on account of sin, so that we will all feel ourselves to be your sons and daughters.[30]

The prayer evokes the guilt of the members of the church, as well as the desire to heal the wounds of the past errors and to embrace a new spirit of the Christian family where all are truly brothers and sisters. Unfortunately, the progress in this regard has been slow. Many Christians still think and comport themselves along the lines of the racist mentality and stereotypes inherited from the Enlightenment. Western Christians still treat their brethren from the younger churches, especially Black Africans, as mentally, morally, and spiritually inferior, like immature babies that are incapable of contributing effectively to the important discourses of the adults. They seek support in the divergence in the ages of the church in the various parts of the globe.

For example, while people from the younger churches are praised for their ready and undiluted obedience to established authority, they are treated as less capable of living the evangelical counsels of chastity and poverty. A gesture that, for a Westerner, is considered a normal expression of affection is immediately stigmatized as an immoral misdemeanor when it comes from a Black African. Until the shocking outbreak at the turn of this twenty-first century of the scandals of pedophilia and abuse of minors by members of the clergy in some Western countries, many in the West wallowed in the ludicrous conviction that infidelity to the commitments of celibacy and chastity was a thing of the poor and immature Christians from the younger churches, especially in Africa. Many Christians, particularly the religious and members of the clergy, still tend to arrogate to themselves a certain maturity that shields them from or elevates them above the fragility of the ordinary persons.

Often children in the West are exposed only to grotesque depictions of Blacks as depicted in their history books: the slave, relegated to hard work indoors and outdoors, often with nude torso made muscular by the labors, and not infrequently brought to satiate the urges of their masters and mistresses. Such children grow up with the culpably truncated idea of the dark-skinned person as someone limited to physical exertion and given mainly to venereal delectations. When administrative responsibilities in the church are put in the hands of persons imbued with this mindset, they tend to implement policies that exclude or disadvantage people from the younger churches considered incapable of proffering useful initiatives.

It must be affirmed that the church in the West has produced an army of men and women who distinguished themselves in the love of God and their neighbor. Many of them are duly remembered and celebrated in the spiritual readings and liturgical traditions of the church. A special mention should be made of those men and women who, in the prime of their youth, left the comforts of their homes and the company of their peers, and traveled to mission lands to bring to the local populations the gospel of Jesus Christ. Unlike the political, colonial masters and the commercial adventurers, these missionaries had no economic goals. Yet, they were not deterred by the news of strange diseases, the death of their predecessors, and the probability of their own death in the new mission. Moved by the Christian love of neighbor, some of them sacrificed their health and their lives, sometimes soon after their arrival in the mission lands. For Christians of the younger churches, these are their heroes of Western Christianity.

Yet, despite the specific missionary formation they received before leaving their homes, these great men and women were not always clean of the remnants of a certain autoreferential and condescending mindset inherited from the Enlightenment. They presented God, Jesus Christ, the angels, the saints, and all the heavenly beings as white or light-skinned like themselves, while the devil and the evil cohorts were painted Black. This mentality would be subtly imbibed by many of the newly evangelized who, because of their darker skin color would consider themselves inferior. It is disheartening to imagine how pernicious this mindset can become. It engenders prejudice and discrimination not only between persons of different ethnic origins, but also pollutes the minds of persons who share the same parentage, that one feels a complex of superiority over the other for possessing a lighter skin color. Unfortunately, this warped mentality has remained until now and not much is being done to correct it.

Sometimes, Western secular society seems to be more advanced than the church in the West in the efforts to eschew the residue of the racist mentality inherited from the Enlightenment. For example, many exponents of the church in the West tend to remain excessively autoreferential. They see the church as essentially belonging to the West. Consequently, they speak of a crisis in church membership and vocations to the religious life, when the reality is a geographical redistribution of the numbers of churchgoers and vocations. Instead of trying to understand the providential design behind such demographic redistribution and taking advantage of it, they abolish pastoral structures and policies that have served the church for centuries and try to invent new ones of questionable efficacy.

In Western secular society, when businesses lack the necessary human resources to remain alive and productive, they seek and import the labor force from that part of the world where it is available, give it the necessary training and adjustment, and integrate it accordingly. On the contrary, the autoreferential church in the West prefers to shut down its parishes or lump them together under a few pastors. Little or no consideration is given to the option of turning, in an organized way, to those young churches that are currently reaping abundantly the fruits of the sweat and sacrifices of the Western missionaries. Agreements could be reached with these younger churches, which have seminaries and convents teeming with vocations, from where the necessary pastoral workforce could be obtained. As in the secular business world, those involved would be given the necessary formation and orientation before incorporating them into the pastoral plan of the churches in the West. This approach was adopted in the formation of the missionaries who left for the developing world, when the West had the vocational and churchgoers' demography in its favor. Moreover, if it has been used with success in secular economic affairs, why won't it work for the church? There is no doubt that the missionaries, who spent their lives to sow the seed of the gospel in the mission lands, would feel honored when the fruit of their sacrifice is employed in the spirit of authentic ecclesial communion to supply for the temporary pastoral shortfalls in the West until the tides turn again.

More could be said. When God wishes to oblige a person to discover a passage hole in the wall, God gradually closes all other doors and windows. What if the fall in the quantity of vocations in the West is how God wishes to oblige the churches in these countries to open, accept, and pastorally integrate their brethren from the younger flourishing churches as full members of the same family?

MY AFRICA

Racial discrimination against Black Africans, persons of African descent, and Blacks in general has been the most widespread and devastating. It is found even among groups who themselves have been the objects of racial persecutions. A case in point may be the difficult integration of the Jewish Black Falasha population among other Jews in the State of Israel.

For centuries, Black Africa served as slave mines in which Arab and European merchants, with the complicity of some Africans themselves, scavenged for the human merchandise they delivered to waiting slave owners. On the one hand, racial ideologies, which accorded Blacks less human dignity than their Western or Arab counterparts, provided the justification that these merchants needed for their trade in Black Africans. On the other hand, at the same time, the slave trade bolstered the racist mentalities of the slave dealers and their clients. The effects of this situation have been devastating. The abolition of the slave trade and slavery, with the consequent emancipation of former slaves in various parts of the world, began an important healing process. However, much still needs to be done to untie the centuries-old knots of the racial construct.

Centuries of subjugation to treatments emanating from the racist mindset created in many Blacks a certain slave mentality, shattered their self-esteem, and replaced it with an inferiority complex. Many Blacks unconsciously came to consider and treat themselves and those like them as inferior to other lighter-skinned persons. The slave masters propagated the idea that the Blacks were only physical muscles and no brains, incapable of challenging speculative research and scientific knowledge, as well as inadequate for sporting activities involving high strategic and mental calculations. This idea was so widespread that in 1993, the daughter of a European diplomat in Cote d'Ivoire reiterated it and challenged me to cite one thing that had been invented by Blacks for the good of humanity. I could only refer the young lady to some types of music. My ignorance was no better than hers.

Yet, that humiliating challenge enticed my curiosity and led me to the surprising discovery of various outstanding inventions and contributions made by Blacks that have been absent from the common history books but are now available on the internet. I came to read of Otis Boykin, who invented electrical resistors used in computing, missile guidance, and pacemakers (patented in 1959); of Alexander Miles, inventor of the automatic elevator doors (1887); of Frederick McKinley Jones, father of the roof-mounted refrigeration system for long-haul trucks and railroad cars (1940); Lewis Latimer, who discovered the carbon light bulb filament (1881), to mention just a few. The list of things invented by Blacks is amazingly long and includes many essential things that have affected the quality of our daily lives, like the clothes dryer (in 1892 by George T. Sampson), the automatic gear shift in motorcars (in 1932 by Richard Spikes), and the three-light traffic system (in 1922 by Garrett Morgan). As recently as 1986, Patricia Bath invented a laser cataract treatment device called a Laserphaco Probe. Most recently still, in 2022, Dr. Philip Emeagwali was acclaimed for having invented the world's fastest computer.[31]

Regarding sports, when the German Nazis were singing their superiority over everyone, a Black man, Jesse Owens, soared above them to win four gold medals in track and field events (100m, 200m, 4x100m, and long jump) at the 1936 Summer Olympics held in Berlin. He would be followed by a long queue of Black Africans and people of African descent who, these past decades, would dominate professional and amateur athletic track and field events. Again, when tennis was regarded as a white man's game, the African American Arthur Robert Ashe Jr., went on to win three Grand Slam singles tennis titles, namely, the Australian Open, the U.S. Open, and Wimbledon. If anything was still left of that myth regarding tennis, the Williams sisters (Venus and Serena), with their prowess in the game, have surely put an end to it. In the same vein, who would have imagined that in all-around gymnastics, hitherto dominated by Caucasians, a Black, Joe Fraser, would emerge as the gold winner at the 2022 European Championships, becoming the first British citizen to achieve that feat? Similarly, in response to those who think that mountaineering is beyond the reach of Blacks, on May 12, 2022, a group of seven African Americans called Full Circle led by Phil Henderson reached the summit of Mount Everest in the Himalayas, consolidating the history made in 1953 by Tensing Norgay and Sir Edmund Hillary.[32] Finally, when all these events are taken together with the inclusion of Mae Jemison as a member of the Endeavour space shuttle crew in 1992, it becomes evident that not even outer space is beyond the reach of Blacks. What Black Africans and Blacks in general need is an equitable opportunity, accompanied by the necessary enabling environment, to measure up to others and even excel in different domains of life.

All this reveals the emptiness and falsity of the supremacist fiction on which racial discrimination, especially against Black Africans and people of African descent, is based. Yet, it is painfully embarrassing that, while this racist mindset and the related practices are being condemned, and many Westerners are making efforts to eschew them, they have found a home as an unholy heritage among some Black Africans and people of African descent. While slavery and the slave trade have been abolished in the West, they have continued to be practiced in various forms among Black Africans. In the same vein, some Black Africans and people of African descent continue to treat their brothers and sisters in condescending manners that are redolent of the racism practiced against them by Westerners. Many Black Africans and persons of African descent tend to show greater trust, esteem, and preference to Westerners over their fellow Blacks who sometimes may even be more qualified or competent in a particular thing.

Racism is always loathsome since it denigrates the intrinsic God-given dignity of the human person, but when it metamorphoses into arrogant prejudice and discrimination between persons of the same color, origins, culture, and language, it is nothing but arrant madness. Unfortunately, this type of mentality is still rampant among Black Africans, despite their cries against the racism they suffer at the hands of Westerners. It is the phenomenon of the vicious victim.

Some people blame this intra-African "racism" on religion. Yet, it would be sheer madness for Black Africans to despise or kill one another because of their religious leanings. The two religions currently followed by most Black Africans are Christianity and Islam. Neither of them was born in Africa. They were both imported to the continent. Both preach peace and fraternal love, and both share in similar criticisms. Christianity was brought to Black Africa by Christian missionaries who came with the colonizers. Islam was introduced into the continent and spread in it principally through violent wars of conquest. Christianity was preached by missionaries from the same West that spread the racist ideologies of the

Enlightenment and supported slavery and the slave trade. Islam was brought by the same Arabs who foraged Black Africa for centuries for human merchandise to be sold to slaveowners in the Arab world and beyond. Incidentally, while slavery and the slave trade have been officially abolished in the West and no Christian denomination currently gives official support to them, some Muslim communities, like the Salafi, continue to support slavery and the slave trade officially.[33] So, when some people argue that Islam is more suited to Black Africans than Christianity, one wonders how they come to their conclusion. Unfortunately, Muslims forbid having any image of the Prophet Muhammed. That makes it impossible to determine how close he was to Black Africans in his physical appearance. Similarly, we do not also know the true skin color of Jesus, as a Jew from the Middle East. We only know that when as a child his life was threatened, his parents fled with him to Africa (cf. Matt 2:13–15). Was it, maybe, easier for him to mix there with other children to escape quick identification? We will never know. What is certain is that Jesus and Christianity are closer to Africa than many would like Africans to acknowledge. Africans are very religious. So, the fight against racism in Africa cannot be done without religion, as a source of peace and fraternal love. Any version of the religions born outside or within Africa that comes to preach and spread intolerance between Africans should be ostracized from the continent.

CONFRONTING THE BEAST

In his 1941 satirical allegory on the rise to power of Adolf Hitler and the establishment of the National Socialist State in Germany, Bertolt Brecht warned against the constant threat of a resurgence of racism: "Although the world stood up and stopped the bastard, the *Kroch* [bitch or beast] that bore him is in heat again."[34] Following his cue, I have, elsewhere, presented racism, ethnocentric and related prejudice and discrimination with the same imagery of a beast that "attacks and invades its victims with the subtleness of a worm or virus and manifests itself with the rage of a lion."[35] It is a beast that must be confronted with sustained will and decision.

It has rightly been observed,

> If, in fact, race defines a human group in terms of immutable and hereditary physical traits, racist prejudice, which dictates racist behaviour, can be applied by extension, with equally negative effects, to all persons whose ethnic origin, language, religion or customs make them appear different.[36]

In this regard, the African or Afro-descendant who discriminates against another based on the person's ethnic origin, religion, or other perceived differences is no better than the worst white supremacist or racist from the Western world. The racist and the perpetrators of ethnic or related forms of discrimination are moved by the same mindset and the inability to accept or manage differences, as well as the resultant superiority or inferiority complex, and the concomitant fear of the different. Fighting racism, therefore, should involve a sincere introspection on the part of those who decry it. Otherwise, many people will continue to live in denial while pointing fingers at others.

Since racism and other forms of discrimination are primarily products of a mindset, combatting them should, above all, be focused on the education of the mind. It is on this basis that other measures, like legislation and affirmative action, are to be built. The aim should be to remove culpable ignorance and fear in the face of diversities, to dismantle all supremacist myths, and to teach the common humanity and dignity of all human beings. As countries and communities introduce laws and concrete actions against racism and discrimination, they need to accompany them with due formation in families and communities, in law enforcement agencies, the police, immigration offices, and security forces.

The family is the first place of emphasis where children should be taught to appreciate the beauty of differences and to overcome the temptation to fear or despise the other who is perceived as different. This formation in the family is to be strengthened by the adoption of balanced academic curricula in centers of formal education. Students should be exposed to the contributions of people of different backgrounds, skin colors, and cultures to scientific and human advancement, the common good, and well-being. In this, sincere efforts are to be made to make equitable opportunity and environment available to all students in society.

It happens that some persons lose the excellent training they received in their families and schools when they are exposed to bad habits and ideologies as they try to embrace certain professions or public offices. Such habits and ideologies sometimes circulate among the ranks of members of the law enforcement agencies and security forces. Aware of the enormous powers entrusted to them and the protection accorded them to enable them to carry out their duties effectively, these public officers, who must constantly deal with strangers and those considered different, are the most tempted to exhibit racist and xenophobic misbehaviors in their job. Their training, therefore, should be made to integrate a strong human rights dimension, underlining the equal dignity of all human beings and the elimination of every presumption of impunity.

The church plays a central role in forming the mind. It is a custodian of culture, arts, and moral formation. As already noted, the church has done a great deal to fight racism and related forms of discrimination, but it needs to do more. It is not the fault of the West that it preached a Christianity with a "white face." After various centuries of its reception and existence in the West, it was normal for the good news to assume a certain Western countenance or tinge. Efforts have been made to mitigate that situation, especially with the emphasis which the Second Vatican Council placed on the inculturation of the gospel. Unfortunately, there remains a lot of diffidence in the face of initiatives that might moderate or diversify the colors in the church. For example, it is still very uncommon to find churches in the West with representation of dark-skinned saints. Many in the West still unconsciously consider sainthood a prerogative of Westerners. Only a rare and lucky few from the mission lands, especially if they are dark-skinned, may be admitted into the "club." The faces of Jesus, Mary, the apostles, and the major saints must be kept white, they think. More needs to be done to change this mindset. Decisive steps should be taken to enlarge the repertoire of ecclesiastical artistic representations to include the few recognized saints from the mission lands, especially those with a dark skin color. Church initiatives should clearly reflect that the Black is not regarded as inferior, and that quality, worth, and competence do not depend on a person's origin or skin color.

The Bible offers an important tool in this regard. While the Christian Holy Book shows that, already in the biblical times, there existed persons with a racist mentality, it also indicates how clearly God abhors racial discrimination. An instance is found in Numbers 12, where Miriam and Aaron criticized Moses for taking a dark-skinned wife:

> Miriam and Aaron spoke against Moses because of the Cushite woman whom he had married (for he had married a Cushite woman); and they said, "Has the LORD indeed spoken only through Moses? Has he not spoken through us also?" (Num 12:1–2)

It is not necessary, here, to go into the debate regarding the correct translation of the Hebrew word *Kûshîy*, which some scholars give as "foreign" while others simply transliterate it as "Cushite." The application of the word *Kûsh* to the foreigner does not change the thrust of this argument. In the Bible, the stranger usually depicts the person who is different, and who alongside widows, orphans, and the poor, is typically in need of help (cf. Deut 24:17–21; Jer 7:6; Zech 7:10).

However, the Greek Bible, the Septuagint, translates the Hebrew feminine word *Kûshîy* with *Aithiopissēs* (Ethiopian), composed of *aithein* (to burn or scorch) and *ōps* (face or eye), with the likely meaning of "burnt look" or "scorched face," in other words, "dark-skinned." Evidence of a skin-color connotation for the word *Ethiopian* is found in the Bible itself. The prophet Jeremiah seems to have this in mind when he asks, "Can the Ethiopians change their skin or leopards their spots?" (Jer 13:23). Moreover, the reaction of God to the criticism of Miriam and Aaron suggests that the skin color of the wife of Moses was the issue at stake. The text indicates that "the anger of the LORD was kindled against them [Miriam and Aaron]" and Miriam became "leprous, as white as snow" (Num 12:9–10). It was as though God wished to tell Miriam, "You mock the dark skin, now have your white skin!" Moses had to intercede with God for the restoration of her skin.

The church should be courageous enough to follow the example of God by showing zero tolerance toward racial, ethnic, or related forms of prejudice and discrimination, especially among its members. The manifestation of a racist mentality or comportment should be clearly added to the conditions that would impede the beatification or canonization of Christians. No one who denigrates the image of God in their fellow human being, through racist thinking and actions, should be elevated to the altar as an example and guide for other Christians to follow. Such a clear stance will be an excellent witness to the fruit of the sacrifice of Jesus Christ, which St. Paul succinctly states in his Letter to the Ephesians:

> But now in Christ Jesus you who once were far off have been brought near by the blood of Christ. For he is our peace; in his flesh he has made both groups into one and has broken down the dividing wall, that is, the hostility... that he might create in himself one new humanity in place of the two, thus making peace, and might reconcile both groups to God in one body through the cross, thus putting to death that hostility....So then you are no longer strangers and aliens, but you are citizens with the saints and also members of the household of God. (Eph 2:13–16, 19)

8

DECONSTRUCTING RACIALISM

The Ethno-racial Language of 1 Peter 2:9–10

Paulin Poucouta

> *You, on the other hand, are the chosen race. But you are a chosen race, a royal priesthood, a holy nation, a people for acquisition so that you will go and announce the wonderful actions from him who from darkness has called you toward its amazing light. You, once, were not a people, now instead you are the people of God.*
>
> 1 Peter 2:9–10; *au. trans.*

These two verses of the First Letter of Peter have attracted attention because of the controversies they have aroused about the priesthood. Indeed, in the sixteenth century, relying on this passage, Luther denied the existence of a special sacrament of holy orders; all Christians because of their baptism are priests.[1] The Constitution *Lumen Gentium* builds on this text to emphasize the importance of the ecclesial responsibility of every faithful (*LG* 34–35). The synod on the mission of the laity referred to it to recall that the laity participate in the threefold mission of Christ: priest, king, and prophet.[2]

Today, we are rather sensitive to the sociopolitical context of the recipients of the letter, to the discrimination of which they had been victims. In this perspective, should not attention be paid to the ethno-racial language of the author of these verses?[3] What ecclesiology do these verses propose? What impact does it make in the fight against racism?

To answer these questions, we will first address the question of exclusion and identity in the context and organization of the passage, before dissecting the ethno-racial language used to indicate the church as a race of God's children. After all, are Christians not called to contribute to the deconstruction of any racialist ideology?

FROM EXCLUSION TO ELECTION

A Community of the Excluded

In the absence of the photograph of the author of the First Letter of Peter, we must, with almost all critics, be satisfied with a robotic portrait—that of an anonymous author, witness of the Petrine school, and influenced by the figure of the Apostle Peter, especially after his death.[4]

According to the opening verse (v. 1), the letter is addressed to Christians of multiple ethnic, cultural, and religious backgrounds. In addition, they are scattered in the immense territories of Asia Minor, mainly in five of its provinces: Pontus, Galatia, Asia, Cappadocia, and Bithynia. They are familiar with the Scriptures, which they read in the Greek translation of the Septuagint.

These Christians, most of whom come from modest communities, are asking themselves the question of their identity. Like the Jews in Babylon once, they live in the diaspora.[5] They are even more vulnerable because their socioeconomic situation is fragile. Many of them are slaves or housekeepers.

The First Letter of Peter is the first writing of the New Testament to address *in extenso* the problem of the relations of Christians with non-Christians, the other writings only alluding to it. In this sense, even if the clues in the letter are not numerous enough to deal exhaustively with the problem, several testimonies show that the Christians of Asia Minor lived in a painful situation. We can think of a beginning of hostility that hardened into persecutions, either of Nero (64–67) or Domitian (81–96). The epistle speaks of a fire: "Beloved, do not consider strange the fire that rages in your midst to test you" (1 Peter 4:12). But is this not a metaphor to designate the daily hostile environment that manifested itself in calumnies, suspicions, accusations, and threats of condemnation? The letter insists on the verbal aggressions that seem to be the daily lot of Christians. In the world of Asia Minor, this harassment is more important than in Rome. In the provinces, political or administrative officials are tempted to be more zealous than their colleagues in the capital. They seek promotions!

Moreover, in Asia Minor, the various cities enjoyed a certain autonomy in the management of their affairs. Unfortunately, this freedom is sometimes the occasion for many intrigues. Associations in the name of religion formed sociopolitical pressure groups and disrupted the life of the city. Some, knowingly or unknowingly, equate Christian communities with these groups. This is why the author asks Christians to distance themselves clearly from such groups so as to avoid confusion and provocation: "Let none of you suffer as a murderer, or a thief or evildoer, or as an informer" (1 Peter 4:15).

Finally, in the name of their faith, Christians refused to participate in many activities that were part of social life, such as festivals linked to sacrifices and orgies. Thus, their life choices called into question and condemned prevailing pagan practices. This attitude and conduct cost the Christians dearly. But Christians had to endure it: "You have already spent enough time in doing what the Gentiles like to do, living in debauchery, passions, drunkenness, orgies, carousing, and illicit worship of idols. In this regard, they find it strange that you no longer join them in the same excesses of dissipation, and so they blaspheme" (1 Peter 4:3–4).

The Status of Christians

This marginalization of Christians undermined their identity. They felt alienated, as expressed by the two terms: *paroikoi* and *parepidēmoi*. Etymologically, the first word means "far from home" and designates a resident foreigner; the second word translates as "transient, nonresident." Furthermore, Christians of Jewish origin gradually distanced themselves from Judaism, especially after the Jewish War of AD 70 and the Jamnia Congress that had excommunicated them. Those of "pagan" origin also distanced themselves from traditional religions. Gradually, all Christians were considered as "misanthropes," an entirely separate species, or better still, a non-race. In the words of Marie-Louise Lamau, "Christians were really a threatened species"[6] in their physical integrity and in their identity.

This question of identity emerges in the organization of the letter. It is essentially built on baptismal theology and catechesis. In those critical moments, it was important to remind Christians of the foundations of their identity. Baptized, they are now of the *race of God's children*.

In other words, the author does not resort to a doctrinal exposition, in the manner of Paul, but to a series of homiletic exhortations. It is there that we understand the structure of the letter. Indeed, the letter gives the impression of being disjointed. We move from one exhortation to another. For this reason, commentators believe that the text is composed of a series of small, isolated thematic units.

However, we have literary and thematic clues of a rather rigorous structuring. First, let's consider 1 Peter 2:10–11. Verse 11 begins with a solemn and classical introductory expression: *Agapētoi parakalō*. For their part, 1 Peter 1:3 and 1 Peter 2:10 form an inclusion using the nominal and verbal forms of the term: ἔλεος (*eleos*). In 1 Peter 4:11, the doxological formula εἰς τοὺς αἰῶνας τῶν αἰώνων, ἀμήν ("To him belongs the glory and the power forever and ever. Amen") indicates the end of a section. In 1 Peter 4:12, the interpellation *Agapētoi* (Ἀγαπητοί) announces the beginning of another section, which also closes with the solemn doxology: αὐτῷ τὸ κράτος εἰς τοὺς αἰῶνας, ἀμήν ("To him be the power forever and ever. Amen"; 1 Pet 5:11).

These formal elements are expressed, however, in different structures, according to different commentators. For our purposes, we see the letter organized in a tripartite structure. Accordingly, beside the opening verses (1:1–2), and the conclusion—the final greetings and benediction (5:12–14)—the letter is divided into three parts that reveal the status of Christians and its requirements:

- the race of the elect (1:3—2:10)
- the race of the elect in a pagan environment (2:11—4:11)
- the race of the elect amid trials (4:12—5:11)

Election in Jesus

The election (call) of Christians is anchored in that of Jesus. This is underlined in our text (1 Pet 1:3—2:10), which is developed in three stages. Christians are called to holiness (1 Pet 1:13–25). They are rooted in Christ, the living stone (1 Pet 2:1–8); and they are members of the chosen race (1 Pet 2:9–10). This is the first part of the presentation of the identity and the lot of the Christian, and it is the heart of the question of identity that Christians who have the status of the *elect of God*[7] ask themselves. This is confirmed by John Elliot, who notes the parallelism between verse 1:3, on the one hand, and verses 2:9–10, on the other hand; the mention of Christ as the chosen one underlies the glorious status of Christians as a *chosen race.*[8]

Many authors intrinsically relate verses 9–10 to the subset 1 Peter 2:1–10. It is true that the conjunction δὲ (Ὑμεῖς **δὲ** γένος ἐκλεκτόν) can simply indicate a progression and translate as "but." However, here we have strong opposition. With good reason, some commentators translate the word δὲ, as an adverbial phrase "on the other hand." It is no longer a question of Christ, but of the identity of the church that is expressed by the expression ὑμεῖς δὲ that opens our passage. This formula also shows that the author speaks directly to Christians who are challenged by daily experiences of life that question their status as *the elect of God.*

Apart from the minor variant at the end of verse 9, indicated by the *Novum Testamentum: Graece et Latine,*[9] which Metzger does not consider useful, the verse has no textual problem. On the semantic level and to express his ecclesiology, the author refers to his audience with four predicates that are interconnected like a chain—*γένος, ἔθνος, ἱεράτευμα, λαὸς* (race, nation, priesthood, people)—and they occur three times throughout the letter. Three of the predicates are qualified by adjectives: γένος *ἐκλεκτόν* (a chosen race), ἔθνος *ἅγιον* (a holy nation), *βασίλειον* ἱεράτευμα (a royal priesthood), and one, λαὸς, is qualified by a prepositional phrase, *εἰς περιποίησιν* (a people for [his] possession).

Here, as in all the verses of 1 Peter 2:4–10, the author's argument finds its source in the experience of Israel, but he uses these literary words in an original way. Thus, apart from 1 Peter 1:2, 9–10, there is no association of the four nouns or their joint application to Israel in the Old Testament.[10]

THE CHURCH IN ETHNO-RACIAL TERMS

A Chosen Race

In the Old Testament, the term γένος evokes generality, species (cf. Gen 1:11—12:21) or tribes (cf. Lev 20:17–18). But, often and especially from the second century BC, γένος referred to the people of Israel, especially in times of persecution (cf. Exod 1:9; Isa 22:4).[11] The term then expresses the prerogative of Israel as God's chosen people (cf. Ps 14:5; Ezra 9:2).[12]

In the New Testament, γένος designates gender, family, kinship, species. It is a set of created beings with a common origin: the race of gods, men, animals, and things. The term appears twenty times in the New Testament. On fourteen occasions, it refers to people groups, as a religious category, as is the case in 1 Peter 2:9.

The adjective ἐκλεκτόν (chosen, elect) accompanies the whole history of the people of the Bible in their very special relationship with their God. Abraham's adventure begins with a calling, a choice (cf. Gen 12:1–2). The history of Israel is one of God's free choice:

> It was not because you were more numerous than any other people that the LORD set his heart on you and chose you, for you were the fewest of all peoples. It was because the LORD loved you and kept the oath that he swore to your ancestors, that the LORD has brought you out with a mighty hand, and redeemed you from the house of slavery, from the hand of Pharaoh king of Egypt. (Deut 7:7–8)

In the New Testament, the adventure of the apostles begins with their choice by Jesus, who calls them. Moreover, in the priestly prayer, Jesus will say to them, "You did not choose me but I chose you" (John 15:16). Thus, Christians enter the adventure of the Father's love that started at the beginning of time. Yet, the election is not a privilege, but a gift. Being part of the chosen race does not entitle one to any privileges. On the contrary, it is a very demanding mission.

A Holy Nation

In contrast to γένος, the word ἔθνος designates non-Israelites in contradistinction to Israelites: the nations, the Gentiles. Thus, in the Greek text of Exodus 1:9, we read, εἶπεν δὲ τῷ **ἔθνει** αὐτοῦ Ἰδοὺ **τὸ γένος** τῶν υἱῶν Ισραηλ (Pharaoh spoke to his *nation* about *the race* of the sons of Israel). Nevertheless, in later writings, ἔθνος is also used for Israel. In the New Testament, the word is used 162 times, very often in the sense of pagan nations, distinct from the Jews. It is only in Matthew 21:43 and 1 Peter 2:9 that it designates Christians, thus marking an evolution in the perception, language, and reality of Christian identity.

The noun ἔθνος is accompanied and qualified by the adjective ἅγιον. In the Old Testament, God is said to be the Holy One par excellence, separated from us, perfect, and making us share in his perfection. This is why Israel is called "holy." By his election, Israel is a people taken from among the nations and set apart. It must bear witness to God's holiness: "You shall be holy, for I the Lord your God am holy" (Lev 19:2).

Mostly from pagan origins, Christians now form a nation that no longer lives in ignorance, which is a feature or a characteristic of paganism in the Scriptures: "Like obedient children, do not be conformed to the desires that you formerly had in ignorance" (1 Pet 1:14). Further, the author insists, "You know that you were ransomed from the futile ways inherited from your ancestors, not with perishable things like silver or gold" (1 Pet 1:18).

A Royal Priestly Community

The word ἱεράτευμα can be translated as priesthood or the exercise of the priesthood. This unusual formula has a collective meaning and designates a priestly community. In the Old Testament, Israel is called a "*priestly kingdom*" (Exod 19:6). The Sinai covenant makes it a *priestly nation*. The exercise of the priesthood is part of the exodus. Israel is freed from slavery to become a *priestly people*. Certainly, at the beginning, the priestly function was exercised by the heads of families or kings. But gradually, it was limited to members of the tribe of Levi, descendants of Aaron (Num 3:5–7; 18:6ff.). The priest receives his priesthood by heredity. He is the guarantor of the religious institution and traditions. He represents the religious community.

Moreover, in worship, the people celebrate the covenant concluded between God and the whole of Israel. This presence of God is a gift freely given that invites the people to faithfulness. The priest serves the faithfulness that the people must live before God. He is also the man of sacrifices that signify the gift that Israel (the believer) is to God. The priest identifies with his offering and gives himself to his Creator. He acknowledges and accepts God's claim on him. As an intermediary between God and his people, the priest is the minister of God's presence among his people and leads the people in the celebration of the covenant.

The adjective βασίλειον that qualifies ἱεράτευμα means *royal*, the *dignity* linked to the royal palace and to royal functions. In the Book of Exodus, the noun *basileia* designates either royal dignity or the exercise of a royal function. Used of a people, as in this case, it emphasizes its dignity, as Rabbi Eliezer ben Yose of Galilee suggests: "Every Israelite will have as many sons as those who came out of Egypt (Ps 45:16–17)...true kings and true priests." Emerging from slavery in Egypt, Israel acquired a royal dignity. The term will apply to Christians by reason of their sharing in the kingship of Christ.

By contrast, then, with the empire of the Caesars that was built on pride, violence, and loose morals, an image that the author of First Peter may have had in mind, Christians are presented as forming or constituting a spiritual kingdom rather than a political one. All become a people with dignity, as children of God. Their precarious situation within the empire should not lead them to despise themselves. Jesus gathers the baptized from among the nations where they are scattered and where they suffer vexations.

Like Israel, Christians play a priestly and liturgical function,[13] but it takes the form of the spiritual sacrifices that Paul speaks of in Romans 12:1–2. This is the priestly service that baptism inaugurates and that is accomplished by the offering of life. Christians belong to the kingship of Jesus, the priest, whose priesthood is summed up in the gift of himself. Christians are a *race* and a *nation* of witnesses, founded on service and love. Thus, the priesthood of Christians is a responsibility to transform the daily events of history with the witness of their lives.

A People of His Acquisition/Possession

Finally, in the Old Testament, *λαός* is the most common word used for Israel. This rare term in *koine* can mean a *crowd*, a *multitude*, or a *community*. In its noblest sense, *λαός* designates an *elite* (group). This term, then, expresses the religious honor of Israel. It emphasizes the special attachment of the sons of Abraham to their God.

In the New Testament, *λαός* (*laos*) is used extensively, especially in the corpus of Luke–Acts, to refer to the people of Israel. From there, *laos* was taken over by the church to apply to itself as the special people of God, as the assembly of those who believe in Christ.

In our passage (1Pet 2:9–10), the term λαός comes up three times: all at the end of the chain of the four predicates, like a summary; and to express the significance of the threefold use of the term (*laos*), the author uses a very strong double opposition:

> between ποτε [in times past, formerly] and νῦν δὲ [now on the other hand], and
>
> between οὐ λαός [not people, nonexistence] and λαὸς θεοῦ [people of God].

Those who were considered nothing are now God's special people; and this is precisely the sense that the qualification of λαός by the prepositional phrase (εἰς *περιποίησιν*) conveys. Derived from the language of commerce, *περιποίησις* can mean *acquisition, possession, property*, but also *salvation*, wherefore the prepositional phrase, εἰς *περιποίησιν*, may be translated as *for the purpose of acquisition/through acquisition, for one's property, for possession*, but also *for salvation*. In the latter sense, εἰς *περιποίησιν* may have an eschatological connotation, as in 2 Thessalonians 2:14; Hebrews 10:38; and 1 Peter 2:9 may well have a soteriological scope.[14]

The context and thrust of the First Letter of Peter, however, highlight more the ecclesiological scope of the appellatives of the early Christians under study. The expression γένος ἐκλεκτόν, corresponds with λαὸς εἰς *περιποίησιν*, and they reinforce each other. Both expressions emphasize the exclusive belongingness of the people to their God, as Clement of Alexandria also believes.[15] The verbal root *περιποιέω* expresses exclusivity and means "to acquire/gain/own something for oneself." It expresses that which "belongs only to someone." The phrase εἰς *περιποίησιν* emphasizes God's special relationship to his people, who are especially his—his exclusive good or possession.

The author is inspired here by the books of Exodus and Deutero-Isaiah. Liberated from Egypt, Israel realizes that it is a people apart and distinct from all others. God has consecrated it to himself and has made it his own possession: "Now therefore, if you obey my voice and keep my covenant, you shall be my treasured possession out of all the peoples. Indeed, the whole earth is mine" (Exod 19:5).

In the same way, God reminds Israel, sorely tested by the painful experience of the exile, that it could not disappear. Israel must recall its history. If God had not made it a people, it would have remained a collection/juxtaposition of tribes. If it now stands tall before the powerful nations that surrounded it, it is because the Lord formed it: "For I give water in the wilderness, rivers in the desert, to give drink to my chosen people, the people whom I formed for myself so that they might declare my praise" (Isa 43:20b–21).

In this sense, Christians are formed in the adventure of the Father's love from the beginning of time. They have become a *race*, a *nation*, a *priestly community*, a *people born of God's mercy and tenderness* (v. 10). "Once you were not a people, but now you are God's people; once you had not received mercy, but now you have received mercy" (1 Pet 2:10).

THE *RACE* OF GOD'S CHILDREN

Another *Race* in Jesus

It is through the painful experience of suffering and oppression that Israel is called to be God's γένος; it is through this experience of suffering that γένος takes on its full meaning. Accordingly, the early Christians—"the exiles of the Dispersion in Pontus, Galatia, Cappadocia, Asia, and Bithynia" (1 Pet 1:1–2)—are called γένος ἐκλεκτόν amid their experience of mistreatment and abuse as *paroikoi* and *parepidēmoi*. They were stigmatized as a community by outsiders (non-Christians). Thus, using the ethno-racial language of identity inherited from the Jewish experience, the author of the First Letter of Peter seeks to help his community of Christians to develop and to be filled with a positive sense of ecclesial identity. Despite their deplorable socioeconomic and political situation, namely, without recognition and nonexistent to the authorities, and amid a society that denied them any status and respect, the early Christians, "the exiles of the Dispersion," were encouraged not to live with their heads bowed.[16]

First Peter uses the strategy of "social creativity." It urges the community not to be integrated in the negative and reprehensible conduct of the *outsiders* (non-Christians). On the contrary, the community must have the posture of mind and the assurance of those who bear the status of a "chosen race"; for they have been brought out of the shadows into the light (cf. 1 Pet 2:9). The presentation of Christians as having emerged out of darkness into light derives from a popular imagery in the Scriptures of the opposition between *light* and *darkness*. In Proto-Isaiah (Isa 8:22—9:1ff.), for example, the prophet likens the defeat of Israel by the Assyrians on account of their sins (2 Kgs 15:29), as "the Lord, who is hiding his face from the house of Jacob" (Isa 8:17). The consequent experience of misery, destitution, and anguish, and the temptation to consult ghosts and spirits is likened to a *people* who "will see only distress and darkness, the gloom of anguish; and they will be thrust into thick darkness" (Isa 8:22). The subsequent experience of God's salvation is likened to the people who "have seen a great light" (Isa 9:1ff.) and are walking in light. Jesus referred to this passage in his ministry, applying the opposition between *light* and *darkness* to how people responded to his call to conversion (cf. Matt 4:15–16). Being "called you out of darkness into his marvelous light" was a designation of the early Christians whose sense was both soteriological and ecclesiological: the resident aliens of the diaspora were a people who were saved and made members of the Church, truly, a γένος ἐκλεκτόν.

In 1 Peter 2:9, therefore, the early Christians are presented in terms that express both the sociohistorical context of their call and their vocation to new ethical standards of living. Through their conversion, Christians come out of the darkness of their old conduct into the light of new life. To bear witness to this, Christians must come out of the *shadows* and assume the courage of visibility: hence the exhortation: "Always be ready to make your defense to anyone who demands from you an accounting for the hope that is in you; yet do it with gentleness and respect" (1 Pet 3:15–16).

These Christians and members of the church of First Peter are presented variously as a *race*, a *nation*, a *priestly community* as well as a *people*. These terms and notions are not quite synonymous with the Jewish experience. *Race* and *nation* mean different things; but in First Peter, the two realities are now the same.

The church is the *race* initiated by Jesus, the living stone. While in the Book of Exodus, the people of Israel could not draw close to the rock of Mount Sinai, apart from Moses (cf. Exod 19:21), Christ is the new rock, the cornerstone to which Christians can approach without fear, and in whom their priestly vocation is rooted: "Come to him, a living stone, rejected by mortals yet chosen and precious in God's sight" (1 Pet 2:4). It is he, the stone rejected by the builders, who has become the cornerstone, the one that holds the entire edifice together. He is the "firstborn within a large family" (Rom 8:29).[17] He inaugurates the new *race* where people gather "from every tribe and language and people and nation; you have made them to be a kingdom and priests serving our God" (Rev 5:9–10).

For the author of Hebrews, Jesus is the founder of a *race* from which slavery is banished (cf. Heb 2:5–16). He is the path of true liberation.[18] *Race* is therefore no longer a place of division or oppression, but a space of existence and communion.

Γένος among the Fathers

The First Letter of Peter is at the "crossroads of New Testament theologies," in the words of Albert Vanhoye.[19] However, it did not attract the attention of the church fathers. We have only traces of it in the writings of Clement of Rome, Polycarp, the Shepherd of Hermas, and Justin. The *Muratorian Canon* does not mention it.[20]

Regarding our passage, we find in Clement of Rome a reference concerning the call to pass "*from darkness to light, from ignorance to the full knowledge of his glorious name*" (cf. 1 Pet 2:10; 1 Cl 59:2). This reference does not prove a direct literary and theological relationship but draws attention to the theme of knowledge, so important in the Greek world; and it was to affirm that true knowledge is in Jesus.

The perspective of Clement of Rome is rather ethical and parenetic, with this inclusive call in the first person plural ἡμεῖς (we) instead of the second person ὑμεῖς (you). Clement insists on conversion which, as in Hellenistic Judaism, is a call to pass *"from darkness to light, from error to truth, from death to life."*[21]

The first explicit testimonies of the reception of First Peter appear at the end of the second century in the writings of Irenaeus of Lyon and Clement of Alexandria. Thus, Irenaeus inserts 1 Peter 2:9 in a chain of quotations that show that the apostles invited the pagans to renounce the idols and practices of the past (*Adv Haer* III, 5, 3), to be integrated in the *race* of "sanctified people." Later, Irenaeus refers to 1 Peter 2:10 to draw attention to the theme of divine mercy: *"It is not of pneumatic men that he speaks, but of man, who, after disobeying God and being rejected from immortality, then obtained mercy through the Son of God"* (*Adv Haer* III, 20, 2).

Clement of Alexandria repeatedly quotes the two verses of 1 Peter 2:9–10. Thus, in the *Protreptic* or *Teaching to the Greeks,* he quotes them almost verbatim:

> ὑμεῖς δὲ γένος ἐκλεκτόν, βασίλειον ἱεράτευμα, ἔθνος ἅγιον, λαὸς εἰς *περιποίησιν*, ὅπως τὰς *ἀρετὰς* ἐξαγγείλητε τοῦ ἐκ σκότους ὑμᾶς καλέσαντος εἰς τὸ θαυμαστὸν αὐτοῦ φῶς. οἵ ποτε οὐ λαός, νῦν δὲ λαὸς θεοῦ, οἱ *οὐκ* ἠλεημένοι, νῦν δὲ ἐλεηθέντες.[22]

Clement combines the two verses for his purpose. Indeed, faced with traditional cults and Greek philosophy, he must take a position as a convinced Christian, but as one also very knowledgeable of Hellenism. In his use of the source text, he extends the sense to apply to himself: he inserts himself in the text, changing the second person plural pronoun (ὑμεῖς) to the first-person plural pronoun (ἡμεῖς). Moreover, Clement qualified the reference to Christians as γένος ἐκλεκτόν with a definite article: τὸ γένος ἐκλεκτόν. Christians now constitute not only "*a* chosen race, but *the* chosen race"—the people who belong to Christ and whose behavior is now completely distant from pagan mores. This *chosen race* also has as its requirement, a life of permanent prayer, always and in all places.[23]

Additionally, in his opposition to Valentinian Gnosticism, Clement referred to 1 Peter 2:9 to show that the *chosen race* is the one that is endowed with the true knowledge of God.[24] It walked not on the slippery paths of evil, but on the royal road, which, according to Philo, is that of reasoning and goodness, of which Abraham is the example (Gig, 64).[25] In short, Christians are a "*holy people*" (1 Peter 2:9), renewed, undefiled and purified of all vice.[26]

Deconstructing Racialism[27]

The experience of the First Letter of Peter and of the fathers, such as Irenaeus and Clement of Alexandria, shows the wealth of meaning that the expression γένος had in the early church. For Paul, who was born a Jew, trained in Judaism and Hellenism, and then became a Christian, *race* had the three senses of being a Jew, a pagan, and a Christian; the apostle of the Gentiles combines all three. Christianity had the sense of a *third race*, to which converts belonged.[28] In First Peter, therefore, the Christian *race* faces the non-Christian. This is also the perspective of Clement of Alexandria. Are we not, then, in the deconstruction of racialism?

Indeed, as with any people, socioethnic identity is a construction linked to history. This is how Israel was built as a people. Using the vocabulary of Jewish *self-identity*, First Peter wanted to help Christians to build their identity as a Christian community and deconstruct any form of racialization. The Christian faith is not linked to skin color, but to conversion and to the radical demands of membership.

Love L. Sechrest judiciously notes the dual strategy used by the author, that of *opposition* and *inclusion*. *Opposition* is the recognition of the difference between the race of the people of the new alliance and *outsiders*. It is not possible to dilute the Christian identity in society by adopting prevailing mores. Christians must maintain their convictions and their witness against all odds.

Nevertheless, this *opposition* is by no means a barrier. The church is a "race" that thrives on *inclusion*. It is open to all "nations." Christians do not have to lock themselves up in a dead-end marginalization. That is why they must be involved in society by behaving responsibly in the city and as a family. They must leave the catacombs for the agora where they meet and welcome every person, as a member of the *race of brothers and sisters*, governed not by any privilege, but by divine gratuitousness, mercy, and tenderness. The church is in the sign and the leaven.

In this sense, the main driver of *inclusion* is conversion. It is hope for the advent of new solidarities. This dynamic marks the whole letter. Didn't Christians themselves change their "race" through their conversion? Thus, hope refuses to confine the other to a given racial, ethnic, or even ethical category. Let us quote Justin of Rome, who paraphrased Isaiah and Micah (cf. Isa 2:4; Micah 4:3):

> We who were filled with war, murder, all evil, have on earth transformed the instruments of war, the swords into ploughshares, the spears into tools of the field, and we cultivate piety, justice, philanthropy, faith, the hope that comes from the Father himself through the crucified.[29]

CONCLUSION: A NEW SOCIETY

The tragic death of the African American George Floyd in the United States in May 2020 recalled the centuries-old question of race, whose etymology is dubious and whose use is applied without basis. Indeed, one may categorize the human species according to the color of the skin[30] or eyes, according to the size or the tribe.[31] In fact, isn't racial stigma fueled by supremacist ideologies, exclusion, and violence? Moreover, some go so far as to seek in the Bible a guarantee for all forms of discrimination.[32]

Indeed, a fundamentalist reading of the Bible helped justify slavery, colonization, and apartheid. Today, it leads to condoning wars and their atrocities. However, the word of God deconstructs all these ideologies and practices contrary to the divine plan. By removing its discriminatory venom, it deracializes the notion of race and gives it a meaning consistent with the project that God proposes to all humanity. Any true biblical pastoral care is necessarily a force of contestation against discriminatory practices and ideologies, without any compromise.

This is why, without falling into anachronism, the text of 1 Peter 2:9–10 contributes to deconstructing any form of ethno-racialism. Now, by vocation, the church is the sacrament of a world where all persons recognize themselves as members of the same race, all chosen, all called.

By welcoming the word of God into the depths of our hearts, our collective unconscious, the text of 1 Peter 2:9–10 helps to uncover all these tendencies to racialism that are linked, in fact, to political, economic, social, cultural, and religious sorting. "Indeed, the word of God is living and active, sharper than any two-edged sword, piercing until it divides soul from spirit, joints from marrow; it is able to judge the thoughts and intentions of the heart" (Heb 4:12).

By making this passage one of the foundations of the apostolate of the laity,[33] the Second Vatican Council recalls the mission of every Christian to deconstruct everything that in its language, its structures, and its practice still bears traces and seeds of all forms, sometimes unrecognized, of racism and racialism. In fact, as the "a chosen race, a royal priesthood, a holy nation, God's own people" (1 Peter 2:9), the church contributes to bringing about

> a new society based on the service of others more than on the desire for domination, a society based on sharing with others what one possesses more than on the selfish struggle of each one to accumulate as much wealth as possible; a society in which the value of being together as human beings unquestionably takes precedence over belonging to any other smaller group, be it family, nation, race or culture.[34]

9

COMBATING RACISM

Trajectories, Resources, and Strategies

Teresa Okure

SYNTHETIC PRINCIPLES

This chapter presents a "task force on racism." A task force is a small group of experts sent into the field to explore possibilities or perform a task for the needs of a group. It is "a temporary group of forces and resources for the accomplishment of an objective."[1] The objective of this chapter and task force is to discover ways of effectively combating or coping with racism for the service of humanity.

Members of this task force consider it a duty to alert humanity, through their various research fields of expertise, to awareness of racism as an evil in their midst, despite the 1947 UN Declaration of Human Rights. This Declaration proclaimed that all peoples are born equal, thus no one should be discriminated against based on race, nationality, color, religion, and so forth.

The work of this task force will be undertaken through conversation, where different but connected issues about life will emerge. The conversation style will depend on each member of the task force and the issues raised extend beyond the members and impact the entire human race.

In this chapter, the words *combating, coping with,* and *addressing* are used interchangeably as key actions in the struggle to rid humanity of the evil of racism. The life context of my conversation is the faculty course "Sex and Gender in the Bible and in Extra-biblical Cultures," which I taught almost exclusively to postgraduate seminarians at the Catholic Institute of West Africa (CIWA) for about thirty years.

The underlying principle of the course, which also applies to racism, is that culture forms a people; it is the DNA of a people. It is received or learned and transmitted from generation to generation. By itself, culture is neither right nor wrong; it simply is. Culture reveals its strong and weak elements when it encounters other cultures and meets values in those cultures different from its own. It can choose to use those values to renew and enrich itself or ignore them to its own impoverishment. The highest cultural value that each culture needs to encounter, be open to, appropriate, and benefit from is the gospel culture, a pure gift from God. We will return to this later.

Racism is rooted in and sustained by culture. Culture exists wherever human beings exist, and racism is embedded in it. The aim of the course was to awaken and help students to come to grips with issues of sex and gender in the Bible as a book rooted in cultures: the cultures of its different authors and recipients in their different epochs, and in the cultures, especially African, of the students, themselves. The same trajectories, resources, and strategies used in addressing sex and gender in the Bible and in human contexts can also help to address, in a gospel manner, the issue of racism, which, like sexism, is embedded in culture and imbibed by humans in and through their cultures in a process of reception and transmission.

This chapter has two main aspects: (1) resources and strategies from nature—what can be observed in humans and their societal, cultural practices irrespective of ethnicity, biological sex, nationality, and so forth; and (2) resources and strategies from Scripture—what God's revelation says about God and about human beings and creation. Our aim is to use the results from both these resource avenues in finding a way of combating, coping with, and addressing racism.

An underlying understanding of this chapter is that Scripture speaks or knows of only one human race, though we humans speak of the white, Black, and the colored race (made prominent by the apartheid regime in South Africa). I have never seen a white human being, though I have seen a Black one;[2] Black being the basic color from which other colors emerge. I may recall here a conversation I had with a young man sitting beside me in a flight from Port Harcourt to Lagos, Nigeria. I cannot remember how the conversation started, but

I remember very well him saying to me, "Sister, we Africans are the original color."

"What do you mean?" I asked.

"The Bible says that God created Adam from the dust of the earth." Then, stretching out and pointing to his arm he said, "This is the color of the earth. We are the original color." That was, for me, a brand-new exegesis of Genesis 2:7 worth pondering. But let's leave that aside for now.

KEY TERMS

Trajectories imply what is thrown to be caught or to arrive at a given destination. In biometry, the term applies to "the curve that cuts all of a given family of curves at the same time"; "the path of an object through space, or the path of life that a person chooses." What is said in this chapter on racism cuts equally across the whole human family and race without exception. At the same time, it is intended to encourage humans to eschew racism by redirecting or reorienting their minds and attitudes toward a true, God-centered perception of the human race.

Resources are "what can be looked to for support" or serve as an aid; "a supply that can be drawn from when necessary; ability to handle a situation effectively, a means that can be used profitably." Hopefully the outcome of this task force will serve as a multifaceted rich resource for humanity to cope effectively and profitably with racism.

A *strategy* is originally a military term; "the art, science of identifying a plan for large-scale combat operations." Tackling racism is surely a large-scale combat operation for humanity. Every human being needs to come on board if the fight against racism is to be successful, because racism is a humanity issue; it affects every human being and requires each to take necessary actions to eradicate it from their hearts, minds, attitudes, and life.

Combating something is "to try to stop something unpleasant or harmful from happening or increasing," for example, making every effort "to combat poverty and illiteracy"; it is "to take action to reduce or prevent (something bad or undesirable)"; for example, "an effort to combat drug trafficking."[3] "Combat stresses the forceful or urgent countering of something, e.g., disease. Its synonyms are:

oppose, resist, get rid of."[4] Racism is seriously harmful to humanity. It needs to be stopped by a collective energy or force and prevented from growing and waxing strong among men and women; its continued spread has dire consequences as we saw, for instance, in the murder of George Floyd in 2020, the Rwandan genocide in 1994, and more recently in the politically and economically motivated tribal wars in many parts of Africa, especially in Kenya, Nigeria, and the Sudan, fueled by selfish Western interests.[5]

In sum, this conversation on trajectories, resources, and strategies for combating racism aims at throwing out resources that can effectively and strategically be used in combating racism. We will now examine what is rooted in nature and what is given, revealed in the Scriptures. Finally, we will highlight some fruits of our exploration to impact and energize a humanity determined to rid itself of racism.

TRAJECTORIES, RESOURCES, AND STRATEGIES IN NATURE

The resources and strategies presented here and used in my course on sex and gender in the Bible and extrabiblical cultures mentioned earlier were also shared in conversation within my congregation, the Society of the Holy Child Jesus, to help us cope with the issue of racism within the congregation. Racism with its related practices, tribalism and nationalism, kept surfacing in the reports from the Society-wide conversations that preceded our 28th General Chapter.[6]

These "ism" words—racism, tribalism, sexism, nationalism, and so on—are common to humanity, irrespective of where one lives, though they may take different forms and have different intensities. They affect every human being whether at the giving or the receiving end.

For the sake of clarity, and briefly, sex, here, is understood as God's creation of humanity as male and female (Gen 1:26–27; 5:1–2); while gender is how society decides what belongs to a human being based on their God-given biological sex as male or female. My Ibibio language does not have an abstract word for sex. Human beings are either male (*owo eden*) or female (*owo anwan*). The following exercises do not address issues of LGBT. When applied to racism, the same exercises can help all human beings to become vividly aware of what is at stake regarding racism—an issue of humanity; consequently, whatever affects humanity as a species or cuts across the human family, inevitably affects them personally.

Exercises in Awareness

The course generally starts with groundbreaking exercises aimed at helping the students to understand, become deeply aware of, and come to grips with what is at stake in the issue of sex and gender, and to realize that, though a societal issue, sex and gender issues affect them personally and is part and parcel of them. The same exercises can help all humans deepen their awareness of issues at stake in racism, to become aware that racism is endemic in them in one way or the other.

Exercise 1. In the first exercise, I ask the students, "Which of you decided that you were going to come into existence?" Some first put up their hand; then they hear the question and put it down. I continue, "Come into existence as a human being rather than as a dog, goat, cow, and so on?" Their hands-down response indicates that they understood the point of this question.

Lesson from the Exercise. The truth is that no human being brings oneself into existence. Parents may pray for a child, may desire a boy or girl. But the child cannot pray or cause or will itself into existence. Life is God's pure unmerited, undeserved gift. This truth helps us to understand the fundamental meaning and nature of grace. Life in all its ramifications is the foundational grace and gift from God, not based on any human consideration or "because of works of righteousness that we had done" (Titus 3:5). We contribute nothing and add absolutely nothing to our coming into existence. The only response we can give is to say "thank you" to God for the gift, the pure unmerited grace of existence.

Exercise 2. I then ask the students, "Which of you decided when you came into existence that you would be male rather than female, a boy rather than a girl, man rather than woman; tall rather than short, fair rather than dark; African rather than European or American or Chinese; Black rather than white (to use conventional racist terms); Ibibio, Yoruba, Hausa, Igbo, rather than Ewe, Akan, Fanti, Angas, Tiv, Zulu, Kikuyu, etcetera?" The answer is nobody.

Lesson from the Exercise. The question raises further awareness that we contribute nothing to our being male or female or to such circumstances as our nationality by birth, color, tribe, ethnic group, culture, mother tongue, and personal features.

Exercise 3. I ask the students from different language groups to come to the front of the class, one from each language group. In addition, I ask those who know other languages not represented by those who have come out—for example, Italian, German, French, Swahili, Ewe, Fanti—to join them. I could get as many as twelve Nigerian languages alone in a class of about thirty Nigerian seminarians, and in the last few years one or two sisters. Then I ask each of them to say, "Good morning," or "How are you?" in their language. When they finish, I ask the class "Which of the greetings is right and which is wrong?" "Which is superior, and which inferior?" They burst out laughing. So, they get the point.

Lesson from the Exercise. We inherit our cultural identities from and are socialized into the culture, language, and worldview of our birth. The fact that the circumstances of my birth are different from another person does not make my circumstances superior and vice versa. Each person is different; each shapes and conditions us into the human being that we are. It is against the will of the Creator God to consider the purely gratuitous circumstances of my coming into existence as a human being superior to another person simply because we are different. The fundamental human error is to view differences in terms of superiority and inferiority. This is hierarchism, something foreign to God's creation.

All "ism" words arise from making one category the norm and judging, belittling, looking down upon, and condemning the others, using one's own as the norm: nationalism—my nation is superior to yours; racism—my race is superior yours inferior (though Scripture knows only of one race), or because you are not like me, you are not a human but a beast, monkey (so I can use, abuse and enslave you as subhuman, or beast of burden); sexism—the male sex is the norm and the female inferior (or according to Aquinas, "misbegotten males," human beings who did not quite make it to being fully human, a reason that woman could never be regarded as capable by nature of imaging Christ, the perfect humanity).

Exercise 4. This exercise is written; it aims at guiding the students to consider specific issues of sex and gender in the Bible and in extrabiblical cultures, starting with their cultures; the church straddles both the biblical and extrabiblical cultures; the biblical culture straddles all ages and cultures.[7] The students go into their own cultures to identify those practices and stipulations—the do's and don'ts—that society assigns to a boy and girl, man and woman, husband and wife, on the sole basis of their God-given biological sex (and we may add color). They are to put these roles and stipulations in two parallel columns with the headings: boy/girl; man/woman; husband/wife. Write down in the appropriate column what society assigns to or expects from each group.

When they have done that, they are to reverse the column headings such that all that society assigns to the young boy now belongs to the girl; to the grown man now belongs to the woman; and all the rights and privileges of the husband now belongs to the wife. For example, traditionally and still in some cultures, a young boy by nature has the sole right to inheritance and to education, while a young girl has no such rights. In the revised headings, the girl has the right to inheritance and education, while the boy has none. Racism would require the headings: black boy/girl—white boy/girl; black man/woman—white man/woman also done in reversed order.

After the reversal of roles, the students write a reflection on what happened within them as they did these exercises; they then do a theological or scriptural reflection on their experience remembering that each person, male or female, Black or white (to use conventional terms) is created by God in God's own image and likeness. Therefore, what is said derogatorily or honorably of the female or male is said of the God who created the female and male in God's own image and likeness. What is said of both together is said of the God who deliberately and deliberatively ("Let us," Gen 1:26) created humanity male and female in God's own image and likeness and conjointly "named them humanity," *adam* (cf. Gen 1:26–27; 5:1–2); that which is taken "from the dust of the ground," *adamah* (cf. Gen 2:7).

The male by himself does not fully image God; the female by herself does not fully image God. Only the male and female, humanity, as one entity fully image God. What is said of the Black person or white person is equally said of God who created them that way. The diversity of peoples in their different cultural and other human settings are flowers in God's garden.[8]

It is amazing, sometimes heartrending, to see what the students write in this last exercise, as they recall what happened to them, when they were growing up as boys, and to their mothers and sisters in their culture. Some weep deeply to recall the treatment their mother suffered when their father died; and the contrary treatment of their uncle when his wife died. Others see themselves as deprived human beings, because as boys, they were forbidden to undertake domestic chores like cooking that they later discovered to be a great disadvantage when they were in situations where they had to fend for themselves.

All could not imagine themselves to be disinherited or denied education, simply because they were born as female, something that was not of their making. What shocks them most as seminarians is the awareness that if they had been born female, they would automatically, by that very biological fact, be excluded from the priesthood. They would not stand the chance of God calling them to the priesthood, though, theologically, both women and men, girls and boys, and young and old, are born and configured on equal terms (pure grace) into Christ at baptism, by God's own gratuitous act of begetting them, not by their merit (cf. John 1:12–13).

When we have completed these exercises, we enter the heart of the course, exploring how these practices, human stipulations, and "isms" play out in the Bible, in our cultures, and in the church, which is rooted in human cultures and feeds from the unevangelized cultures in the Bible. A fifteen-week semester is never enough to complete this task.

Finally, we explore how Jesus, the "new humanity" (cf. Eph 2:15) has redeemed all: male and female, boy and girl, man and woman, and husband and wife, from these belittling, diminishing gender roles. Liberation from racism is Scripture's fundamental groundbreaking liberation where election theology and the discriminating racial attitude of Jews toward Gentiles is thrown out the window. This then leads us to the second part of this chapter: scriptural trajectories, resources, and strategies for coping with racism.

Racism Is Learned

Before exploring scriptural trajectories and resources for addressing racism, it needs to be stated that racism as a human construct is learned, not endemically inherited. Three brief examples illustrate this.

1. Since last year, a video clip has been circulating on WhatsApp of a white/Caucasian American woman who says, in an interview, that to be a white American and not racist would be a miracle because racism is deeply entrenched and built into the very fabric, structure, and value system of the American society. People understand that they are born into and grow up in the society with it. The Israelites experienced the same attitude toward the Gentiles based on their election theology that both Peter (cf. Acts 10:38) and Paul (cf. Rom 3:22–23) later overthrew when they saw and witnessed God's action in themselves and among the Gentiles. The same is true of racism and other anthropological "isms"—tribalism, ethnocentrism, nationalism. Only "the truth," Jesus and our discipleship of Jesus, can set us free in this matter (cf. John 8:31–36).
2. The second case was narrated by a mother, the wife of a Western diplomat in Lagos, Nigeria. Their son at the international school that embraces children of well-to-do Nigerians and diplomats was to have a birthday party. The child asked the mother if he could invite his friend to the party. The mother wanted to know whether the friend was white or Black and did all she could to explain what she meant. The child could not understand her. So, she called the Nigerian domestic staff and, putting the hand of the child next to hers, asked, "Does your friend's color look like yours and mine or like that of the domestic staff?" The child reflected, then said, "Mummy, I don't know. When I go, I will look." The friend turned out to be a Nigerian. The mother who told the story had a great shock. The boy saw a human being, a friend; the mother who had been socialized into a racist way of thinking and viewing human beings saw color, not a human being. This recalls the 1967 movie, *Guess Who's Coming to Dinner*. It is possible that from then on, the child would see

people in terms of colors, similar to or different from his, and not as human beings.

3. The third experience is personal. When I was studying in the United States, I entered a shopping mall in New York City. A white mother was shopping with her little boy who liked exploring what was in the mall. He picked up something and turned around, and I was the nearest person to him. So, he came forward to show it to me and to talk about it. As we were conversing, the mother turned around and saw that the child was conversing with me, a Black woman. Angrily, she dragged the child away and gave me a very nasty and contemptuous look. I felt sorry for her and for the child who didn't understand her racist reaction. These examples suffice to show that racism is learned, but it can also be unlearned.

TRAJECTORIES, RESOURCES, AND STRATEGIES FROM SCRIPTURE

I have written much on this aspect.[9] Here I will highlight some trajectories and resources for further exploration. The strategies will follow. Here, we will treat

- the issue of race is linked to racism,
- God's creation of humanity, and
- how God in the person of Jesus demolished the barriers and walls of racism and other "isms."

Scripture's View on Race

Scripture is very consistent and clear that God created only one human race. So even the term *racism* is an error, since it is untrue to creation to say that *racism* makes one race the norm and judges and condemns other races based on a perceived sense of racial superiority. Scripture would see *racism* as a human behavior born out of ignorance of God or as simply an anti-God view of God's creation.

First trajectory. In the creation accounts in Genesis, God created humanity, *adam* "male and female" in God's own image and likeness (1:26–27). We leave aside what this image and likeness could mean, though the most obvious is to be God's partner in engendering human beings, in response to God's command: "Be fruitful and multiply and fill the earth and subdue it" (Gen 1:28), and in caring for the earth, as Pope Francis has reminded humanity.[10] To underscore the point that the creature, *adam*, is humanity—male and female (not the male exclusively)—the biblical author repeats it in his introduction to the genealogy of the human race (*adam*): "When God created *adam*, he made *adam* in the likeness of God. Male and female he created them, and he blessed them and called them *adam* when they were created" (Gen 5:1–2). This emphasis *adam* is lost in English translations, though such versions as the New Revised Standard Version try to substitute "humankind" unsuccessfully for *adam*.[11]

In my Ibibio language and in most, if not all, African languages, this problem does not arise. *Owo* is exclusively used for "human being"; *owo eren* (contracted: *awuden*) is a human being who is male, and *owo anwan* (contracted *awuwan*) is a human being who is female. In no circumstance can *owo* be used for the male to the exclusion of the other. The genealogy of *adam* that begins Genesis 5 is not that of the male only, as commonly understood, especially in patrilineal cultures, but of humanity, made up of male and female. This truth that *adam* is humanity has deep implications in the use of English language in African contexts and its continued theological colonization in Anglophone African countries.

The author of the creation account in Genesis 2 underscores the intrinsic oneness of man and woman as husband and wife joined inseparably as one by God (2:24). The emphasis on the same stock is embodied in the fact that the man and woman come from the same creature from the dust of the ground (*adam* from *adamah*). The difference in biological sex (*ish* and *ishshah*, 2:23) is a second step; it does not nullify the oneness of the source and nature but rather presupposes it, in that the creature *adam* was not like any of the animals named or identified by their nature (cf. 2:19–20).

In the biblical narrative, God deliberately use this strategy of differentiation to make it clear that both the man and woman are of the same substance and nature. The creature recognizes and proclaims, "This at last is bone of my bones and flesh of my flesh" (2:23); "bone of bone and flesh of flesh" is a cultural expression of persons who share the same descent or ethnicity, as the Israelites said to David: "We are your bone and flesh" (2 Sam 5:1; cf. 19:12–13; 1 Chr 11:1).

Second trajectory. The same emphasis on one stock or race, one creation, occurs in the account of the flood. Noah is instructed to take into the ark everything that God had created, "clean and unclean" (labels that did not exist at the time of creation, Gen 1:1—2:4a); "male and female" (Gen 6:17–22); so that they can continue to propagate their kind after the flood (6:19–20; cf. 8:16–18). After the flood the injunction given at creation: "Be fruitful and multiply and fill the earth" is repeated (Gen 1:28; 9:1). God then makes a covenant with Noah, his family and the entire creation, everything that exists: "all flesh [human and animal] that is on the earth" (Gen 9:16–17). The emphasis is not only on one humanity, but also on God's one creation. God's covenant is "between me [God] and the earth" (9:13), which embraces "every living creature," "of all flesh" (9:12, 15). The initial emphasis that humanity is one, and that creation is one, is here repeatedly affirmed.

The beginning of *racism* is narrated in Genesis 11, the episode of the Tower of Babel, as a prelude to the choice of Abraham (Gen 12:1–3); and the beginning of the nation becomes the beginning of races. The derogatory attitude toward other races then emerge as if any people or nation created itself. The Jews were not alone in viewing people of other races as inferior to them. In the New Testament period, Colossians (3:11) for instance, speaks of "barbarians and Scythians" alongside "Jews and Greeks," the Greeks considered themselves as super human beings, the civilized ones compared to the rest who were barbarians. A Greek mortified author laments that the ancestors, the Bacchiadae, would turn in their graves to see Corinth, the once "flower of Greece" now inhabited by "a pack of scoundrels," referring to the freed slaves that Julius Caesar settled in his rebuilt Corinth; though they were not the only inhabitants of Corinth.[12]

Racial antagonism is still with us today, even though Jesus put an end to it with his body on the cross as we will see shortly. Pentecost reversed the scattering that humanity, "all flesh," brought on itself by the project of the Tower of Babel. At Pentecost, God poured out God's Spirit, "God's life principle" (cf. John 6:68; 1 John 3:9) "on all flesh" (Acts 2:1–21, v. 17).

Third trajectory. In his speech on the Areopagus (Acts 17:26), Paul cites the biblical belief that God created the entire human race from "one stock" ["one blood," in some witnesses], alongside everything on earth. As a result, even Greek poets, nonbiblical authors, could recognize and proclaim that all humans have their habitat in God: "In him we live and move and have our being" (v. 28).

This biblical emphasis on one human race is buttressed by archaeological findings and the effect of climate on Africans who have lived abroad for ages. The Museum of Origins in Johannesburg hosts the cave where the skeleton of the first *Homo sapiens* and *Homo erectus,* male and female, are found. It is further believed that the mitochondrial gene (core DNA) of every human being alive today can be traced to an African woman who lived over two hundred thousand years ago.[13] Variations in color are the result of billions of years of the separation of the huge landslides from the motherland, Africa, landslides that eventually became other continents. Moreover, even now, Africans who stay continuously in Europe or America for many years acquire a lighter skin color. I personally experienced this when I lived in England for seven years without a home visit, and later in the United States and Israel for the same length of time. The effect of the sun on the human being, or lack of it, is not neutral to one's color, which explains why people do suntanning. When the color change lasts for billions of years it becomes endemic, and deep-seated and resists weather effects on one's skin color.

Jesus, God-Word Become Flesh

God in Jesus dealt a decisive blow on *racism,* first by becoming a human being "flesh" (cf. John 1:1–2, 14); then by breaking down all anthropological barriers "by his body on the cross" (Col 1:20; Eph 2:11–22); making all "one" in him (Gal 3:28). Giving us the enabling power, the Holy Spirit, life-giver, God's life principle (cf. 1 John 3:9), is one "who causes to live" (John 6:68), to become God's flesh and blood children, thus establishing "a new creation" (2 Cor 5:17), and sending town criers, his followers, to carry this good news to "all nations till the ends of the earth" (Matt 28:16–20). The New Testament message and mission concerning humanity is clear: God's destruction of *racism* and all other "isms" in Jesus is the core of the gospel message.

The significance and mystery of the God-Word becoming flesh goes beyond his having two natures in one person, as is traditionally emphasized (cf. John 1:1–2, 14). He, "the word became flesh and pitched his tent among us" (John 1:14 NRSV adapted), signifies that he inserted himself into the fabric of our human reality and became substantially, consubstantially, and inseparably one with us.[14] The Letter to the Hebrews states that "we have one who in every respect has been tested as we are, yet without sin" (Heb 4:15), sin being what separates humans from God. Jesus himself emphasized this reality when he preferred to refer to himself as "the child of a human being" (*hyios tou anthrōpou*, *ben adam*, *bar enosh*, *eyen owo*), what is usually translated in English as "son of man."[15] First and foremost, his reconciliation, substantially uniting humans to God, was in his person, in-carnation, his becoming flesh, a human being. That reality programmatically changed the status of human beings from creatures to children, his siblings according to the flesh.

In the second place, through his death on the cross, Jesus broke down all racial and other anthropological barriers. The most outstanding barrier in his time being *racism*, between the Jew and the Gentiles. By his death and resurrection, Jesus became the "new humanity" (*kainos anthrōpos*, Eph 2:15), the "new *adam*." He made all one in his person, incorporating them into his own body. As he became substantially flesh, so did he give humans who believe in and receive "the enabling power [*exousia*] to become substantially his flesh and blood," "children of God," his siblings and siblings of one another (John 1:12–14).[16]

In short, Jesus—the "new humanity (*adam*)"—ushers in "a new creation" (2 Cor 5:17) where all the barriers that humans have built up and sustained against one another from time immemorial are destroyed once and for all. This, it is worth repeating, is the core of God's good news for humanity, the realization and acceptance of which sets all humans free from racism to become a new creation in Christ.

Racism and the Gospel

Over the centuries, have we carried out Jesus's mission to proclaim this good news to "all the nations" (cf. Matt 28:20; Mark 16:15) as did the first disciples? It cost the Jewish disciples greatly to break out of their centuries-long Torah-based inheritance and creeds that emphasized their uniqueness as an elected people—a belief entrenched in their covenant with God on Sinai (cf. Exod 19—24)—to embrace the gospel and embrace Gentiles as siblings. Because they did that, we today can call ourselves Christians, with varying degrees of understanding what that signifies or requires of us. The first disciples gave themselves or were given this name "Christians" (cf. Acts 11:26) to help them grow out of the mentality and culturally ingrained habit of viewing and labeling one another by derogatory racist terms—Jews, the circumcised; Gentiles the uncircumcised, dogs—and to see themselves as brothers and sisters: one in Christ.

It would seem that when the gospel came to Europe and later to America, it fell into the service of the empire; and the old covenant, rooted in election theology, which Jesus abolished by his body on the cross, was used as a criterion in the colonial power and domination-seeking ventures that had nothing to do with the gospel.[17] Blacks and whites have been socialized into a distorted view of human beings. What is needed is for each to realize that *racism* is bad for them individually, a fake self. Socialization into *racism* makes it natural for one to define self falsely as white and Black. The first casualty in *racism* is the racist; the second is the one discriminated against; the third is the whole of humanity. Those who fight against *racism*, wherever it is found, are friends to humanity.

STRATEGIES AND WAYS FORWARD

This last section is an attempt to highlight some of the fruits of the trajectories and resources for combating *racism* that have surfaced in the foregoing sections. It is understood that this conversation is ongoing. The immediate conversation partners (members of the task force) and the group (humanity, for whom the task force is carrying out its work) will continue the reflection and map out concrete sustainable strategies for combating *racism*, which does nobody any good. With this proviso in mind, we list the key strategies that have emerged from this chapter.

The need to make sustained efforts to bring to awareness that all human beings are created equal by God in the one human race. *Racism* is learned; it is evil, and nobody is created or born a racist.

The three stories told earlier illustrate this truth. Other life-centered stories and personal experiences illustrate this fact.

There is a need to cultivate, promote, and encourage personal responsibility to become aware of and address the *racism* in one's heart, mind, and attitude. Because we are born alone and die alone, each human being has the ultimate responsibility to eschew *racism*; to seek and pursue that authentic self, given by God, in God's own image and likeness; to steer away from the socializations into *racism* and from promoting the same in others. We do not determine what we inherit; but we can responsibly do something to what we inherit so that those who inherit from us can have a better life and world.

The primary casualty in *racism* is the racist. Often, the racist does not even know they are racist, because it is so deeply and culturally embedded in them. That is why the exercises in awareness mentioned earlier are capital. Individuals enter the exercise, not with regard to how *racism* affects others, but with the primary purpose of discovering how *racism* affects them, at the psychological, attitudinal, and emotive levels.

We need to dispel the darkness of *racism* with the light of the gospel. Racial culture gets transformed and liberated when it allows itself to be exposed to the light of the gospel, Jesus, "the light of the world" (John 8:12; cf. 1:5, 9). Any other way will not lead to genuine and authentic liberation of humanity. The truth remains that Jesus is the only name "under heaven...by which we must be saved" (Acts 4:12), authentically and irrevocably liberated from *racism*, because in him each human being is destined by God to become "a new creation," with the old passing away (cf. 2 Cor 17).

Unless humans awaken to the fact that *racism* dehumanizes us personally, and consequently want to be liberated from it, to become children who "remain in the house forever" (cf. John 8:34–36; Heb 12:22–23), no task force will succeed in making the change. The kind of exercises that we outlined earlier can help even diehard racists to come to deep-seated awareness of what their unevangelized cultures have done to them by initiating and socializing them into racism, making them proud of something they should be ashamed of and avoid.

We need to proclaim faithfully and boldly the core truth of the gospel. This core truth is that Jesus came to break down all anthropological barriers of *racism* ("Jew or Gentile"), class ("slave or free"), and sex (male and female) and make all "one" in himself (cf. Gal 3:28). One is one, otherwise it is a fraction, half, third, quarter, and so forth. In him, we assume a Spirit-filled courage not to deny, play down, shield, or decorate *racism* and tribalism among us nor get unduly hung up by what we have lived in the past, and so remain enslaved to, and hinder our liberation from *racism*.

Instead, like Paul, forgetting the past, individually and as a human family (cf. *Fratelli Tutti*), we commit ourselves to forge ahead in the liberation from *racism* that God has opened our eyes to see though this conversation. We press on with God's energizing Spirit "for the prize" which God has captured us in Christ Jesus (cf. Phil 3:13–14) by making us God's children, siblings of Christ and of one another, either by baptism or as his siblings according to the flesh.

Tasks to Combat Racism

As members of the task force on *racism*, we *can do the exercises mentioned earlier* to help us deal with *racism*, tribalism, nationalism, color-ism, and other "isms" within ourselves. In that way, we also strive to become a new creation. Jesus first became a human being before he could incorporate us in himself as a new humanity in the new creation.

We can *encourage others with whom we work*: students; colleagues; institutions, over which we have guiding and supervisory authority; members of the same religious community, especially international communities and even church dicasteries, *to do these exercises*. We can encourage these groups or any mixed groups of humans to write out what they say, hear said, and believe about people of other cultures, color, and nationality, and how they see themselves being given the same derogatory tags and treatments they give to or receive from others.

The worst affected human being is the racist because they do not see that they are racist, blind, and in need of help, as Jesus tells the self-righteous Judeans: "If you were blind, you would not have sin. But now that you say, 'We see,' your sin [blindness] remains" (John 9:39–41). It is a great liberating moment or grace for one to see and admit that they are racist, because then they can do something about it.

We can expose racism wherever it exists. As members of the task force, we need to be bold enough to expose *racism* and tribalism wherever they exist; not to shield it or speak of it behind closed doors or pretend that it is not what it really is by using flowery language or even by claiming that it is part of our culture. We need to know and help others to know that to do so is to choose to remain imprisoned, enslaved by this anti-God, anticreation, antihumanity, and anti-Christ evil. We need to call it evil, no matter where it is found. Evil named, exposed to light, is evil overcome (cf. John 3:20–21). Once exposed to the light of truth, it is deprived of its covert power to operate and be cherished in the hearts of God's children, or even be protected by them, as the immune system protects the HIV virus, thinking it is part of them; yet while the protection lasts, the virus of *racism* continues to gnaw away at God's children, destroying them and their human family.

We can promote and cultivate appreciation of human diversity. We need to encourage people to see and know that the diversity of human beings on earth is like flowers in God's garden, each adding its beauty and grace; if only all could have or cultivate God's eyes, not our culturally deformed human eyes, to see it. Since only the truth sets us free, the task force can commit itself to live and proclaim this core liberating truth of the gospel by all possible means.

We can be ready to pay the price for self-liberation from racism. A key task is for each one to discern how they have contributed and continue to contribute to promoting *racism* and the attendant tribalism and ethnocentrism in church and society and make every effort to eschew it. This will require each person to do violence to themselves, to wrestle out of the cage of ingrained racism, tribalism, nationalism, and sexism outlined earlier.

We can attend to whom we associate with spontaneously. A practical concrete gauge to how racism-free we are is to identify who we prefer to be with, share with, and connect to spontaneously. Paul's real conversion happened in the house of Lydia, who challenged him to put his body where his theology was (cf. Acts 16:11–15, v. 15). The brethren in Jerusalem had no problem that Peter baptized Cornelius and his household. But how could he and they—God's chosen people—mix with, physically share table fellowship, oneness with the uncircumcised, the unclean, the Gentile dogs (cf. Acts 11:17)? God told Peter that he had no right to "call unclean" what God had sanctified (cf. Acts 10:9–16, v. 15) by creating them "good" (the refrain in Gen 1). Peter thus realized that to be racist is "to stand in God's way" and that humans have no such right, starting with himself. By his example, he won over the brethren (Acts 11:1–18). They learned how to grow in their understanding that God has reconciled them, all humanity and creation to the divine self in Christ Jesus (cf. Col 1:20; Eph 1:10) with no merit on the part of anyone (cf. Col 3:23).

"The kingdom of God is subjected to violence and the violent are taking it by storm," the same violence that Paul did to himself when he wrestled out of the cage of his Jewish upbringing with its election and Torah-based theology and covenant, and counted all that previously stood to his credit (a proud and exceptional law abiding Jew) as loss, "rubbish," compared to the supreme worth of knowing Christ and being "found in him" (cf. Phil 3:4–11); he cultivated this "place in Christ" by relating to Gentiles as his "siblings" with fondest tenderness, as in the church at Philippi (cf. Phil 4:1).[18]

Paul writes, "For freedom Christ has set us free" (Gal 5:1). So, we stand firm together in Christ refusing to be enslaved by our societal and cultural anti-Christ ideologies, socializations, and conditionings. We find our true, God-given worth in Christ as pure grace, given equally to everyone; not in our unevangelized cultures with their racist and tribalistic ideologies and superiority complexes that promote a proud, ethnic, tribal, and racial false sense of superiority.

Jesus destroyed all anthropological barriers in his person; created in himself one new humanity and creation by his death on the cross and resurrection. The oneness happened in him, in his person. We become one with him at baptism that we renew at the Easter vigil. This oneness must also happen in each of us, in our person, attitude, mindset, and reality, or it will remain an impossible dream.

In conclusion, the core truth that has emerged through this conversation is that *racism*, tribalism, and all other "isms" are learned, inherited from the moment of our birth into a particular unevangelized culture, society, class, and worldview. Racism benefits nobody—neither the racist nor the one who is racially discriminated against and subjected to racist ill-treatment. Racism like sexism and other "isms" is, dare we say, an enemy to a crime against individuals and humanity at large, and a contempt of the Creator God.

To drive home this truth, we return once again to the exercises outlined earlier. No human being determined the circumstances of their birth, color, tribe, or nationality. We realize that we have nothing which we did not first receive. Consequently, having received all as grace, we do ourselves much damage by "boasting" (1 Cor 4:7) and discriminating against others, and thus, impoverishing ourselves. That realization, if personal and deep-seated, can set humanity free from racism. Once every human being places him- or herself on the track of genuinely wanting to get rid of the old self of racism, the aim and purpose of this chapter, conversation, and indeed, work of the task force on racism would bear the desired fruit.

10

THE STORY OF NOAH AND CANAAN

A Contribution from Patristic Exegesis[1]

Peter Kodwo Turkson

For the Church to receive Holy Scripture with an authentic, fully sapiential attitude, the study of patristic exegesis is fruitful, necessary, and unavoidable. *Lectio Patrum* is not a hermeneutic exercise extrinsic to the understanding of Holy Scripture; it is intrinsic to it. The *Catechism of the Catholic Church* (*CCC*), in fact, includes it in the Tradition of the Church among the fundamental criteria for reading the Bible: "According to a saying of the Fathers, 'Holy Scripture is written principally in the Church's heart rather than in documents and records' (*Sacra Scriptura principus est in corde Ecclesiae quam in materialbus instrumentis scripta*), for the Church carries in her Tradition the living memorial of God's Word, and it is the Holy Spirit who gives her the spiritual interpretation of the Scripture ('... *according to the spiritual meaning which the Spirit grants to the Church*')" (*CCC* 113).[2]

The importance of the patristic interpretation of Scripture is also mentioned in the apostolic exhortation *Verbum Domini*, published after the Ordinary Synod of Bishops of 2008 that was dedicated to the word of God in the life and mission of the Church: "*We learn from the Fathers that exegesis 'is truly faithful to the proper intention of biblical texts when it goes not only to the heart of their formulation to find the reality of faith there expressed, but also seeks to link this reality to the experience of faith in our present world'*" (VD 37).

Theology, where critical reflection is based on Revelation, is very careful in its approach to patristic exegesis, precisely because it considers Scripture to be the "veiled soul" of its own identity and is inspired by it, thus avoiding the double-edged sword of neglecting patristic teaching and connecting the Bible to the contemporary situation of the Church that is always changing and can lead to arbitrary updates.[3]

Based on this methodological premise, we will examine a passage of Scripture that has undergone misleading interpretations in the history of Christian thought, to the point of being used paradoxically to justify the legal institution of slavery: the curse imposed by Noah upon Canaan, the son of Ham, when the latter found the patriarch lying drunk and naked in his tent and went to tell his brothers about it. Out of respect and pity, Japheth and Shem then covered their father's nakedness with a cloak, while looking away:

> Noah, a man of the soil, was the first to plant a vineyard. He drank some of the wine, became drunk, and lay naked inside his tent. Ham, the father of Canaan, saw his father's nakedness, and he told his two brothers outside. Shem and Japheth, however, took a robe, and holding it on their shoulders, they walked backward and covered their father's nakedness; since their faces were turned the other way, they did not see their father's nakedness. When Noah woke up from his wine and learned what his youngest son had done to him, he said:
>
> "Cursed be Canaan!
> The lowest of slaves
> shall he be to his brothers."
>
> He also said:
>
> "Blessed be the LORD, the God of Shem!
> Let Canaan be his slave.
> May God expand Japheth,
> and may he dwell among the tents of Shem;
> and let Canaan be his slave." (Gen 9:20–27; NABRE)[4]

Among the Church fathers who commented on this episode and on the specific passage concerning the curse of Ham, we will focus on Origen, the exegete par excellence, and on some representatives of the "two lungs" of the Church—the Eastern lung of the Syriac and Greek-speaking churches, and the Western lung of the churches of the Latin Rite. In other words, we will examine the interpretations given by Justin Martyr, John Chrysostom, Ephrem Siro, Ambrose of Milan, and Augustine of Hippo.[5]

ORIGEN (CA. 185–253)

Origen's interpretation of the Bible is always fascinating. His unmistakably original hermeneutic "genius," his capacity to penetrate the text and his amplification of the meanings obtained and obtainable from it make him truly unique in the history of ancient Christian thought. The passage of Genesis that we are about to examine does not occur very frequently in his extant works.[6] Some references are found in the exegetical context of other Bible passages.[7] One of the characteristics of Origen's *ratio hermeneutica* is the juxtaposition of different passages of Scripture, linked by a common word or image, so that one passage explains the other: *Scriptura illustrat Scripturam*.[8]

In his *Homilies on Numbers*,[9] the character of Ham is allegorically interpreted as a figure of the soul capable of doing evil in the future. His son, Canaan, is thus the symbol of a sin that has been committed and is thus the object of the curse.

> This is perhaps why even the child Canaan is cursed before he was born, as a figure of this mystery. For Ham his father had sinned, and Noah, while prophetically indicating each of the excellent things for each of his sons, when he comes to Ham, says: "Cursed be the child of Canaan." Ham sinned, and Canaan his offspring is cursed and was cursed. And therefore we must pay very keen attention and be on the lookout, that our soul not produce anything that deserves to be cursed. Even if it has not yet fulfilled the deed, yet by the very fact that it is willed and intended, an offspring of this sort will be cursed.[10]

This passage features a theme that is very dear to Origen's thought: free will, which he vigorously upheld against the Gnostic determinism of his time.[11] The dynamism of the soul that freely conceives the action and subsequently puts it into practice is allegorically and, I would say, plastically represented in the father-son succession. The audacity of the allegorical procedure, commonly used in ancient thought, which was more inclined to synthesis than to analysis,[12] might seem foreign to current exegetical sensitivity. Yet, Origen's exegesis anticipates and resolves the question of Canaan's alleged lack of responsibility and the iniquity of a punishment inflicted on him for his father's sin. Thanks to Origen's reinterpretation, the biblical text is elevated to a higher level, to suggest an anthropological theme that enhances man's dignity, will, and freedom.

The use of *etymological explanations* is another exegetical method typical of Origen.[13] It abounds in his *Homilies on Joshua.*[14] While commenting on the episode of Rahab, whose name he etymologically interprets as "breadth," he introduces a digression on Canaan. Here, too, the master theologian of Alexandria overcomes the materiality of the text and the trammels of unsatisfactory literalism and reinterprets the curse on Ham's son from a theological viewpoint, as a providential, benign act of God who, using punishment pedagogically, purifies, redeems and saves even those who sin.[15]

> Japheth, in a similar manner, is interpreted as "extension." Certainly he, too, was a sign of the people who are saved "out of the nations." The boy Canaan is a servant subjected by his father to Japheth and to his brother Shem, who symbolizes those who are saved from among the circumcised. We must admire the kindness and providence of God in this. Wishing to offer a remedy to the sinner Canaan and to bring salvation to him, God made him a servant to his brothers, just as Esau was made to serve his brother Jacob; certainly not so that he might be destroyed, but that he might gain salvation by obedience to his betters. For it is much better for wicked persons and sinners, who are ignorant in the ways of self-government, that they not entrust themselves to themselves, but become servants to holy persons and be subject to their betters. Thus they will

> not be directed by their own bad thought, but by the good one of others.[16]

As is customary in Origen's exegesis, Canaan, the historical character mentioned in the biblical narrative, is transformed into a "figure" representing something else, that is, the moral life of those subjects who, to avoid leading an existence miserably dominated by unbridled passions, need to be supported by the example, testimony and guidance of their more virtuous brothers. Origen's exegesis of the biblical passage follows a typically Hellenistic anthropology, substantiated by the centuries-old philosophical tradition developed both by the great intellectuals of previous centuries and by his contemporaries. Based on this tradition, our task is to combine the three psychological dimensions—concupiscible, irascible, and intellectual—letting reason guide the sovereign powers of his soul.[17] According to the definition contained in the text we are examining, sinners are people "who are ignorant in the ways of self-government." God offers a medicinal remedy for this "cursed" behavior: spiritual "servitude" to their betters. Basically, it is the Pauline precept according to which the "strong" help the "weak." Canaan is, therefore, the sinner whose weakness is corroborated. Instead of being the cause of a curse, he partakes in a greater blessing.

Furthermore, it should not be forgotten that Origen's text that we are commenting on belongs to a homiletical cycle. It is a transcription of the preaching intended for a liturgical assembly of believers, in Caesarea in Palestine, made up of "ordinary people," who are shown a lofty but attainable goal of Christian life. The ancient Greek-speaking Christians of that community in Roman Palestine would easily have been able to identify with Canaan, recognizing that their actions were often based on a *sensu malo*, on lust and disordered desires, and that they needed the support of wise, strong guides, of whom there were many and who, according to Origen, were to be sought among the *didáskaloi*, the masters of thought and life, the authentic catalysts of Origen's Church.[18]

Two main meanings can thus be drawn from Origen's interpretation of the episode of the curse of Ham: the affirmation of free will, and the help that good people offer to sinners. Nor can this double interpretation exhaust the inherently inexhaustible richness of the biblical text. Indeed, according to the *mens origeniana*, the exegete paves the way for the discovery of the pluriform spiritual meaning of Scripture.[19] Readers and listeners have the task of continuing this search.[20]

AUGUSTINE (354–430)

After the loftiness of Origen's spiritual interpretation, Augustine's reading of the biblical text concerning the curse of Ham might, at first glance, seem rather poor. In fact, he seems exclusively concerned with justifying the apparent incongruity of the punishment inflicted on Ham's son for the sins committed by his father. He thus resorts to the thesis of the punishment suffered by descendants for the crimes committed by their ancestors, typical of the most archaic biblical religiosity, in the context of Greco-Roman civilization, and powerfully expressed in tragic literature. In Augustine's vast corpus, we find the following:

> Can anyone count the many passages in Scripture where sons are bound by the sins of their parents? Why did Ham sin and vengeance was declared against his son Chanaan? Why was the son of Solomon punished for the sin of Solomon by the breaking up of the kingdom? (Cf. 1 Samuel 12.) Why was the sin of Achab, King of Israel, visited upon his posterity? How do we read in the sacred books: 'Returning the iniquity of the fathers into the bosom of their children after them' and 'Visiting the iniquity of the fathers upon the children unto the third and fourth generation'? The number here can be taken for all the descendants. Are these statements false? Who would say this but the most open enemy of the divine words? The carnal generation even of the people of God of the Old Testament, which *generates into bondage*, binds children for the sins of their parents.[21]

For a correct understanding of Augustine's text, it is necessary to use a fundamental hermeneutic rule: it must be read in its literary and historical-theological context. The passage examined is taken from one of the most important theological treatises of Augustine's anti-Pelagian thought: *Contra Iulianum*. Julian (386–454), bishop of Eclanum, a city located in today's region of Irpinia, in southern Italy, was an eminent man of his time: he belonged to an aristocratic family and was the son of another bishop, Memor, a close acquaintance of Paulinus, bishop of Nola. He had a vast, in-depth culture, was a late exegete of the Antiochian school, and in his correspondence with Augustine, he entertained a tense controversy on the so-called Pelagian question.[22] It is known, in fact, that, following the teachings of the monk Pelagius, several Christian thinkers adhered to the thesis according to which the nature of humanity remained ontologically good even after the sin of Adam: sin is not transmitted with generation; baptism does not remit any "original" sin; there is no invincible concupiscence that requires divine help; and grace is understood, rather, as a good inspiration that extrinsically accompanies man and his will in the accomplishment of good. It was evident to Augustine that such a theology, no matter how solidly argued and widely expounded by its fierce representatives, undermined the Christian message of the salvation of sinful humanity, thanks to the redemption of Christ operating in the sacramental economy of the Church.[23] Christian anthropology itself was subverted by Pelagianism.[24]

Augustine was an opponent of Pelagianism, of which Julian was a distinguished exponent. With a powerful speculative argument, he "dismantled" his opponent's entire theological structure in *Contra Iulianum*, where biblical exegesis and anthropological meditation neatly fit together.[25] At the end of Augustine's tight argument, right before the conclusion of the entire work, we find the passage that we have just taken into consideration. It belongs to the sixth book of Augustine's treatise that he wrote to respond to the theses that the bishop of Eclanum had expounded in the four books of his *Ad Turbantium*. The fundamental idea that Augustine suggests, responding to Julian, who had denied the transmission of original sin, is that it is demonstrated by the universal redemption brought about by Jesus Christ. Original sin is personal, not *proprietate actionis*, but *contagione propaginis* (not by reason of a personal action but by reason of birth [progeny]). To support his theses, he quotes some biblical texts taken mostly from chapter 5 of the Letter to the Romans and from the Old Testament. Our passage from the Book of Genesis is, therefore, embedded in this biblical dossier that shows the reality of the transmission of original sin and the universal need for baptism, even for infants. In the curse of Ham, the order of nature, dynamically exposed to a process of inevitable corruption, meets the invocation of a restoration in the order of grace. Nature wounded by sin goes hand in hand with an overabundance of healing and perfecting grace: the soul of Augustine's theology is found in the commentary on Genesis 9:25–27. Augustine's interpretation confirms a basic exegetical principle: the *analogia fidei*, according to which the Bible is explained within the harmonious and hierarchical structure of the truths of the *depositum fidei*.[26]

Augustine, however, gives us another important note on the biblical text of the curse inflicted on Canaan due to the fault committed by his father, Ham. Indeed, he includes this verse from the Book of Genesis in the "questions" listed in his book *Quaestiones in Heptateucum*. As he explains in the preface of this very original work, composed during a sabbatical from ordinary pastoral activities while living in Carthage in 419, some passages of the first seven books of the Old Testament do raise questions and appear problematic. They need an explanation to make them intelligible. Augustine's testimony is important: if the material reading of the text, without a gloss, appears necessary for the whole of Scripture, it becomes urgent for some passages that would otherwise be unintelligible. Augustine's "glosses," which are in line with the *Scholia* and with the broader commentaries that the ancients produced to explain the works of the "masters," almost always in the scholastic context, point out the richness of the biblical text that, by raising questions, requires the exegete's commitment to a broader understanding in order to overcome the apparent contradictions with other biblical texts or with a correct theology. The following is Augustine's explanation that interprets Genesis 9:25–27 in the light of the entire *historia salutis* (history of salvation) recounted in Scripture. "It is debated why Ham, for the sin of the offense caused, as a father, is not cursed in himself but in his own son Canaan, except because it was prophesied in a certain way that the land of Canaan, after the Canaanites had been driven out and defeated, would receive the children of Israel, who would come from the seed of Shem."[27]

If one examines Augustine's text, the curse translates into a prophecy in the light of the patristic theology of history. In fact, history does not end with a single event but is associated and linked to other facts belonging to the same salvific history, the totality of which becomes the hermeneutic criterion of particular facts. In this sense, the "curse" inflicted on Canaan, precisely because it is inexplicable and unsustainable in the light of the personal responsibility for one's acts, becomes a "blessing" for ancient Israel. This interpretation, however, cannot in any way be bent to nationalistic deviations. For Augustine, ancient Israel, in the light of his replacement theology, is always the figure and representation of the new Israel, the Church, which, in her faith and universality, embraces all the people of the earth.

JOHN CHRYSOSTOM (CA. 349–407) AND AMBROSE OF MILAN (340–397)

The exegetical approaches of John Chrysostom, the greatest representative of the "School of Antioch," and of Ambrose, the great Ambrosian doctor, seem different from those adopted by Origen and Augustine. Indeed, while the latter adopted a purely theological, dogmatic, and spiritual approach, the exegesis of Genesis 9:25–27 performed by the former is moral in character.

In his *Homilies on Genesis*[28] Chrysostom—like Origen and Augustine, as we have already seen—answers the question that spontaneously arises from a reading of the text: Why is Ham's sin atoned for by his son, Canaan? The originality of his explanation is based on his unmistakable ability for psychological penetration and on his direct knowledge of the faithful.

> Ham did not endure less punishment than his son, he too felt its effects. You know well, of course, how in many cases fathers have begged to endure punishment in place of their children, and how seeing their children bearing punishment proves a more grievous form of chastisement than being subject to it themselves.[29]

If this explanation makes the modern reader somewhat uneasy by attributing to God an implacable rigor in inflicting a very harsh punishment on Ham, Chrysostom himself continues his homily by specifying that, in this way, God's original blessing on Ham is not taken away from its recipient, and the providential plan can be fulfilled without being hindered by human infidelities and sin. "This incident occurred"—says John Chrysostom—"so that Ham should endure greater anguish on account of his natural affection, so that God's blessing should continue without impairment."[30] It is not out of place to observe that the fathers, in their reading of Scripture—and this is one of their precious teachings—are capable of combining in God both justice and mercy. In fact, beyond the precise explanation of the text presented here, based on the prayerful and liturgical reading of Scripture, the criteria adopted by the fathers are the cornerstones of their inheritance. What is said of God and of his relationship with humanity can only be consistent with his fundamental attributes. Thus, a virtuous circularity is established between Scripture and theology or, in other words, between exegesis and dogma. This admirable unity, this comprehensive harmony of one and the other, is the appealing legacy of the patristic magisterium that can be enjoyed even when the interpretation of Scripture deals with more complex passages, such as the one we are examining. Furthermore, as we have seen, Chrysostom provides "added value" with his pastoral concern, his psychological sensitivity, and his ability to truly resonate with the hearts of his listeners. His hermeneutic power is consolidated and enlivened by the context of liturgical preaching in which he practices his exegesis.[31]

Ambrose of Milan also refers to the curse of Ham in *De patriarchis*, one of his exegetical-spiritual treatises. Like Chrysostom, Ambrose also draws a moral lesson from this episode: the respect that must be given to parents. In fact, in his short treatise he comments on Jacob's blessings on his sons and of Moses's blessings on the tribes of Israel, presented respectively in Genesis 49:3–27 and in Deuteronomy 33:6–25. At the beginning of his treatise, he makes a key argument: in the Old Testament, the blessings of parents on their children are endowed with a special divine grace that makes them effective. Similarly, curses also accomplish what they set out to do. And it is precisely this effectiveness that instils the sense of honor owed to parents.

> First of all, we learn how much reverence to give to our parents, when we read that those who received their father's blessing were blessed, while those who received the curse

> were cursed. Thus, God granted parents this grace to encourage filial affection. The prerogative, therefore, of parents is the education of their children. So, honour your father for him to bless you. The loving son honours his father out of gratitude, the ungrateful son out of fear.[32]

The patristic legacy on Gen 9:27 is thus enriched with a further meaning. This moral interpretation is surprising, if we consider the fact that Ambrose ordinarily reinterprets the episodes of the Old Testament from a typological viewpoint.[33] Indeed, inspired by the allegory of Philo of Alexandria, who had already commented on the first books of the Bible, he sees in those episodes a prefiguration of the mystery of Christ. The restrained reference, however, to the curse of Ham is treated from a more historical-literal perspective, as a precept of *reverentia filialis* (filial reverence). Besides, Ambrose's spirituality does not negate his fundamentally ethical approach to life, but rather completes it. A typical exponent of *Romanitas* (Roman sense), Ambrose is a proponent of human and Christian virtues united in a solid construction that includes the cornerstones, that is, fortitude, justice, prudence, and temperance, and the other moral perfections whose roots are inscribed in the natural law and which the profession of Christianity consolidates, from *pietas* to *liberalitas*. These also include *reverentia* toward one's parents. Ambrose refers to this without fail also in *De officiis ministrorum* (Duties of ministers), his treatise on moral philosophy, where the biblical examples he presents are drawn from the stories of the patriarchs: "Isaac was God-fearing, as befits a son of Abraham, and was so submissive to his father that he didn't even refuse death against his father's will. Joseph too, despite dreaming that the sun, the moon and the stars adored him, nevertheless remained scrupulously respectful towards his father."[34]

CONCLUSION

Even this quick, desultory examination of the patristic interpretation of Genesis 9:25–27, and of the curse of Ham in particular, helps us expand the meaning of Scripture to cover broad theological and spiritual meanings, as shown in the following summary table.

Patristic Author	**Work**	**Interpretation of the curse of Ham**
Augustine	*Against Julian*	Original sin
Augustine	*Questions on the Heptateuch*	Salvation story
Ambrose of Milan	*Patriarchs*	Respect for one's parents
Ephrem the Syrian	*Commentary on Genesis*	Prophecy of personal sin
John Chrysostom	*Homilies on Genesis*	Punishment of the father
Origen	*Homilies on Numbers*	Allegory of free will
Origen	*Homilies on Joshua*	Divine Providence

11

CURRICULUM, CONTENT, AND RACISM

The Need for a Paradigm Shift

Dorothy Mensah-Aggrey

As a curriculum design specialist at a higher educational institute, I have observed the developmental shift from a single-focus structure of resources based in the United States to those that are more inclusive and global. Within the past ten years, in particular, other subject areas have begun to shift focus to include global resources. To create a paradigm shift from U.S.-based resources, thus avoiding insularity and chauvinism, to equitable ones for all students, the pervasive discrimination in educational institutions must be decisively addressed.

Recognizing that racism is ingrained in American history and culture is the first step toward sensing its tentacles in other areas such as education, religion, and culture. Even though racism as a social construct began in the seventeenth century in America, its consequences still create ripple effects among people of color, specifically, Blacks and immigrants of African descent (IAD). Racism is prejudice against people of another race based on the belief or assumption that one's race is superior. The pervasive nature of racism creates difficulties in identifying such tendencies within a curriculum, but research provides evidence that it exists.[1]

How racism affects higher education policies is subtle yet complex. Some scholars in the field of anti-racist education have likened the changing dynamics to those of the chameleon. It is common knowledge that elites often determine the rationales that typically drive policymaking to mold higher education strategies in ways that would benefit them. Given that the upper echelons of the United States are disproportionately made up of members of the white majority, it could be argued that the rationale of this group is to preserve power, status, and opportunity for the majority, while limiting access to similar privileges from the marginalized and minoritized populations. Haynes observed that the behavior of such elites has primarily been to restrict access to others. These are "behaviors reflective of a restrictive view of equality focused more on creating equal access to learning by promoting inclusion of the *Other*, which safeguards white supremacy and fuels the reproduction of racial hierarchies in the classroom."[2]

This chapter reviews how racism has hindered educational access and opportunities for students from underrepresented groups, and how such hindrances could be meaningfully addressed for the sake of educational equity for all. Although the chapter references practices within the United States and a few other countries, there are racist tendencies in education in many other countries due to colonialism. Therefore, existing practices in specific countries are included to elaborate on the effects and role of curriculum and content in racism.

WHITE CULTURAL DOMINANCE IN SCHOOLS

For years, education has been utilized to persuade people of color that their culture is inferior to that of the dominant white culture.[3] There were earlier suggestions about the miseducation of Blacks into believing they are of lesser value than whites. Education was perceived as a tool to maintain white dominance by socializing those students to believe they are superior while also instilling in Black students a sense of inferiority.[4]

Clark and Clark researched African American children's racial preferences to explore the above hypothesis.[5] Researchers observed that when Black youth were presented with both black and white dolls and asked to choose which one they preferred, they consistently chose white dolls. According to the research, many Black children exhibit a racial inferiority complex when it comes to whiteness. The researchers believed that African American youth developed inferiority complexes from school circumstances during racial segregation. In the *Brown v. Board of Topeka* case (1954), the Clark and Clark study was used as a critical piece of evidence to support desegregation.[6] The notion that groups of people were inferior has been around for some time, according to Ali, who maintained that "certain founding pioneers like Thomas Jefferson alleged that African Americans were the most generically inferior race on the planet."[7] To make strides in a society that has already labeled its members as inferior is difficult.

Because race relations have improved and schools have been legally desegregated in the United States for several years, Woodson and Clark and Clark's discussions may appear out of date; however, they are still relevant. Although *Brown v. Board* helped people of color gain access to educational opportunities, significantly higher education, it also led to the shutdown of non-white schools. Districts dismissed teachers of color because administrators judged it socially inappropriate for them to instruct white students. Educating children of color was left to white instructors, who did so not because they wanted to, but because they had no choice. When non-white youth were exposed to predominantly white teachers, their psyches and educational outcomes often suffered.

EDUCATION

Carter Woodson is a notable name regarding the education of Blacks. Second to W. E. B. Du Bois, Woodson highlighted the plight of education for Blacks.[8] He drew attention to the miseducation of Blacks, and the vicious cycle that was being produced by the miseducated themselves proceeding to educate others, and themselves also miseducating those under their care. Woodson set an example for others to follow. Brown, in a recent article in the *Washington Post*, underscored the magnitude of Woodson's contribution to inequalities in academia. Even in his time, more than fifty years ago, Woodson could detect that Blacks were at the short end of the stick regarding education.[9] Yet, Blacks have not been the only group of people who have had to undergo such trauma. As has been recently revealed, the Indigenous Peoples of Canada suffered a similar fate through the introduction of the residential school system, also known as boarding schools in Africa. In the case of the Indigenous Peoples of Canada—

the First Nations, Inuit, and Métis people—children were at times forcefully separated from their parents and kept on school grounds for the sole purpose of "educating" them. According to Joseph, the Prime minister of Canada in 1883, John A. Macdonald, made the following comments in a statement to the House of Commons:

> The child lives with its parents, who are savages....Indian children should be withdrawn as much as possible from the parental influences, and the only way to do that would be to put them in central training industrial schools where they will acquire the habits and modes of thought of white men.[10]

Thus, the dominant race (white people), conveniently used education as a tool to repress the Indigenous Peoples of Canada. This tactic worked in other countries.

Curriculum and racism are viewed from different angles depending on who stands at the podium. Sociologists contend that racism is a learned behavior, behavior to suppress a specific race that has sometimes taken place through education—the lack of it, or misinformation in various subjects.[11] Whichever way one scrutinizes education across the board—whether in the Americas (both North and South), Europe, or Africa—racism has played a pivotal role in suppressing various groups of minority races. In addition, during the worldwide pandemic, racism rose to the forefront, considering the disparity of resources between the haves and have-nots even within the United States. Schools with well-established endowments were able to switch to online services as soon as the pandemic hit hard. In contrast, schools with limited resources scrambled to do likewise. This phenomenon was not limited to the United States; it was worldwide, for example, schools in Ghana took a while to transition to online learning due to a lack of resources and technology, while in France, "Ma class à la Maison" was immediately introduced into homes, with similar programs in Portugal.[12]

With the knowledge of racial tensions, especially in the United States and Canada, and the recent upheavals regarding the forceful separation of natives for the sake of education,[13] it is imperative that the records are set straight. It is equally essential that the paradigmatic shift of ongoing race discussions is extended to the educational sector. If education is power, then it behooves religious and political leaders and educators to make this power available to all persons without any hindrances. The most vivid memories of education separating the elitist from commoners are found in South Africa during the era of apartheid—the gap still exists up to this day, so much so that recently, students advocated a change in curricula.[14] It is commendable to note, however, that Georgetown University in Washington, DC, has begun a series of transformational educational initiatives to what many have long been perceived as racist tendencies within the system.[15]

Anthropologically, racism is considered "institutional when it is embedded in the laws, policies, and norms of a society and normalized by pseudo-scientific claims about physical or social differences."[16] Racism, it bears repeating, is prejudice against people of another race based on the belief or assumption that one's own race is superior. It can often be difficult to identify clearly how racism affects curriculum due to the pervasive nature of its unintended behaviors and consequences. Racial bias entails forming attitudes toward certain groups of people based on stereotypes or attitudes.

In education, racial bias has often reared its head when a majority group in power mandates content and curriculum for varied subjects through educational policies. These subjects or courses are taught in a manner that is often foreign to the recipients thereby creating biases and tensions. Examples can be found in colonized countries around the world. For instance, in most British colonized African countries and English-speaking Caribbean Islands, school-age children learned the alphabets in this manner, "*A* is for Apple, *B* is for Boy, *C* is for Cat...*G* is for grape." How many apple trees and grapevines will one find in Africa and the Caribbean Islands? Yet, because Europeans had invaded and colonized these countries, citizens were forced to learn English as a medium of communication. Fast-forward to higher education: the race gap between the (white) privileged and minorities, mostly Blacks, is phenomenal.[17]

Quite often, minority educators point to the fact that the "elite" have the upper hand in designing textbooks and controlling publishers, resulting in the preservation of power, status, and opportunities that benefit a specific class or group of people—the white majority. Harris notes the lack of white persons in acknowledging the problem at hand: "It is both ironic and deeply problematic that white persons forget or refuse an insight into this perversity, which has been visible in the writings of people of color for decades."[18]

CURRICULUM

Curriculum connotes a sense of planned direction, especially in education. Educators may speak of a set number of courses specific to a subject matter, or over a period, with definite goals. In most cases, the curriculum is laid out by a school's administration and teachers are required to abide by the contents of the curriculum. Egan maintains that curriculum is "the study of any and all educational phenomena."[19] Egan's interpretation of curriculum is in line with modern-day education. Young, however, argues that, although curriculum is difficult to define, it can be perceived as "the transmission of knowledge from one generation to the next."[20] Curriculum, I contend, is often systematic with set outcomes that are based on what the designers (of the said curriculum) intend for their learners. As such, one would notice that curriculum content in colonized countries had specific implications: learning the language and culture of the colonizers, period. Everything else to do with the local culture and way of life was shoved aside. It was the reason why languages foreign to many were introduced in schools; there were set goals to be accomplished. As Young noted earlier, certain information was passed on to that generation with the hope that they would, in turn, pass it on to the next generation—a cycle set in motion. Curriculum, therefore, can be defined as a foundation for education in all its variations. The question one may ask is what was behind the curriculum of the Europeans who colonized several countries?

It is almost impossible to discuss curriculum in the American school system (currently) without mentioning Critical Race Theory, which is causing a great deal of consternation in some circles. Critical Race Theory (CRT), coined by Kimberlé Crenshaw, seeks to place the role of race and racism squarely within the legal system that created the construct of racism. By discussing racism in the legal system, and extending it to educational institutions, students can better understand the ramifications of ongoing racial tensions.[21] It is an academic and scholarly practice of critiquing the "social construction of race, and institutionalized racism that perpetuates a racial caste system that relegates people of color to the bottom tiers."[22] CRT seeks to emphasize the fact that, since racism was socially constructed for the benefit of a few as has been noted by sociologists, it can be equally deconstructed for the benefit of all.

As strange as it may seem, the pandemic and its effects have highlighted racist tendencies in school curricula. Too many people have died because of racial violence, and far too many children have been harmed because of discrimination. While eyes on reforming the justice system is important, it is equally essential to reform the educational system, albeit curricula. Changing the educational system is a critical first step toward eradicating structural and institutional racism, for racism has been part of education for far too long.[23]

Since the integration of public schools in America sixty-six years ago, the educational system has not been able to address racial matters properly. Several school districts decry unequal access to opportunities in the form of budgets, and human and learning resources. In addition to the lack of resources, the redlining strategy that was utilized in housing discrimination relegated people of color to low-resource districts, which furthered the gap between the rich and poor. Potter and Burris noted how some foundations are setting out to assist deprived schools with better access to resources that will create sturdy learning environments for students.[24] Obviously, great resources matter, as they boost the morale of students and teachers alike. When schools take steps to replace anti-racist curricula, students become the prime beneficiaries. In fact, all society benefits because, when belief systems change, students who later become leaders in their communities carry with them these changes. Several institutions now offer implicit bias training to human resources as they try to fill positions with qualified personnel who will, in turn, impact the lives of students.

Ali speaks about culturally relevant and value-driven pedagogy (CVD) as a tool for enhancing learning materials for students, similar to Ladson-Billings's cultural relevant model (CRM).[25] Ali further explains that utilizing such models in curricula assists learners to "place a higher value on the lesson or instruction...and create a cultural lens for students to guide, interpret, navigate, and assess their learning experience."[26] Proper use of culturally enhancing learning resources provides students with better opportunities to learn and remember what they learned. Gay describes culturally responsive teaching (CRT) as "using the cultural knowledge, prior experiences, frames of reference, and performance styles of ethnically diverse students to make learning encounters more relevant to and effective for them. It teaches to and through the strengths of these students."[27] How then can educators who have not experienced a culture teach in order to reach the students? Turney, Philips, and Law, who conducted research in Leeds, in the United Kingdom, stressed the intentionality of administration in deconstructing racism, especially in educational institutions.[28] It goes to reason that, when an administration is intentional about such processes, educators often follow suit. Apart from culturally enhancing resources, racially diverse human resources are equally important for institutions that earnestly seek change.

LANGUAGE

Prior to the development of the Romance and Germanic languages, Latin was the language of the learned. In the early centuries, kings and popes established universities that were open only to monks, priests, and laypersons, who studied the medical sciences.[29] Although largely defunct, Latin still plays a role in most Roman Catholic documents that originate in Rome. If indeed the church is interested in reaching the ends of the world as mandated in Matthew 28:20, is this realistic? Currently, how many academicians comprehend Latin, let alone students struggling to make their grades and graduate from college without heaping student loans? Jennings summed up the use of Latin as an elitist language.[30] He asserted that "the comprehensive reach of Latin not only indicated Rome's power but also signaled its monopoly on the channels of official education and scholarship."[31] He added that Latin was the language that scholars had to learn as a means of inter- and intra-communication with church authorities, which again begs the question, How many Blacks could afford such education? In addition, most Blacks who happened to be in Europe and America were transported as slaves who were perceived as unworthy of sharing the same learning space even if the opportunity presented itself. When people have to express themselves in a language other than theirs, there are bound to be issues.

Several witnesses have shared the extent of damage that they suffered at the hands of white people as Native Americans (in the

United States) just like Africans (in Africa) were banned from speaking their local dialects in school. Students who spoke their native tongues were punished severely and ridiculed in school and the community to assimilate them into the European way of life and culture.[32] Jennings reported similar incidents in Africa, where students were called derogatory names and asked to refer to themselves in like manner when they were caught speaking their native dialects. Once again, language was used as a tool to gain the upper hand; language, ergo curriculum, became a divisive tool in the name of education.

The suppression of indigenous dialects is a known fact around the world. Several African and Caribbean authors have written extensively about this heartless treatment by educators who should have known better; a number of them were largely missionaries too.[33] Some have argued that language was used as a hidden agenda. In extreme cases, students were forbidden to speak vernacular at school and in some homes. To progress fast in schools, some parents even preferred the use of foreign languages in their homes. Until recently, Latin, Classics, and the philosophy of Greeks and Romans filled African universities. By studying such and shelving native philosophers and languages, the tacit discernment was that the local language was inferior. Language, therefore, became a powerful tool for subduing certain groups of people by intent. Individuals were considered smart if they were fluent in foreign languages other than their own—to the detriment of their local dialects.

Great educators know that language leads to understanding. Therein lies the problem of using a foreign language to explain biblical concepts which have not always worked well. Language has been linked to religion, and it is interesting to note that Martin Luther, the Augustinian monk whose thesis sparked the Protestant Reformation in 1517, created greater waves in Germany than simply rebellion against Pope Leo X. The Germans were the first to utilize their native language instead of Latin in education, yet due to colonization, the English language became ubiquitous as the years progressed. Whichever way one turns, the unlikely marriage of racism and curriculum go hand in hand, more so via language. It has been said that, once a people's language and culture are dismantled, one can play the puppet strings as desired. Every country that was colonized by a European country, whether in Africa, South and Central America, or Asia, ended up using the language of the colonialists as their medium of communication in schools, and in most cases, in houses of worship. Several African countries, though, are attempting to reverse this suppression by introducing their local dialects into their educational systems.

THE IMPACT OF RELIGION AND THEOLOGY ON EDUCATION

Historians and social scientists have written on the interrelations of religion, theology, and education and how the three might impact one another. This section provides an overview of studies on the impact of religion and theology on educational attainment. Neither religion nor theology is obviously the sole element that has caused the disparity of educational inequities. Several other factors, such as economic, geographic, cultural, and political situations, have contributed to systemic racism found in education.

Past successful trends in educational accomplishments assist in explaining current patterns within certain races and ethnicities. The educational infrastructure of a country determines access to schooling—a stable road to educational fulfillment. In many cases, the infrastructure is constructed on the foundations of religious leaders and organizations to promote learning and to disseminate the faith. Christian monks constructed libraries in the Middle East and Europe, preserving valuable older literature produced in Latin, Greek, and sometimes Arabic prior to the invention of printing presses. These religious monasteries eventually became universities in several instances, with examples in Bologna, Italy (1088), University of Oxford, UK (1096), and Halle, Germany (1502).[34] Notably, some deviated from religion and theology to languages and medicine.

Religious institutions created schools mainly to disseminate doctrine by educating their clergy and lay adherents. Georgetown University, run by the Jesuits, was established in 1789; the University of Notre Dame du Lac, run by the Congregation of Holy Cross, was established in 1842; and the University of Dayton, run by the Marianists, was established in 1850. Although most of these institutions have since become secular, their existence may explain why the (upper-class) populations of the United States and Europe are so well educated.

In addition to their involvement in building infrastructure, religious organizations were crucial in developing public attitudes toward education. It must be noted, once again, that these institutions catered only to whites initially. In October 2020, the *U.S. Catholic* magazine republished an extensive interview given by Fr. Cyprian Davis (1993) on the treatment of Black Catholics in the church.[35] In that interview, Davis did not mince his words when he stated that "the Church in this country reflects the problems of the country, which has yet to solve the question of race; that has been America's tragic flaw."[36] The question of race really has been the universal church's flaw, not just America. Herein lies the paradox of the church's mission of evangelization and discipleship, and a sad, but true contribution to the intersection of religion and racism in general.

Missions had a purpose, and developing theology was part of that purpose. Unfortunately, the *God* of Europeans, who were the main colonialists of Africa and Asia, was presented as superior to the *God* of others. The Christian message was usurped by Eurocentric attachments. Thus, worshipers had to learn a European language, music, and culture to worship. An education based on the religion of the white person involved several factors, such as singing and reading in Latin, no vernacular, and strict adherence to certain behaviors, such as no movements during worship celebrations in line with the social fabric of whites, mostly Europeans. A good example of such a reversal of attitudes is the Second Vatican Council (1962–1965), during which time it was agreed through a simple majority that liturgy could be celebrated in the vernacular across the globe.[37]

By insisting that the faithful learn Latin, Greek, German, Spanish, and English to participate in religious celebrations, indigenes were forced to relinquish certain grounds. Some missionaries looked down on local dialects as students were punished if they spoke their native dialects as if to imply that native dialects did not have the capacity to theologize; only the white person's language has that capacity. So, students were forced to learn to read, write, and speak English to theologize when one thought in a different language. For example, the issue of gender-inclusive language, which is now the order of the day, does not pose any issues in most Akan (Ghanaian) dialects: *Oyankopɔn* (the Greatest Friend), *Ɔbɔadeɛ* (the Creator). Yet, in most languages, one would have to add identifiers for male and feminine nouns that then becomes an issue for some native speakers.

The same attitude (of educating to eradicate indigenous customs and traditions) that was employed among Native Americans and the Indigenous Peoples in Canada was applied in African countries. In July 2021, a missionary from the United States was "recalled" home from Ghana. This missionary (to a Lutheran community) was upset that the Ghanaian students were communicating in a native dialect. He responded in contempt by teaching in German that day to a group of students whose official language was English. He took this a step further and mandated that no one could speak any Ghanaian dialect in the school. Thankfully, the Ghana Lutheran mission got wind of the incident and politely asked him to leave the country since his sense of missiology was obviously warped. Ironically, Presbyterian missionaries to Ghana were the first to translate the Bible into local languages, yet here was a missionary who still carried tendencies of a superiority complex in the field of education. There is a difference between this scenario presented above and what has recently been reported about the plight of Native Americans in the United States and Canada. Here was an individual propagating racist tendencies ,whereas, the situation with Blacks, Native Americans, and Indigene Peoples in Canada was institutional racism. Either way, education propagated racial tension.

Sadly, too many stories are being unearthed, particularly of the Canadian Residential Schools. Students were separated from their families under the pretext of being educated. Whereas there might have been altruistic reasons behind the education of the indigenes, the way some missionaries treated the children has nullified any such reasons. For the Canadian indigenous tribes, the residential schools that have headlined the news of late were places of atrocities. To date, the indigenes blame the government and the church for attempts to force-feed them with foreign materials in lieu of their culture.[38] There have been several apologies to the Indigenous Peoples and their families regarding the unethical treatment of children under the guise of education. The fact is that these situations took place because white people felt the need to replace the culture of the Indigenous Peoples with theirs. This behavior spanned the globe. They were not peculiar to Indigenous Peoples in Canada and the Americas. People have struggled with Christianity not because of its message but because of its messengers. The message of Christianity is credible based on the credibility of the messenger. Christians perpetrated such atrocious acts in African and South American countries that, to date, some are opposed to anything bearing the name of Christian. Christianity has a lot in its closet, and if it will gain grounds in any sector, thorough cleaning of the closet is a must.

Current-day writers continue to perpetuate falsehoods about certain ethnicities. An example of Africans being cannibals, according to Fritz, sustains this crass mindset of the dominant culture in the United States.[39] When students read such appalling materials in class (and youth ministry of all places), how can there be a change of mindset? Below is a rather lengthy excerpt from his book. Note the number of times that Africans are referred to as cannibals (emphasis mine):

> Imagine that an island—previously uncharted and unknown—is discovered off the coast of Africa. On this island is an ancient tribe of *cannibals* with its own customs, music, dance, food, dress, value system, and way of life....The Catholic Church decides to send missionaries to this island....The four missionary priests immediately identify the chief of the *cannibal* tribe and approach him. They...explain to the chief that *cannibalism* is wrong.... They distribute the Latin prayers and invite the members of the tribe to join them for...Holy Mass. What's going to happen to those missionaries? The *cannibal* tribe is going to eat them for dinner. But why?[40]

This book is still in use by youth ministers in the United States and Canada. It came across my desk for a course development for a Canadian diocese, and no attempt on my part to switch to a healthier version of the portrayal of Africans was accepted by the powers that be. This is only one example, yet it begs the question as to whether educators are ready for real systemic change.

CULTURE AND MUSIC

Culture, according to the American Sociological Association, is the summation of a people's way of life—language, belief system, rules of law, music, and customs that give meaning to their very existence. Given this definition, it is understandable that one group of people imposing their way of life on any other group would not necessarily yield the best results. Yet, the phenomenon of majority groups shoving their way of life down the throats of minority groups continues to exist. The plight of colonized countries that still bear marks of castles and language corruption goes to prove the point that to control a people, one only has to change their culture.

By far, the most truthful statement or attempt to reverse the plight of Blacks in the United States has been recent acknowledgments of past wrongs and genuine efforts of reparation. Walli, Williams, and Kelly drew people's attention front and center when they stated,

> As anthropologists, we feel a responsibility to speak out against injustice and destructive harm of racism because we recognize that our discipline has been complicit in perpetuating pseudo-scientific ideas about racial inferiority. As museum professionals, we also recognize the injury and cultural violence museums have done by harmful and inaccurate representations of the world's cultures and unethical collections practices.[41]

It seems that the science of eugenics, which propagated inferiority complexes of certain races, is finally beginning to acknowledge the harm that has been done, and which needs to be unknotted. Hopefully, if anthropologists have come to this realization, an interdisciplinary effort will soon begin to reshape the narrative that has for so long created stumbling blocks for certain groups of people. This acknowledgment could be the watershed event onto which textbook publishers and curriculum designers could latch and reverse systemic racism. It is no secret that part of the dissemination of institutional racism is due to publishers of textbooks who for so long have maligned minorities by derogatory remarks and information. Not only history, but journalism has also played a role in the portrayal of people of color and indigenes as less than. Such portrayals in various news media outlets have not augured well for certain groups of people.

Gone are the days when certain music genres were anathema in concert halls. Individuals had to patronize orchestral concert halls to be considered cultured; that is, high culture. In fact, in most African schools from the 1960s to 1990s, music consisted of Western music legends, mostly classical composers. I was a product of that era; I need not look far. For my Ordinary Level Certificate examinations, I studied the baroque, classical, and romantic periods and knew more about Johann Sebastian Bach and Frederic Chopin than I knew about any local musician! These days, several traditional African, Asian, and South American musicians have been part of European orchestral ensembles to showcase diversity and inclusion. Hopefully, such inclusivity will eventually be the norm.

A ROAD MAP TO PRACTICAL SOLUTIONS

Anti-racist education is being demanded in many institutions, particularly by students, while educational institutions are promoting strategies to deconstruct academic racial inequity. Several well-established universities have created offices of diversity and inclusion to tackle matters of racism. Georgetown University in Washington, DC, and Leeds University in the United Kingdom are two examples. A simple Google search will provide interested persons with a plethora of institutions that have created such offices and strategies within the past five years. Turney, Phillips, and Law designed a tool kit for training administrators and educators which highlighted outcomes, taking responsibility for curriculum, and long-term evaluations based on research that they conducted in Leeds. One of the questions they posed, which is key for transformation in any educational institution, was "Does your institution's curricula reflect the changing needs and views of a modern, diverse society?"[42] A group of administrators and educators could very well spend a day's development training based on findings of such a question. Teaching students about anti-racism could have a positive impact on their mental health, albeit personal life. If anti-racist policies and curricula are implemented in institutions, the face of racism could very well be replaced with understanding and enormous growth in all areas of education.

Unfortunately, discussions regarding race are sometimes uncomfortable, and many will end in conflict, but change is never easy or comfortable. It is important to confront racism to deconstruct the system that created and supports it. Pollock listed four possible scenarios that institutions could utilize to promote and maintain academic equity. The fourth particularly caught my attention. He states,

> Everyday antiracism in education involves equipping self and others to challenge racial inequality...actively challenging the widespread tendency to see racial disparities in opportunity and outcome as "normal"...proactively reminding students of color...that they are equally intelligent and potentialed...reminding white students that they are not naturally superior, but rather privileged by an intricate system that they, too, can make more equitable for others."[43]

The goal is to eliminate racism from the educational system and offer a safe environment for all learners. This goal can certainly be attained through curricula and the leveraging of empathetic human resources. Only by continually identifying and describing racism—and then dismantling it—can racism be undone. It is critical to review course materials and content to make sure that course designs are expressly and actively anti-racist. Whiteness as a superior race must be eliminated in courses where race is a topic or curriculum focus, and different perspectives and voices must be represented throughout such courses. The University of Dayton's Institute for Pastoral Initiatives embarked on such a project several years ago, and courses are still under revision. It was not so much the racist remarks that needed attention; rather, course materials depicting the universality of the students who participate in these online courses. Using "Discussion Board" questions, students can interact with one another comfortably without interference to learning, thus ensuring that all voices are heard. To help students develop critical awareness, it behooves educators to offer students opportunities to analyze their prejudices. In relation to these opportunities, it is also critical to create a classroom environment that allows for such reflection and investigation. Students have a wide range of views and understandings about various topics, and in some cases, experiences that they may willingly share with their peers.

CONCLUSION

Where racial tensions are concerned, education at all levels can be the beacon of hope for change. Education can transform lives and situations; it has in the past and has potential for the future. Administrators, faculty, and staff can make lasting positive changes that will eventually eradicate racism, which is a social construct. Curriculum and content, therefore, play pivotal roles in education; thus, it is critical to be intentional about how learners are formed. Obviously, the foundation that is provided to learners is that which will bear fruit in the future. Bearing this in mind, it is important to educate all persons about systemic and institutional racism to break the cycle that has long repressed persons of color, the minority.[44] The development and growth of any country hinge on good and well-rounded education, ergo, curriculum and content. The urge to deconstruct white supremacy systems in education does not correlate with reversing racism, as some have insinuated. Rather as evidenced by the Truth and Reconciliation Commission of South Africa, reparation is possible through education. South Africa set the standard for such possibilities of educating persons of color who had been relegated to the back bench due to racist regimes. Canada is following suit with regard to Indigenous Peoples. Other countries can learn from these two. Equity and empowerment in education must be applied to all races, and at all educational levels, not a few, certainly, and not one group only. It is incumbent upon educators to rethink consciousness and collective action in radical, deliberate, and practicable phases. Academic equity will decide posterity for humanity. This is a fact with which educators must contend.

Innovative changes in curricula can provide pathways to educational equity. With foresight, policymakers can create better learning spaces, resources and environments that will enhance opportunities for minority groups. One must be intentional about education; in particular, curriculum, for curriculum is the content that shapes learners. Changing the educational system is a critical first step toward eradicating structural racism.

12

RACISM, THE CHURCH, AND STRUCTURAL SIN

Paulinus Odozor, CSSp

Racism has been described as "any prejudice against someone because of their race, when those views are reinforced by systems of power."[1] As a document of the United States Conference of Catholic Bishops points out, "Racism arises when—either consciously or unconsciously—a person holds that his or her own race or ethnicity is superior and, therefore, judges persons of other races or ethnicities as inferior and unworthy of equal regard." The bishops add that "when this conviction or attitude leads individuals or groups to exclude, ridicule, maltreat or unjustly discriminate against persons on the basis of their race or ethnicity, it is sinful."[2] The question of race question, therefore, is a question of belonging, that is, of inclusion and exclusion. It is also a question of power that focuses on skin color as the primary determinant for who is in or out, who belongs and who does not belong, who gets to sit at the table and who sits at what point at the table when they are invited at all. As a question of power, racism is a power play in which certain people feel superior to others simply based on the color of their skin. Usually, it is the case where the light-skinned members of the human community feel that they are superior to people of darker skin, it does not matter whatever else is at stake or whatever the others bring to the table.

RACISM IN THE CATHOLIC CHURCH

After the death of George Floyd in Minnesota, in 2020,[3] I wrote two pieces: the first was based on an interview I gave in June that same year for CruxNow.com, an independent Catholic news site based in Rome; the second was an article for *Church Life Journal*, an online publication from the McGrath Institute for Church life at the University of Notre Dame, Indiana.[4] In both articles, I argued that the incident regarding the death of George Floyd has shown that the question of race was no longer just an issue for the United States, but that the protests that followed indicate that it had become a worldwide question that, for many reasons, needs sustained attention from the church.

After the publication of my article in *Church Life Journal* on September 8, 2020, I received many reactions from some Africans in the United States about their experiences of racism, especially, within the Catholic Church. Here are some stories that have been edited for this presentation. Although each of these stories are from the United States, they contain patterns that I have also heard or witnessed in other Western countries.

The first story is from a Cameroon-born philosophy professor at a large university in the Midwest. He wrote, "I have had very bitter experiences within the Catholic Church. When I was in Milwaukee, I went to a church in one of the suburbs where we were the only Black people. We sat in a pew and other people refused to sit with or close to us. During the 'sign of peace' people refused to shake our hands. I complained to the priest, but he did nothing—or appeared irritated that I would raise the issue. I wanted to join a committee in the Church, but I was 'cut out' from the committee—they would call and hold meetings without inviting me. Father, I wish I could discuss this with you at some length."

Another person wrote, "The first thing that hit me when I walked into a Catholic Church in this country was that I was a minority. I had never felt different that way in the church. I became conscious of my minority status. This feeling was reinforced for a very long period by people's attitude toward me and my family. Few people dared to sit close to us in church. It was as if we had a wasting disease. Sometimes it seemed difficult for some people to share the kiss of peace with us." This person concluded by saying that "he felt he was just being tolerated as a member of his parish and that many Catholics in his situation feel very alienated as members of their parish communities."

These stories echo some stories I have heard in the past on the question of racism and the church in the United States of America.

A few years ago, an African literary scholar who was educated at convent schools in her country wrote to inform me that, when she moved to her new parish in the university town where she had just been hired to teach, she went to the parish office to make inquiries about enrollment and to see how she could be involved. The parish secretary who met her at the door immediately told her that they had no aid to give her. She did not ask who she was or what she wanted. As soon as the secretary saw her come out of the cold in her winter dressing, she assumed she must be looking for a handout. The African woman insisted on seeing the parish priest. When the priest came out to see her, he would not let her talk but rather pointed out that there was another parish in town where he thought she could fit in better. Of course, after attending this all-white parish for a while it became clear that she was merely being tolerated here. She would have left the Catholic Church at that point but decided against it for the sake of her children.

In another story, a Nigerian literary scholar who had been a deputy vice chancellor at the University of Nigeria, Nsukka and a very devout and knowledgeable Catholic told me about his experiences in a certain parish in Boston where he had been hired at that time to teach at Harvard. He had been sick for a while. However, he willed himself to attend Mass on this Sunday since it was Easter. As he entered the church, his parish church, he was stopped at the foyer by an usher who kept on showing people to their seats while he left him there and ignored him. Whenever he tried to go to a seat, this bulky usher stood in his way. Here he was, on Easter Sunday morning, sick, and being treated in a very un-Easter-like manner. This incident ruined this man's Easter completely; he felt terribly upset, turned around, and went home. After this incident, my correspondent felt he had to change parish. Prior to this Easter Sunday treatment, the professor and his wife had been receiving very degrading treatment from the pastor of this same parish. The priest used to stand at the door of the church to greet parishioners at the end of Mass. But, as soon as this Black couple approached him, he would turn away and refuse to extend his hands or even acknowledge them. This went on for a long time, until after that Easter Sunday event, the family decided to move out of the area and into a new parish.[5]

The incidents here may seem minor, but they are not. Actions speak louder than words. For people who are already suffering all other forms of discrimination in the wider society, such negative actions within the church are too much for them to take. They shake people's faith to the core, and many people who experience these types of actions have left the church. In the case of the two families above, the only reactions, thankfully, was that they left their respective parishes and neighborhoods in search of more receptive parish communities.[6]

IDEOLOGICAL AND PRACTICAL ASPECTS

There are two important aspects to the phenomenon of racism that must be pointed out. The first is the ideological aspect. Racism has been nurtured and fostered through strongly held and argued philosophical views. From the time of the Enlightenment, people have been taught that the Caucasian race is superior and on the top of the human ladder. Other races follow from this in varying orders of importance. Down on the lowest rung of the ladder are Black or dark-skinned peoples.[7] The ideological aspect is not the most lethal, for people can think whatever they want; it is what they do that really matters as the above stories illustrate. Ideology comes to life in the daily practical aspects of our lives—in the institutions and practices that form the bases of our lives, the places where we live, and move, and have our being such as the arts, entertainment, politics, and religion. It is in these places that racism seeps into everything we do and becomes a structural and a very destructive force. It is at this level that people are denied job opportunities, refused entrance to the schools and clubs they desire and deserve, refused mortgages for some spurious reason, refused promotion for a position for which they are qualified, talked down when they nurture ambitions for leadership, hunted down like animals by law enforcement officers whose job is "to serve and to protect," or by fellow citizens who find it unbearable that a Black person is jogging through their neighborhoods, and so on. Sadly, too, it is at this practical level that a devout Catholic, even one who is a prominent international scholar might not be allowed to participate in the affairs of his local church. It is at this level, too, that people would not sit close to a fellow Christian at church. It is at this level that a human being who is coming to her church would be held outside of the rectory and directed to another place where they would be given handouts, even though they were not coming to beg alms. It is at this level, too, that a diocese might refuse to harbor a Black priest because he speaks with a certain accent or even allow him to officiate a Sunday liturgy for fear of offending some members in the parish who do not find him normative as a priest. The list is long.

THE CATHOLIC CHURCH ON RACISM

The modern Catholic position on racism has evolved over two hundred years. It struggled on the philosophical, theological, political, and social aspects that have characterized the life of the church throughout this period. The church's position has crystalized in recent times in the teachings of recent popes from John XXIII to Francis and of the Second Vatican Council. In his important book on continuity and change in Catholic teaching, a *Church That Can and Cannot Change*, the late great American jurist and moral theologian John Noonan demonstrates how the church struggled with the question of slavery over centuries, with some church institutions sometimes owning slaves or at other times issuing declarations against the practice and even joining in practices against the institution of slavery. Central to the institution of slavery was the question of race. Thus, whatever the church thought about this ended being also important for its position on race, especially since the slaves involved in the transatlantic slave trades were mostly Black.[8]

A study of racism in the church "involves excursions to various planes of analysis, much of which until recent times were connected to the question of the Jews in Europe—precisely the question of antisemitism."[9] John Connelly has shown that Catholic responses and reaction to racism (particularly in its antisemitic form) was varied. He states that "not only were there racists and antiracists in the same Church, but they could even cite the same Catholic authors to support their divergent views. Critics are impressed by the institutional Church's own pretext of representing unchanging wisdom, but in the Jewish question oversees fantastic transformation within a few decades. Diversity among Catholics at any time is matched by changes over time."[10] Regarding racism as a universal problem, the church has grown consistently, even if slowly to an awareness of the very evil character of this phenomenon.

The Catholic Church found a united and universal voice regarding race from the pontificate of Pope St. John XXIII. He begins his encyclical *Pacem in Terris* with an affirmation that has become one of the pillars of Catholic social doctrine for this issue:

> Any human society, if it is to be well ordered and productive, must lay down as a foundation this principle, namely, that every human being is a person, that is, his nature is endowed with intelligence and free will. By virtue of this, he has rights and duties of his own, flowing directly and simultaneously from his very nature. These rights are therefore universal, inviolable, and inalienable. (no. 9)

This passage presents several ideas that are essential to human rights discourse in Catholic moral teaching, namely the personal character of the human being manifested in intelligence and freedom, and the personal nature that is the source of rights and duties. It is also to be noted that the Catholic rights doctrine "aims to be universal and not particularistic in both its foundation and its application."[11] The human rights doctrine proposed by John XXIII in *Pacem in Terris* goes beyond the United Nations Universal Declaration of Human Rights and is far more extensive than anything that has gone before it, even in the Catholic Church.[12] This doctrine even goes further in two key documents of Vatican II, namely *Gaudium et Spes* and *Dignitatis Humanae* and in many other magisterial documents since. Although there have been discussions on the human person in various papal writings from Leo XIII onward, the development of an elaborate theological anthropology in *Gaudium et Spes* far supersedes them.

GAUDIUM ET SPES

The dignity of the human person serves as the cornerstone of *Gaudium et Spes*. In chapter 1 of that document, the Council presents a set of elaborate anthropological constants that define the human person, such as creatureliness, sociality, duality of being, sinfulness, grace, and redemption. In various parts of the document, the Council fleshes out the details of its teaching on the human person. According to *Gaudium et Spes*, "God has a parent care for *every individual* and has willed that all should constitute a single family treating each other as brothers and sisters. All have been created in the image of God who 'from one ancestor made all nations to inhabit the whole earth' [Acts 17:26], and all have been called to one and the same end, God Himself" (*GS* 24). The Council acknowledges that the human is superior to everything and should be helped to lead a truly human life: "Everything should be rendered to a person which is required to lead a truly human life, such as food, clothing, education, shelter, the right to free choice of one's state of life and found a family, to work, to one's good name, to respect, to appropriate information, to act in accordance with the right norm of conscience, to the protection of one's private life and to a just freedom, including religious freedom" (*GS* 26).

Gaudium et Spes continues to speak in further ways that respect must be shown to every human person (cf. 27). Here, we find the paragraph made even more famous later by Pope St. John Paul II in *Veritatis Splendor* about matters and conditions that not only are not in accord with human dignity properly understood but, in fact, diminish the human person in many ways. The document states,

> Whatever is hostile to life itself, such as any kind of homicide, genocide, abortion, euthanasia and voluntary suicide; whatever violates the integrity of the human person, such as mutilation, physical and mental torture and attempts to coerce the spirit; whatever is offensive to human dignity, such as subhuman living conditions, arbitrary imprisonments, deportation, slavery, prostitution and trafficking in women and children; degrading conditions of work which treat laborers as mere instruments of profit and not as free responsible persons: all these and the like are a disgrace, and so long as they infect human civilization they contaminate those who inflict them more that those who suffer injustice, and they are a negation of the honor due to the creator. (*GS* 27)[13]

This paragraph was made more famous later by Pope St. John Paul II, who, in *Veritatis Splendor*, refers to matters and conditions that are not only in accord with human dignity properly understood but, in fact, diminish the human person in many ways.

Gaudium et Spes also presents a key to understanding the teaching of the Council on racial equality. Important in this passage is the restatement of a refrain that is found throughout the document to the effect that all men and women possess a rational soul and are created in the image and likeness of God and therefore share in the same image and the same origin and have been equally redeemed by Christ (cf. *GS* 29). They all share "the same divine calling and dignity," and thus the basic humanity that they all share needs to be increasingly recognized. Although people differ in their mental and physical capabilities, and even in their moral resources, this should not be the ground for the denial of the equal personal dignity that belongs to every human being as a human being: "Every type of discrimination affecting the fundamental rights of the person, whether social or cultural on grounds of sex, race, color, class, language or religion should be overcome and done away with as contrary to the purpose of God" (*GS* 29).

The Council further insists that we must work to remove the "curse of ignorance" that shrouds our vision on the matter of human dignity and equality:

> There is a most appropriate duty for our age especially for Christians, to work for basic decisions to be taken in the economic and political fields and at national and international levels, to recognize and implement throughout the world the rights of all the human and civil culture appropriate to the dignity of the person without discrimination on the grounds of race, sex, nationality, religions or social condition. (*GS* 60)

Given all that has been stated so far, there are three important theological notions worth highlighting that underlie recent Catholic moral discourse on racism. These include the notion of structural/social sin, Christian anthropology, and the understanding of racism and God's will.

STRUCTURAL/SOCIAL SIN

The Catholic tradition speaks of sin in two ways. In the first instance, sin is considered as an offense or transgression against God and against the moral order. Here an action is a sin if it is bad, the individual knows that it is a bad, and the individual consents to act on it. This is the notion of personal sin that is familiar to many.[14] When we sin this way, we feel obliged to go to confession and to receive absolution for our actions. In this situation, it came to be accepted by many Christians that "it was possible to respond to the Gospel and yet be unconcerned with social responsibilities. Although love of neighbor was always seen as basic to Christian life, effective social action, and involvement to implement that love through the works of justice was not considered a necessary requisite."[15] In contemporary times, Catholic moral teaching also puts emphasis on *social* sin. The idea of social sin follows the biblical emphasis on sin as more than just an act. Sin is also viewed as "as a stance, orientation, direction, attitude rather than deed, incident, transgression."[16] Individual sins, as the name indicates are the products of individuals making willful decisions to do evil actions. Social sin, on the contrary, arises out of group biases, malice, and blindness. Social sins arise within social structures and are embodiments of the sin of injustice that constitute structures of sin. Social and structural sin thus give rise to each other and, in turn, feed off each other.

When we speak of structural sin, we speak, in the words of John Paul II, of "the sum total of the negative factors working against a true awareness of the universal common good, and the need to further it, gives the impression of creating, in persons and institutions, an obstacle which is difficulty to overcome."[17] Structures of sin arise, according to the pope, through "the concrete acts of individuals who introduce these structures, consolidate them, and make them difficult to remove. And thus, they grow, spread, and become sources of other sins, and so influence people's behavior."[18] Gregory Baum, the famous Canadian theologian, also like John Paul II, speaks of social sin as constituting "the injustices and the dehumanizing trends built into the various institutions—social, political, economic, religious and others—which embody people's collective life." As people in such institutions go about their daily tasks, "the dehumanizing trends built into the institutions which guide their lives will damage a growing number and destroy their humanity eventually."[19] Thus, social sin and the structures they engender arise usually out of inattention and neglect because, although the reality of injustice and dehumanization are evident for all to see, people close their eyes and minds and refuse to "see" them. And, although these situations of injustice and oppression may not be blamed on many contemporary individuals, they thrive due to the neglect of and by the people of the present age because these people have chosen not to see what is going on or have decided to go along with the present ethos because they are benefitting from it, or simply because it does not concern them. This is where social sin then becomes a *personal sin of omission*. In the Catholic tradition, sins of omission, that is, those sinful situations—sometimes big, sometimes small—that one can do something to remedy but refuse to, are no less sins for which one should be held accountable by God. Therefore, although, as has often been pointed out, structural sin are sins by analogy, they become real and actual sins for which one bears responsibility, just like actual individual sins, due to neglect and inattention, especially when one can do something to present or ameliorate or even eradicate the impact of the structures in question but fails to do so on account of a number of factors.

One refrain that runs through every Catholic theological discourse on racism is that racism is a sin. In their 1979 seminal text on race, the United States Conference of Catholic Bishops (USCCB) insist that

> racism is a sin; a sin that divides the human family, blots out the image of God among specific members of that family, and violates the fundamental human dignity of those called to be children of the same father. Racism is a sin that says some human beings are inherently superior and others inferior because of races. It is a sin that makes racial characteristics the determining factor for the exercise of human rights.[20]

In that same document, The US Catholic Bishops speak of structures of society as being racist:

> The structures of our society are subtly racist, for these structures reflect the values which society upholds. They are geared to the success of the majority and the failure of the minority. Members of both groups give unwitting approval by accepting things as they are. Perhaps no single

> individual is to blame. The sinfulness is often anonymous but nonetheless real. The sin is social in nature in that each of us, in varying degrees, is responsible.[21]

Furthermore, they add that "all of us in some measure are accomplices," since "the absence of personal fault for an evil does not absolve one of all responsibility." The only way to absolve us from the sin of racism is to seek to resist and undo the injustices built into our social structures lest "we become bystanders who tacitly endorse evil and so share in guilt in it."[22] Racist social structures "reflect the values which society upholds" and "are geared to the success of the majority and failure of the minority," with the "unwitting approval" of the majority.

What the bishops were driving at in issuing this document is that racism is a social sin. In theological terminology, racism is a structural sin. It is, in some ways, a different conception of sin that we will discuss below.

THE SIN OF RACISM WITHIN THE CHURCH

Racism goes against everything we stand for as a faith community. In the church, we believe that God makes everyone in his image and likeness. Everyone bears the divine imprint, equally and really. God did not make any counterfeit materials. The implications of this fact are huge. First, creation in the image of God confers equal dignity on all, regardless of social status, one's bank account or attainment. The Second Vatican Council speaks of the human being as the only creature God willed for himself. This truth applies to everyone. Joseph Ratzinger notes that at the heart of Christian anthropology is the truth that

> emperor and beggar, master and slave are all ultimately one and the same person, taken from the same earth and destined to return to the same earth. There are not fundamentally different kinds of human beings, as the myths of numerous religions used to say, and some worldviews of our own day also assert. There are not different categories and races in which human beings are valued differently. We are all one humanity, formed from God's one earth.[23]

Second, racism fundamentally contradicts another Christian belief, namely, that Christ died for us all and for our salvation. In his writings, St. Paul invites us all to understand that through his death, Christ has molded us all into a new humanity, a new Adam, as he puts it often. We have become one body, the body of Christ. St. Paul reminds us in his Letter to the Ephesians: "There is one body and one Spirit, just as you were called to the one hope of your calling, one Lord, one faith, one baptism, one God and Father of all, who is above all and through all and in all" (Eph 4:4–6). In his Letter to the Galatians, he further asserts that, for the Christian, belonging in Christ means the end of all divisions based on pedigree, race, ethnicity, or gender: "There is no longer Jew or Greek, there is no longer slave or free, there is no longer male or female; for all of you are one in Christ Jesus" (Gal 3:28).

Racism wounds the body of Christ in another painful and important way. It so scandalizes many among us that it makes it difficult for them to continue to believe. Here are a few facts to consider:

a) A good number of the persons who have come to the West as faithful and practicing Catholics in Africa have stopped going to church completely for various reasons related to racism (and liturgy in the Western churches).
b) Many of those who are still active as Christians have left the Catholic Church and joined a church where they feel welcome and at home.
c) Many Catholics who came to the West as married Catholic couples are now divorced and sometimes remarried, sometimes because no one was there to help them in their moments of crisis or pain. Where they do not divorce, family breakdowns occur and could have been avoided if they had received adequate support from their caring pastor or from their local Christian community.

WHAT MUST WE DO?

Since contexts and manners of manifestations of racism differ greatly in the church, one can only speak in generalities. The first thing is to do whatever is possible to find out the extent of this issue within the local church. This can be done first, by inviting the minorities in your local church to speak about their experiences in a candid and nonjudgmental way, and second, by inviting the wider diocesan community to think about the issue together, just as many churches did immediately after the death of George Floyd. Sometimes, many well-meaning persons are not aware of racism and alienation that is happening around them or of the way they are contributing to the alienation of other members of the community. Many of the visible minorities in the churches in the Western are immigrants. But most are indeed people who were born in these countries or have become naturalized citizens in those places. Despite this situation, we must recognize the truth that all of us, our racial affiliations notwithstanding, live in various cultural caves that give us identity. Such identities, when properly nurtured, can enrich the community by forming a rich and beautiful tapestry.

Second, many of the minorities are still at heart strongly attached to the cultures and modes of worship from where they come. The reason many Africans leave the mainline Christian churches for the African-themed Pentecostal churches that are plentiful in the West is because they find worship in Western Catholic churches very starchy and boring. It is important therefore that every diocese with minorities from these areas pays attention to this fact. What they do about it should be decided in consultation with the groups concerned. The intention is not to create a different Catholic Church but to find ways to keep the church catholic.

Finally, it must be noted that wherever peoples of various ethnicities and nationalities are gathered, there will always arise the question of fairness, justice, and equality. We have the example of the New Testament dispute between the Hebrew and Hellenist members of the church. It took very bold leadership by the apostles to resolve the matter, just as was the case on the matter of conditions for membership in the young church. The lesson from this is that church leadership at whatever level must be very vigilant in making sure that every group within the community feels welcome and appreciated.

13

CORROSIVE RACISM

Subterfuges and Preliminaries

Pius Ngandu Nkashama

The African diaspora community faces complex situations caused by the emergence of extremist groups or right-wing parties for whom *racism* is commonplace. Sometimes, it manifests itself openly where no one expects. Despite all appearances, racism is a fundamental fact. It manifests itself in unexpected and unpredictable places, including the church, and the hierarchy of the Catholic Church cannot escape mention in these preliminary critical observations. In fact, the number of priests from African countries serving in Europe and North America grows every year, and these priests suffer the contradictions of doctrines of love and tolerance and the most basic signs of rejection and non-belongingness.

This chapter does is not limited to denouncing certain reprehensible acts or wrongdoings; it seeks rather to propose strategies of protection against those harmful consequences that often ruin human relations among communities. The experiences drawn from three places that I have lived, separated far from each other—Algeria, France, and the United States—make it possible to corroborate the logistics of presumption as well as the reflexes of self-defense. It is necessary to show an exceptional courage to avoid yielding to the temptation of despair or outright violence or debacle.

The criticisms that are made against racism are generally done one-sidedly, from what is denounced in the media. It must be admitted, however, that the actual incidents become offensive or virulent when victims suffer them either voluntarily or involuntarily. A media source or presentation of an offensive action does not allow one to react easily, and the inactivity or lack of reaction that is displayed in the face of instances of ignoble acts leads to lethargy on the part of those who then resign themselves to a consented silence; the recurrence or repeated instances of an offense diminish their offensiveness and then transformed into unreasonable mimicry.

The people who are subject to these misfortunes often close themselves up in opaque shells that disintegrate their consciences, dehumanizing them. Without any defense in the face of misfortunes that overwhelm them, some wounded spirits seek to dissolve or bury their bitterness and their despair in confused fantasies that allow them to endure hardships in the depths of their being; others manage to sublimate the psychological tortures.

It is becoming increasingly difficult to counteract such frustrations with positive movements. History teaches us that obtuse circuits reinforced by parallel propaganda often tend to exonerate the vectors of silences that make the paradoxes of endurance hermetic when caused by such frustrating circumstances.

However, the reaction must not correspond to the illusory antagonisms of consent by equivocal passivity, before preserving them indefinitely to the point of inconsequential turmoil. Hostile racism is never overcome by defeatism, much less by complicit fatalism. Such attitudes conceal acquiescence by brooding over one's own weakness.

On the contrary, deficiency evolves when it inspires clumsy pretexts. Clever subterfuges end up distorting it into a patched-up theory of the hierarchy and inferiority of humankinds. The doctrine of defects that holds certain categories as assigned to genetic castes reinforces the valorization of species and divides epistemological criteria into Manichean components: good/bad; superior/inferior. Through the cynical equation thus formulated, those who consider themselves superior manipulate the laws that manage communities and set the rules of legitimacy for the lives at stake, to the point of objectifying (reifying) those who are excluded and discriminated against.

Legislated experiences make it possible to return to the roots of limiting a priori. They intensify the supposedly irreversible antitheses.

ALGERIA: VICTIM OF INDUSTRIAL MIRACLES

For eight consecutive years, between September 1982 and February 1991, the passage through Algeria marked the confrontation of cultures of protection against "racism" in a singular way. The colonial metropolis, namely France, made it possible to better grasp the raw dimensions of the emergence of a mentality of discrimination. The challenges imposed necessary criteria to assess the conflictual parameters, in the face of instinctive opposition against Africans from south of the Sahara. A climate of stubborn suspicion still prevailed, likely to limit delusions to the limit of collective hysteria.

Indeed, during our first contact with a formal contract issued by the Algerian State for teaching at the University of Annaba, we discovered a new nation, enriched by intervals of deadly battles. The city of the "Jujubes" was rebuilt in total cooperation, thanks to the Africans, without any confrontation of face.

In most higher education institutions, subjects were taught with the participation of foreigners. The latter came mainly from the "Eastern countries," mainly Russia, but also the satellite states at the time—Romania, Poland, and Czechoslovakia. An important system supports the oil industry or that of other raw materials, such as natural gas, iron, hydrocarbons, and petrochemical derivatives. The superstructures of the numerous factories in the east (Annaba) and Mitidja come mainly from the above-mentioned countries. It became imperative that the training of future engineers should be provided exclusively by their nationals.

At the outset, it was worth noting the preliminaries of the injunctions issued by Frantz Fanon, according to which the anticolonial struggles had to reach a broader objective, to preserve it from the oversized contradictions of the consecutive imperialism: "the total liberation of the whole of Africa." A weekly newspaper in the country still bears the name of a work by Fanon that managed the precepts of confrontation, the *African Revolution*. The herald he represented sought to lead this "revolution" from the Mediterranean shores of Algiers to those of the Atlantic in Cape Town, in the subtle footsteps of those of Che Guevara in the Americas.

The continental ambition was too visible in the stratagems put in place since the postulates of the "National Liberation Front"

(NLF), especially during the regime of Houari Boumediene from June 1965 to December 1976. He died on December 27, 1978. The number of Africans participating in the government's work provided the intellectual guarantee of such collaboration that was essential for the proper functioning of the system. The nationalist movements for the whole continent had an upscale headquarters on the outskirts of the capital. They were composed of militants of Mandela's African National Congress (ANC), the guerrillas of the "Kamerun" led by Ruben Um N'Yobé, and local guerilla fighters in brigades against the Negus-Emperor Haïlé-Sélassié and their clumsy killers around the enigmatic Mengistu.

Congolese Lumumbist militants were survivors of the 1960 massacres that had killed their hero in a planned assassination. The companions of Patrice Lumumba were welcomed with great respect. They held comfortable positions in the local administration and had been well received here.

A painter from Algiers known for his works, exhibited, and celebrated in European capitals, had presented in frescoes and beautiful colors my collection of poems, *Nuptiales en fragments* (The poet's wedding). Colloquia and numerous seminars brought together authors who had come from the countries of Africa. The events gained historical momentum!

The "future" writers passed through Algiers. They were welcomed with many honors: Ahmadou Kourouma, Moussa Konaté, many Haitian intellectuals or "African Americans." Artists, including musicians, actors, painters, and sculptors from all over the continent were highly esteemed. Big festivals were held regularly in stadiums and public places in the interior of the country. They drew considerable crowds during the performances. The Algerian Ministries had at their disposal advisers from "Black Africa" in impressive numbers. We ourselves have participated in "think tanks" on national university education policies without any trace of discrimination, especially when Frantz Fanon had to be celebrated in a major colloquium held in Algiers in 1985.

At the level of universities and higher institutes, the share of African teachers was preponderant: more than 150 individuals throughout the national territory. The working conditions were excellent from every perspective—salaries, interpersonal relations, statutory promotions, and guaranteed housing. Teaching both at the

University of Annaba (Bône) and at Constantine, I was often part of the Juries of Theses in Algiers or Oran, with much conviction and self-esteem.

Islam was practiced in a restricted, almost confidential way. It was not a "state religion." The number of mosques was limited to privileged places: there were none on the university campus. The ostentatious wearing of canonical beards and veils (hijab) seemed almost nonexistent among female students and the public reading of the Qur'an was rare. However, other religions were widely tolerated. Catholic priests or Protestant pastors of all confessions worshiped indiscriminately in perfect openness, because the state guaranteed a serene atmosphere that ensured total harmony.

In addition, it was possible to travel day or night without worry throughout Algeria by road, using the regular daily bus services, or by air. We crossed the desert without any apprehension. We were received in all communities with enthusiasm. I only remember that my father back home was worried about my security: He overwhelmed me with letters of caution: "Never let your children walk everywhere, for the Arabs are enslavers of Blacks." It was difficult to calm down these untimely attitudes of panic.

But then, from 1987, this country that had been sheltered from the burdens of racism began to experience the vagaries of economic complications. The ups and downs of basic infrastructural failures affected everyday life. They fuelled the terrible "hunger marches" regularly put up by a distraught youth.

Precisely, the system that had appeared to be well balanced was built on an "illusion of history" and elaborate lies. The fateful ramblings of a masterful "socialism" were an informal caricature and imitation of the Soviet Union. They could hardly withstand socioeconomic constraints and pressures. As soon as the International Monetary Fund (IMF) put its nose into the crevices of the façade, the discovery of the concealed deviations became catastrophic.

The dark propaganda of the One Party watered down lies about the "foreign debt." It gave credence to the principle that "Algeria was the only country in the world to know no suspicion of foreign debt. The figures disclosed, however, were staggering. The masquerades of the civil service supported by the swindles of a despotic administration were based only on the ramblings of the false "fighters" of the war. The vertiginous amateurism of the latter meant that they were merely camouflaged cowards without any history of combativeness. Most of them sneaked under the false masks of family members proclaimed as surreptitious heroes. Besides, by means of scabrous tricks that had been cleverly crafted, they had physically eliminated the real, original "mujahideen," or forced them into exile in distant lands, like Mohamed Boudiaf, one of the founders of the revolutionary National Liberation Front.

The representatives of the One Party themselves showed febrile incompetence, supported by scams of indomitable fanatics. Incessant frauds and embezzlement of public funds took place in the intoxication of a dictatorial power that had ended up invading the mechanisms of collective dilettantisms. The short-lived dictatorship of Chadli Bendjedid complicated the equation in dramatic proportions.

To wash away such turpitudes, they concealed the disaster by resorting to the nefarious movements of the Muslim Brotherhood. Suddenly, at the dawn of 1987, euphoric Islamists emerged from nothing. They subtly took over the most prominent functions of the state. At the university, delinquents were appointed to positions of responsibility: from the indelible rector to the deans of institutes, from directors of departments to members of the management staff. In the finance department and in the personnel office, people had been appointed exclusively based on their membership of the Muslim Brotherhood movement. With gluttony, they pocketed emoluments and fantastic sums.

The students also did not remain unaffected. To benefit from scholarships to advantageous studies, or to pass an examination effortlessly, it was necessary to wear the prefabricated beard, to wear a djellaba of occasion, and to brandish a borrowed Qur'an. Mosques were hastily built. Improvised imams suddenly emerged with the mission of spreading messages diverted from the Holy Books. Very quickly, falsified Hadiths turned into calls to hatred against other religions embodied by foreigners, among whom we found ourselves—people from Black Africa, and mostly Christians, Catholics and Protestants. These malleable opportunists did not admit an Islam that was tolerant, such as the Islam that was practiced in the regional countries of Senegal, Mali, and Niger. Now, we became traitors who prolonged the abominable French colonization. The punishment that hit the *métèques* ("foreigners") was insidious. It affected salaries and administrative conditions of stay in the country.

The marriages that had been contracted between Black African and Algerians were beginning to dissolve in general panic. The secular music of orchestras was abolished, and the practice of Islam was the only law allowed in the community. Overnight, the neighbors with whom we had shared unforgettable moments, facts, and gestures of conciliation, turned into inveterate xenophobes. They held indecent parables about us and in public, imbued with vindictive hatred and unalterable violence. Humiliating rhetoric spread among academic circles amplified by overtones of aggressiveness. They entertained the apology of a chauvinism with cannibalistic appearances.

The mechanisms of widespread segregation developed through servile discrimination based on the doctored doctrines of Islam. They claimed an insidious interpretation of the Quranic messages exasperated by the promotion of heretical ideologies.

By the time the parliamentary elections were held in 1991, the Islamists had won the votes hands down, because the people had finally adhered to their pompous well-established propaganda, insofar as they held the levers of all administrative powers. However, the central authority was caught off guard and succumbed to an uncontrollable panic. They rejected the results obtained through normal elections. This led the Muslims to take refuge in the clandestine maquis and develop dangerous extremisms. The insurrections worked their way down the spiral including the murders perpetrated first within cultural circles against writers and artists, then against practitioners of other religions. This later led to caliphates in Syria and other places.

Racial intolerance was rigidly reinforced. It drowned the interstices of internal revolts to the point of provoking senseless sectarian reprisals. They ransacked the battered territories of Sahelian Africa and destroyed the social fabric to insane proportions. Indiscriminate attacks finally reached the countries of Europe.

The last few decades, however, have shown signs of appeasement. They influence interpersonal relationships. Above all, they augur that Algeria can experience a real "cure" of the evils that have distorted its face as a welcoming country. This is a real "exorcism," because the insolent malevolence was beginning to take on the proportions of a real common curse.

FRANCE: "LIBERTY, EQUALITY, FRATERNITY"

The speeches and writings disseminated by France mostly bear the indelible character of anti-racism. They sublimate tolerance to the point that certain gestures are at odds with intellectual tools. Consequently, living equivocal attitudes that shine through the most flagrant acts are a well-formatted performance. Rather, it would take a tempered character to confront the most deleterious attitudes to overcome the panic capable of progressing toward ease and assertive balance. As a result, a type of discrimination is discovered even more pernicious, because it turns out to be intransigent and devious in its outrageous demands.

Admittedly, the humanitarian principle is enshrined in the institutional acts governing "immigrants" at all levels of official services. The debauchery of violations of the rule reverses the trends, to the point of intentionally blurring the social burdens of the outrages maintained.

On three occasions, by means of compliant legislation, we were granted regular stays in France. The circumstances of these translocations are recalled because they appear to be weighed down by the incoherence of the iniquitous words that occasionally support them.

In 1973, France granted "scholarships" to the assistants of the National University of Zaire (Congo-Kinshasa) with the intention of enabling them to prepare doctorates for promotion in their respective fields. Until then, it was concluded that these stays were organized within the Belgian institutions on behalf of the former colonial metropolis. When it was necessary to change countries, the consular authorities of France dealt with all the formalities with suspicious promptness. They carried out the process from obtaining long-stay visas to granting patronizing funding for favorable conditions of settlement (stay) on arrival.

It was proposed to us that we bring with us members of our small or extended family, without any specific clause. So much so that most of the boarders, apart from a few rare exceptions, never presented the supposed doctorates at the end of the periods prescribed by the required conditions. On the contrary, they took advantage of these accommodations never to leave France and to take advantage of the living situations facilitated by these providential circumstances.

After the defense of a postgraduate thesis, when it was necessary to opt for the return to the "native country," the ensuing outcry among colleagues prolonged the ephemeral contritions. Recriminations were raised against those who felt betrayed by such an interruption perceived as a clumsy defection.

At that time, acts of racism seemed rather insidious. It manifested itself, especially, in the choice of research topics. The specialists that were consulted in various universities where we wanted to register often repeated to us, including the eminent scholar, Étienne Étiemble, that "African literatures," on which we wanted to write doctoral theses, "did not exist." In fact, it was claimed that we were not allowed to propose topics on the sociology of the peoples of Africa, because the inevitable methods used were similar to the beginnings of ethnology, the "science of the savages without writing."

Some of these "pundits" had even sent angry letters to the Ministry of Cooperation that was responsible for our stay and study, stating that our behavior belonged to the infamous category of strange crooks with excessive ambitions. Obviously, we had behaved like scammers who abuse French generosity to take advantage of free tuition. Some colleagues found a way of counterattacking; they preferred to present their work in Belgian universities, since France clearly and deliberately did not want it.

The second stay took place while I was preparing for a State Doctorate at the University of Strasbourg (1980–1981), the highest degree in the field. Religiously locked in a monastic-looking student room, I did not endure the demands of persistent racism. In addition, the country had overflowed with popular jubilation during the debonair election of François Mitterrand (May 1981): an unexpected deliverance to the immigrants at all levels.

It should be imagined that the successive governments of the magnanimous left had granted beneficial status to foreigners, to the point that in the years 1985 to 1995, residence visas were granted as free gifts to nationals of French-speaking countries. The formality was accomplished without requiring any compensation, including under the reign of an intolerable man of the "right," like Charles Pasqua in the Department of Interior.

The avowed and unannounced objectives were, however, of a sinister malfeasance aimed at the reckless contribution of an easy and exploitable workforce for the benefit of factories or vehicle industries. We have been able to travel to France many times without interruption, to acquire privileged status, to stay there as many times as we wanted. In such a context, I settled advantageously in Essonne, with a prestigious position of cultural advisor to the Ministry of Culture and the "General Council." However, the experiment failed miserably to the chagrin of all the partners in this exceptional operation. The circumstances of this eventful stay were the most pernicious and also the most atrocious. Despite holding a degree of *Doctorat d'État* (State Doctorate), it was not possible to find suitable employment other than that of sweeper and subordinate in casual hires. A book was inspired by the ill-silenced wrenches during this execrable period: *Vie et mœurs d'un primitif en Essonne quatre-vingt-onze,* in which racism plays a preponderant role.

The French turpitudes forced us to apply for a remote position in Algeria. The pilgrimage continued under other horizons, but at the rhythm of identical tribulations and infallible compromises. The subterfuge of the free residence visa allowed us to return to France and stay there in even more uncertain conditions. Immigration laws were becoming more and more demanding and burdensome. It was necessary to resign oneself to teaching in secondary schools around Brive-la-Gaillarde, before recovering a drifting position at the University of Limoges.

As a humorous side story to this situation, in 1981, on a famous French literary television program called *Apostrophes,* an episode attracted the attention of attentive observers. Bernard Pivot, the program's host known for his humanist positions, had invited a Black Haitian writer, Jean Metellus, to discuss his novel, *An Etching* (1983). The work chronicles the life of a pure white native, a Swiss painter. But when Metellus had been introduced by the press services and arrived on the set, the star host rebelled against such an untimely "intrusion." To the astonishment of the invited author, he cried out, "He cannot be the author of this novel: Blacks do not understand anything about the psychology of whites!"

Metellus calmly replied that he was a psychoanalyst in a large Parisian hospital. The relevant cases he frequently dealt with often went beyond the clinical episodes described in his novel. The famous host ended up getting tangled up in hasty excuses.

In 1986, I applied for a teaching position at the Australian University of Tasmania. The selection committee had requested letters of recommendation to decide on the case. I took the liberty of adding the name of a professor of the University of Paris XII-Créteil, whom I considered a loyal colleague. The file was returned with the singular mention of rejection, along with the handwritten letter of this professor. He said with his hand on his heart: "To my knowledge, I do not believe that there is a single black African who can properly teach in a European-type university, not even this candidate for whom I have a lot of esteem."

The first manifestation of obsequious racism was a phone call from a grandmother of one of the students, when she had learned of my assignment in the Grammar in Linguistics class. With an unusual defiance, she questioned me about my ability to speak the French language well. She questioned the "nerve" I had in wanting to teach it to children of France: "Do you speak French well, Mr. African? Can you give proper lessons to our French children?"

I had to berate her, in turn, and threaten to report her to the police for hostile harassment. She had to address her complaints to the president of the university who had hired me according to criteria accepted by the central administration. No one has ever repeated the misdeeds of such a bad kind.

From Limoges, I managed to climb to the Sorbonne Nouvelle, Paris-III. A remarkable position of Francophone Literatures obtained after a long struggle, the first of its kind in the history of the teaching of African authors in France. I did it to the best of my ability. From the first day, the authorities of our faculty warned me without embarrassment: "Do not dare to apply for a position of responsibility. Whenever the students are dissatisfied and show their bad mood, they will resort to shameless rhetoric since you put the Africans (they did not dare to pronounce the word "Negroes") at the direction of a French university, nothing works. You can imagine the damage!"

Other misunderstandings ensued amid irremediable litigation when I had to supervise the defense of a doctoral thesis: where I was considered the recipient student and never as the president of the jury. Furthermore, some of my colleagues, whenever they passed me in the teachers' room, intelligently claimed that I confused the place of the student with that of the professor.

In 1996, I returned from a successful summer school at the University of Portland in Oregon, the capital of the Trail Blazers. I brought back in the luggage many sports products, T-shirts, and basketball shoes. The arrival at Roissy in France proved tumultuous. The customs officer kept me for more than five hours wanting to understand why I was so overloaded and with what money I had acquired these expensive items, despite my explanations of being a "visiting professor." One of them babbled nonchalantly that there was only one motivation that could allow a Black African to go and work as a teacher in an American university: during this period of the Olympic Games in Atlanta, I could only claim the shabby title of "sports teacher."

The most macabre aspect of this simultaneous malevolence appears more truculent in the circles of the churches, both Catholic and Protestant. Priests who rush to France are always solicited by various ministries in the parishes of the capital, Paris, as well as those of the provinces. They allow themselves to be exploited by unscrupulous parishioners, as much as the European confreres. The case of Father Kadima Kadiangandu seems to be indicative of these manifestly racial perspectives. With an introverted spirituality, he arrived in France without a scholarship. Despite this inconsiderate handicap, he intended to undertake postgraduate studies in psychology.

Assigned to the diocese of Versailles in the parish of Sainte Marguerite du Vésinet, he found himself entangled in inextricable imbroglios. The flock belonged to a religious community situated in one of the municipalities of the suburbs of Paris, populated for the most part by one of the most pathetic financial bourgeoisies. It was composed of rich bankers, wealthy entrepreneurs, and business leaders. Among other hassles, his talents as a brilliant preacher had won him the sympathy of the Christians. They deserted the Sunday celebrations of the parish priest, to jostle for the eleven o'clock Masses that he celebrated with moving rhythms. The affluence was accompanied by various donations in quests, generous offerings, and abundant alms.

He then ran into trouble for the ecclesiastical authorities did not look favorably on these donations. The local bishop himself meddled in the insidious quarrel and decreed that the priest in question behaved like a perfect crook, protected from evil intentions to divert the liberalities of innocent Christians. He had abused them with a parody of devotion for a purpose: to enrich himself and undertake commercial actions in his home country, Africa. He received me personally to explain the validity of such ill-considered predispositions.

He sent voluminous correspondence to the officials of the diocese of origin requesting the priest's unconditional repatriation.

A copy was reserved for the French services in charge of formalities for immigrants. The undisciplined Father Kadima was bluntly excluded from the parish of Vésinet and his misfortune in an inhospitable Paris was dragged on for more than three consecutive years. There he met no benevolent attachment. Endowed with an unshakeable will and by dint of an admirable spirit of self-sacrifice, he managed to persevere in his studies toward his defense of a State Doctorate under heroic conditions. Finally, Benedictine nuns convinced him that he was welcome at the Abbey of Faremoutiers in the suburbs of Paris and where he spent himself until his last days.

Such distressing cases are not uncommon throughout the countries of Europe. Frenzied acts of pernicious racism are numerous. They multiply each day—in Paris and the larger cities of the provinces. Devoted priests suffer abuse, even to the point of supreme sacrifice. They are tortured relentlessly by their unseemly prelates. The fact that they find themselves stuck in a deplorable situation forces them into attitudes of resignation and fatalism to the detriment of their own lives. They submit not for the sake of faith in the church, but because the springs of self-defense have been cushioned by insurmountable trials. They no longer master the mechanisms of resistance nor the necessary energies to resolve conflicts. They constantly face moral tests. Unfortunately, they cannot count on the support of their own churches in Africa.

The official services of the national police further illustrate the audacious, blatant acts of malice when they physically harm both the immigrants and those citizens who have taken up residence for many years. They are badly treated as subhuman, beasts to be slaughtered with total impunity, only because they are "negroes." Unfortunately, these crimes will never be met with a criminal sanction.

THE UNITED STATES: MANNERS AND CUSTOMS

Obtaining a teaching position at Louisiana State University in Baton Rouge was more than beneficial. The laborious circumstances surrounding the move promised a forgiving future. However, self-righteous minds insisted on benevolent premonitions, and realities confirmed the first opportunities for hypothetical privileges.

Here, the distribution of populations into racial components is rigorously governed by strict legislation. They obey constitutional constraints, and the logic of their application is transmitted through administrative acts. Membership according to the provisions of identities obeys the criteria set by the states. It does not support a noisy interpretation of the disciplines envisaged in the present case.

The management of the university assigned me a number that appears on the regulatory certificates. It corresponds to the rank prescribed in the chronological statutes of employees of equivalent rank, classified according to the order of their racial references: "Caucasian, Native, Spanish, African American (Black), Latin American, Asian." In certain circumstances, codified quotas have been claimed following injunctions at the time of recruitment or the distribution of wages before respecting sociological balances. The criteria are discussed only in special procedures when the constituent arrangements are organized.

The contours of interpersonal relationships, however, do not refer in any way to these legalistic classifications. On the contrary, malicious individuals use the configurations that the "law" allows to monopolize certain specificities of behavior.

During a time when I was mourning the loss of a very close uncle, a colleague of the university, a teacher like me whom I believed sincere in his actions, dared to confront me with an unhealthy casualness. He commented, "I do not understand why you have this awful look and mourn a distant uncle of Africa, when every day on the continent millions of individuals succumb to benign diseases or natural plagues that have been defeated for centuries."

A dull anger came over me that was difficult to suppress, especially since these unworthy remarks were held in front of my students, during a colloquium that brought together hundreds of participants.

On another occasion, an African nephew had married an American "Caucasian" girl. She belonged to a family whose parents were originally from Germany. The ritual ceremony of marriage took place under the shelter of a miraculous decoration: we provided the goats recommended by the dowry according to African traditions, and as many finances in hard currency. There was a spontaneous enthusiasm that accompanied the various stages of matrimonial negotiations. The uncles of the bride hastened to solicit useful explanations concerning these gesticulations that seemed like unusual pageantry, bordering on the presumptuous folklore.

The pomp of the religious celebrations had been organized in the disconcerting decorum of a Protestant church in Lafayette. The celebrant pastor, himself a relative of the bride, had explained the program to the many people who came to cheer them; he had the necessary authorizations and was accredited to combine the ceremonial protocol as well as the legal provisions of a "civil marriage." The spouses signed the required formalities in a solemnity supported by liturgical sequences, all in accordance with American law. They claimed that they would be transmitted later and in all regularity to the official civil registry services, at least we had naively imagined that to be the case.

Several years later, the couple was struggling, despite an offspring of four children who had enriched the union. The difficulties worsened to the point of an unexpected divorce. When they went to bring the documents of the countersigned pact, according to the standards and codes in force, however, it appeared that the documents had never been transferred to the competent authority of the central administration. They were stamped with the seal of disability: null and void.

The parent pastors then provided ultimate arguments: they had never endorsed this "nonstandard alliance." It turned out to be *good* to declare to the bewildered public that there was no question for them that their child, a white woman, would marry, even hypothetically, a "Black African." The separation had to take place outside the law. Since the authentic instrument had never been registered in the manner prescribed by the authorized bodies, the marriage ceased to acquire the characteristics of legitimacy but took the form of a banal concubinage. It could not, therefore, dissolve itself according to normal legislation; it had only ever existed through organized fraud. This meant that the farce concocted from the beginning was a legal vacuum. This distasteful joke had been inspired by a unique (and iniquitous) motivation of primal racism.

CONCLUSION

It is imperative to avoid the likely harmful effects of the numb nonchalance of those who abandon themselves to discouragement. The fight involved requires despotic efforts and weapons equipped for every moment. It's about taming a fearsome monster, a multi-headed hydra. An energetic battle must remain sustained until the prospective triumph. Resignation corrodes consciences, abdication destroys rational balances. Prolific misdeeds disintegrate the structures of judgment and attack the logic of mental constructs.

A worthwhile initiative such as this book edited by Cardinal Turkson helps to consolidate the will for those who still dare to believe in its dimension of redemption. The discrete incidence cannot be measured by visible impacts in the immediate future. However, it has indirect repercussions, because it becomes possible to consolidate the instances of deliberation in the contexts of self-defense precautions. The reconstruction of the imaginary safeguards the supports of intelligence against the ravages of destructive prejudices and dampens our instant immunity reflexes against such devastating stereotypes.

NOTES

FOREWORD

1. See Edward K. Braxton, *The Church and the Racial Divide: Reflections of an African American Catholic Bishop* (Maryknoll, NY: Orbis, 2021).

2. Edward E. Baptist, *The Half Has Never Been Told: Slavery and the Making of American Capitalism* (New York: Basic Books, 2016).

3. See Global Black History, https://www.globalblackhistory.com/the-role-of-the-roman-catholic-church-in-slavery/.

4. See John Strausbaugh, *City of Sedition: The History of New York City during the Civil War* (New York: Twelve 2017), 35, 57, 195.

INTRODUCTION

1. The Greek *adelphos/adelphē* (brother/sister) means "from the same womb." Originating from the same womb, they are equal in dignity (cf. *Fratelli Tutti*, 22, 98).

2. See the Purpose of the UN Sustainable Development Goals (SDGs) as formulated by Ban Ki Moon at the UN General Assembly in 2015 (footnote 22).

3. Amartya Sen, *Development as Freedom* (New York: Oxford University Press, 2001), 291; see also Martha C. Nussbaum, *Creating Capabilities: The Human Development Approach* (Cambridge, MA: Harvard University Press, 2011), 21–22.

4. Cf. *Catechism of the Catholic Church* (Vatican City: Libreria Editrice Vaticana, 1993), n. 357, https://www.vatican.va/archive/ENG0015/_INDEX.HTM.

5. Benedict XVI, Encyclical Letter, *Caritas in Veritate*, June 29, 2009, n. 18, www.vatican.va.

6. This is love of our brothers and sisters in truth (cf. *Caritas in Veritate* 1). Helping to promote the God-given vocation of persons is collaborating with God's plan that precedes creation (cf. Eph 1:4–5).

7. Cf. the Meetings of Popular Movements with Pope Francis.

8. Francis, Address to Moneyval, October 8, 2020, www.vatican.va (cf. *Evangelii Gaudium* 58).

9. Benedict XVI, Address to the Members of the Roman Curia, December 21, 2009, https://www.vatican.va.

CHAPTER 1

1. Perry Anderson, "The Antimonies of Antonio Gramsci," *New Left Review* 1, no. 100 (1976): 15–17.

2. Antonio Gramsci, *Selections from the Prison Notebooks* (London: Lawrence & Wishart 1971), 180–83.

3. A term popularized by Noam Chomsky, though rooted in Gramsci.

4. Gramsci, *Selections*, 416–18.

5. Gramsci, *Selections*, 210.

6. Something that Foucault openly describes as such: Michel Foucault, *Power/Knowledge* (New York: Pantheon Books 1980), 53.

7. Michel Foucault, *The History of Sexuality* (New York: Vintage Books 1978), 97.

8. Foucault, *The History of Sexuality*, 92.

9. Foucault, *The History of Sexuality*, 93.

10. This concept refers to the simultaneous universality and particularity of any local social, political, and economic system. See "Glocalization," *Encyclopedia Britannica*, https://www.britannica.com/topic/glocalization; see also Victor Roudometof, *Glocalization: A Critical Introduction* (New York: Routledge, 2016).

11. This shall be explored later in this chapter and drawing on J. Kameron Carter, *Race: A Theological Account* (New York: Oxford University Press, 2008).

12. Called "exploitation colonialism." Such territories were called "colonies of extraction." Colonial power was devolved to local (often Westernized, sometimes Christianized) chiefdoms who in effect oversaw the extraction of resources on behalf of the colonial political-economic overseers. A classic account that explores this is Walter Rodney, *How Europe Underdeveloped Africa* (London: Verso, 1972/2018).

13. Sometimes called "settler colonialism." In such "colonies of settlement" people from the metropolitan power moved out to the territory and governed it exclusively, often imitating modes of governance in the home country, usually excluding most or all of the native peoples. The "problem" of the native peoples was solved either by (a) full or partial genocide (e.g., United States, Argentina, Chile, Australia); (b) segregation (South Africa, Southern Rhodesia); or (c) a combination of limited assimilation of "West-

ernized" (often mission-educated) chiefs and professionals plus direct or indirect rule over the rest (e.g., Portuguese Africa, French Africa). See Lorenzo Veracini, "Settler Colonialism as a Distinct Mode of Domination," in *The Routledge Handbook of the History of Settler Colonialism*, ed. Edward Cavanagh and Lorenzo Veracini (New York: Routledge, 2017), 1–8.

14. See Stephen Jay Gould, *The Mismeasure of Man* (New York: Norton, 1981); George W. Stocking, *Victorian Anthropology* (New York: The Free Press, 1987); William H. Tucker, *The Science and Politics of Racial Research* (Urbana: University of Illinois Press, 1994).

15. Surveys of its history can be found in J. E. Brady, *Trekking for Souls* (Cedara, Natal: Missionary Association of Mary Immaculate, St. Joseph's Scholasticate, 1952); William E. Brown, *The Catholic Church in South Africa: From Its Origins to the Present Day* (London: Burns & Oates, 1960); Joy Brain and Philippe Denis, eds., *The Catholic Church in Contemporary Southern Africa* (Pietermaritzburg: Cluster Publications, 1999).

16. The best documented case of this prohibition can be found in Guy Tachard, SJ, *A Relation of the Voyage to Siam: Performed by Six Jesuits Sent by the French King, to the Indies and China in the year 1685* [1688, English edition] (Bangkok: White Orchid Press, 1981), 43–80.

17. This anecdote was recounted to me by one of the aforementioned.

18. One sees this, particularly but usually obliquely, in contemporary Catholic publications, whether local publications, like the *Catholic Magazine*, or in missionary journals (e.g., the Jesuit *Zambesi Mission Record*). The tone on race is at best patronizing toward African people, at worst outright racist.

19. For an account of the church's difficult relationship with the "age of revolution," see Owen Chadwick, *The Pope and European Revolution* (Oxford: Clarendon Press, 1981).

20. Thomas Bokenkotter, *Church and Revolution: Catholics in the Struggle for Democracy and Social Justice* (New York: Image Books, 1998).

21. Francis Schimlek, *Against the Stream: Life of Father Bernard Huss C.M.M.* (Mariannhill, Natal: Mariannhill Mission Press, 1949).

22. Paddy Kearney, *Guardian of the Light: Denis Hurley; Renewing the Church, Opposing Apartheid* (Pietermaritzburg: University of Kwazulu Natal Press, 2009).

23. Garth Abraham, *The Catholic Church and Apartheid* (Johannesburg: Ravan Press, 1989).

24. George Sombe Mukuka, *The Other Side of the Story: The Silent Experience of the Black Clergy in the Catholic Church in South Africa (1898 – 1976)* (Pietermaritzburg: Cluster Publications, 2008).

25. George Sombe Mukuka, "The Impact of Black Consciousness on the Black Catholic Clergy and Their Training, 1965-1981" (MTh thesis,

University of Natal Pietermaritzburg, 1996); "The Establishment of the First Black Catholic Clergy in South Africa 1887-1957" (PhD diss., University of Natal Pietermaritzburg, 2000).

26. Lydia Brouckaert, "Better homes, Better Fields, Better Hearts: The Catholic African Union, 1927–1939" (BA Honors thesis, University of the Witwatersrand, 1985); Paul B. Rich, "Bernard Huss and the Experiment in African Cooperatives in South Africa, 1926–1948," *International Journal of African Historical Studies* 26, no. 2 (1993): 297–317; Francis Schimlenk, *Against the Stream: Life of Father Bernard Huss CMM, the Social Apostle of the Bantu* (Mariannhill: Mariannhill Mission Press, 1949).

27. There were indeed a few communists serving in the ICU leadership, but they were expelled from the union in 1926. Cf. Communist Party of South Africa, "On the Expulsion of Communists from the ICU," (1926) at https://www.marxists.org/history/international/comintern/sections/sacp/1926/expulsion-communists.htm.

28. J. B. Brain, *St. John Vianney Seminary: 50 Years of Priestly Training* (Pietermaritzburg: Cluster Publications, 2002).

29. S. A. Catholic Bishops' Conference, "Statement on Apartheid," July 21, 1957, http://www.sacbcoldsite.org.za/wp-content/uploads/2013/05/STATEMENT-ON-APARTHEID-.pdf. Last accessed February 25, 2022.

30. See Peter Walshe, *Prophetic Christianity and the Liberation Movement in South Africa* (Pietermaritzburg: Cluster Publications, 1997).

31. Graham Duncan and Anthony Egan, "The Ecumenical Struggle in South Africa: The Role of Ecumenical Movements and Liberation Organisations from 1966," *Studia Historiae Ecclesiasticae* 45, no. 1 (2019): 1–28, https://doi.org/10.25159/2412-4265/3936.

32. Although they sound incompatible, these groups have, on closer examination, much in common.

33. Cf. Richard Elphick, *The Equality of Believers: Protestant Missionaries and the Racial Politics of South Africa* (Charlottesville: University of Virginia Press, 2012).

34. J. Kameron Carter, *Race: A Theological Account* (New York: Oxford University Press, 2008).

35. Cf. the Chinese Rites controversy, an attempt at inculturation that was centuries before its time. For an example of such an attempt see Matteo Ricci, *The True Meaning of the Lord of Heaven* (Boston: Boston College Institute of Jesuit Sources, 2016). See also Michela Fontana, *Matteo Ricci: A Jesuit in the Ming Court* (Lanham, MD: Rowman & Littlefield, 2011); Jonathan D. Spence, *The Memory Palace of Matteo Ricci* (New York: Viking Penguin, 1984).

36. Laura António Nhaueleque and Luca Bussotti, "The Conceptualisation of Africa in the Catholic Church: Comparing Historically the

Thought of Daniele Comboni and Adalberto da Postioma," *Social Sciences and Missions* 32 (2019): 148–76.

CHAPTER 2

1. Calvin John Smiley and David Fakunle, "From 'Brute' to 'Thug': The Demonization and Criminalization of Unarmed Black Male Victims in America," *Journal of Human Behavior in the Social Environment* 26, nos. 3–4 (2016).

2. For example, as I write this chapter, cemeteries of indigenous children, considered to be of an inferior and uncivilized race, are being discovered in Canada. In the bid to civilize them (bring them close to whites), children were forced to attend residential schools operated by European missionaries. It is estimated that six thousand children died while attending those schools. Their parents were never notified. Hate crimes against Asians is also on the increase in the United States and Canada.

3. John Solomos, *Routledge International Handbook of Contemporary Racisms* (New York: Routledge, 2020); Tania Das Gupta et al., *Race and Racialization: Essential Readings* (Toronto: Canadian Scholars' Press, 2007).

4. Ann Morning, "And You Thought That We Had Moved Beyond All That: Biological Race Returns to Social Science," *Ethnic and Racial Studies* 37, no. 10 (2014).

5. Johann Friedrich Blumenbach, *On the Natural Varieties of Mankind: De Generis Humani Varietate Nativa* (New York: Bergman Books, 1969).

6. Samuel George Morton and George Combe, *Crania Americana: or, A Comparative View of the Skulls of Various Aboriginal Nations of North and South America; To Which Is Prefixed an Essay on the Varieties of the Human Species* (Philadelphia: J. Dobson and Simpkin, Marshall, 1839).

7. Max Weber, *Economy and Society: A New Translation*, ed. Keith Tribe (Cambridge, MA: Harvard University Press, 2019).

8. Weber, *Economy and Society.*

9. Howard Winant, *The World Is a Ghetto: Race and Democracy since World War II* (New York: Basic Books, 2001); Francisco Valdes, Jerome McCristal Culp, and P. Angela Harris, "Battles Waged, Won, and Lost: Critical Race Theory at the Turn of the Millennium," in *Crossroads, Directions, and a New Critical Race Theory*, ed. Francisco Valdes, Jerome McCristal Culp, and P. Angela Harris (Philadelphia: Temple University Press, 2002).

10. Miles and Brown, *Racism*, 2nd ed. (London: Routledge, 2003).

11. Miles and Brown, *Racism*, 9.

12. W.E.B. Du Bois, "Race Friction between Black and white," *American Journal of Sociology* 13 (1908).

13. Anthony Appiah, "The Uncompleted Argument: Dubois and the Illusion of Race," in *Overcoming Racism and Sexism*, ed. L. Bell and D. Blumenfeld (Lanham, MD: Rowman and Littlefield, 1995); "The Uncompleted Argument: Du Bois and the Illusion of Race," *Critical Inquiry* 12, no. 1 (1985); Zack Naomi, *Philosophy of Science and Race* (New York: Routledge, 2002).

14. Naomi, *Philosophy of Science and Race*, 88.

15. Hannah Arendt, *Imperialism: Part Two of the Origins of Totalitarianism* (New York: Harcourt Brace Jovanovich, 1968), 63–64.

16. Patrick Bond, *Looting Africa: The Economics of Exploitation* (New York: Zed Books, 2006), 2.

17. Paul Rabinow, ed. *The Foucault Reader: An Introduction to Foucault's Thought* (London: Penguin, 1991), 75; Michel Foucault, "The Subject and Power," *Critical Inquiry* 8, no. 4 (1982).

18. William B. Cohen, *The French Encounter with Africans: White Response to Blacks, 1530–1880* (Bloomington: Indiana University Press, 1980), 222.

19. Cohen, *The French Encounter with Africans*, 38–39.

20. Georg Wilhelm Friedrich Hegel, *The Philosophy of History*, trans. J. H. Clarke, rev ed. (New York: The Colonial Press, 1899), 93.

21. Joseph Conrad, *Heart of Darknes, Almayer's Folly, the Lagoon* (New York: Dell Publishing Co., 1960), 72.

22. Conrad, *Heart of Darknes*, 74.

23. Christopher Fyfe, "Race, Empire and the Historians," *Race & Class* 33, no. 4 (1992): 3–4.

24. James Brabazon, *Albert Schweitzer: A Biography*, 2nd ed. (New York: Syracuse University Press, 2000), 4.

25. Jan Christiaan Smuts, *Africa and Some World Problems, Including the Rhodes Memorial Lectures Delivered in Michaelmas Term, 1929* (Oxford: Clarendon Press, 1930).

26. Christiaan Smuts, *Africa and Some World Problems*, 152.

27. Mbembe, *Critique of Black Reason* (Durham, NC: Duke University Press, 2017), 152.

28. Mbembe, *Critique of Black Reason*, 152.

29. Mbembe, *Critique of Black Reason*, 179.

30. Mbembe, *Critique of Black Reason*, 47.

31. See Victor Hugo, "Discours Sur L'afrique (1985), 4:1010," in *Actes Et Paroles*, ed. Fizaine Jean-Claude (Paris: Laffont, 1985), 1010.

32. Martin Ewans, *European Atrocity, African Catastrophe: Leopold II, the Congo Free State and Its Aftermath* (New York: Routledge, 2017).

33. Achille Mbembe, *Critique of Black Reason*, 73.

34. Achille Mbembe, *Out of the Dark Night: Essays on Decolonization* (New York: Columbia University Press, 2021), 1.

35. V. Y. Mudimbe, *The Invention of Africa: Gnosis, Philosophy, and the Order of Knowledge* (Bloomington: Indiana University Press, 1988).

36. Frantz Fanon, *Black Skin, White Masks*, Rev. ed., (New York: Grove Press, 2008), 188.

37. Fanon, *Black Skin, White Masks*, 2.

38. "Le colorisme et les crèmes éclaircissantes: ces legs invisibles de la colonisation," theconversation.com, April 25, 2018, https://theconversation.com/le-colorisme-et-les-cremes-eclaircissantes-ces-legs-invisibles-de-la-colonisation-82699.

39. David Dolan, "In Africa, Haircare Becomes a Multi-billion Dollar Industry," August 6, 2014, Reuters, https://news.yahoo.com/africa-haircare-becomes-multi-billion-dollar-industry-113920462.html.

40. Claudia C. A. Juliano, "Spreading of Dangerous Skin-Lightening Products as a Result of Colourism: A Review," *Applied Sciences* 12, no. 6 (2022): 3177; Fatin N. M. Nordin, Atiqah Aziz, Zalina Zakaria, and Che Wan Jasimah Wan Mohamed Radzi, "A Systematic Review on the Skin Whitening Products and Their Ingredients for Safety, Health Risk, and the Halal Status," *Journal of Cosmetic Dermatology* 20, no. 4 (2021): 1050–60.

41. Samara Pollock, Susan Taylor, Oyetewa Oyerinde et al., "The Dark Side of Skin Lightening: An International Collaboration and Review of a Public Health Issue Affecting Dermatology," *International Journal of Women's Dermatology* 7, no. 2 (2021): 158–64; See also Mukhtar A. Yusuf, Nicma D. Mahmoud, Farhan R. Rirash et al., "Skin Lightening Practices, Beliefs, and Self-Reported Adverse Effects among Female Health Science Students in Borama, Somaliland: A Cross-Sectional Survey," *International Journal of Women's Dermatology*, 5, no. 5 (2019): 349–355; Emma K. T. Benn, Andrew Alexis, Nihal Mohamed et al., "Skin Bleaching and Dermatologic Health of African and Afro-Caribbean Populations in the US: New Directions for Methodologically Rigorous, Multidisciplinary, and Culturally Sensitive Research," *Dermatol Ther* (Heidelb) 6, no. 4 (2016):453–459. doi: 10.1007/s13555-016-0154-1.

42. Frantz Fanon, *The Wretched of the Earth* (New York: Grove Press, 1963).

43. Ngugi wa Thiong'o, *The Decolonization of the Mind: The Politics of Language in African Literature* (London: James Currey, 1986), 4.

44. Ngugi wa Thiong'o, *The Decolonization of the Mind*, 3.

45. Mbiti, *African Religions & Philosophy*, 1.

46. Mbiti, *African Religions & Philosophy*, 2.

47. Martin Ewans, *European Atrocity, African Catastrophe: Leopold II, the Congo Free State and Its Aftermath* (New York: Routledge, 2002), 14.

48. Walter Rodney, *How Europe Underdeveloped Africa*, rev. ed. (Washington, DC: Howard University Press, 1981), 153.

49. Rodney, *How Europe Underdeveloped Africa*, 153.

50. Rodney, *How Europe Underdeveloped Africa*, 172.

51. Adam Hochschild, *King Leopold's Ghost: A Story of Greed, Terror, and Heroism in Colonial Africa* (New York: Houghton Mifflin, 1998).

52. Hochschild, *King Leopold's Ghost.*

53. Hochschild, *King Leopold's Ghost.*

54. Hochschild, *King Leopold's Ghost*, 27. Mawuna Remarque Koutonin, "14 African Countries Forced by France to Pay Colonial Tax for the Benefit of Slavery and Colonization," SiliconAfrica.com, January 28, 2014, https://siliconafrica.com/france-colonial-tax/; Antoine Roger Lokongo, "African Nations Can No Longer Afford to Be France's Garden," Global Times, October 22, 2012, https://www.globaltimes.cn/content/739771.shtml.

55. Paulo Freire, *Pedagogy of the Oppressed* (New York: Continuum, 1970).

56. Freire, *Pedagogy of the Oppressed*, 238.

57. Freire, *Pedagogy of the Oppressed*, 238.

58. David W. Lutz, "African Ubuntu Philosophy and Global Management," *Journal of Business Ethics* 84, no. 3 (2009): 313–28. See also Nonceba Nolundi Mabovula, "The Erosion of African Communal Values: A Reappraisal of the African Ubuntu Philosophy," *Inkanyiso: Journal of Humanities and Social Sciences* 3, no. 1 (2011): 38–47.

59. Steve Biko, *I Write What I Like* (Johannesburg: Picador Africa, 1978), 61.

60. Johan Galtung, "Violence, Peace, and Peace Research," *Journal of Peace Research* 6, no. 3 (1969); see also Hannah Arendt, *On Violence* (San Diego: Harcourt, Brace, Jovanovich, 1970).

61. Achille Mbembe, *Brutalisme* (Paris: La Découverte, 2020).

62. Ayodele Samuel Jegede, "What Led to the Nigerian Boycott of the Polio Vaccination Campaign?," *PLoS Medicine* 4, no. 3 (2007): e73.

63. Robert Miles and Malcolm Brown, *Racism*, 2nd ed. (New York: Routlege, 2003), 10.

64. Freire, *Pedagogy of the Oppressed*, 56.

65. Alfred Adler, *The Science of Living*, Psychology Revivals (New York: Routledge, 2013).

66. Robin DiAngelo, *White Fragility: Why It's So Hard for White People to Talk About Racism* (Boston: Beacon Press, 2018).

67. Paul Gilroy, *Between Camps: Nations, Cultures and the Allure of Race* (New York: Routledge, 2004).

68. DiAngelo, *White Fragility*, 1.

69. Stuart Hall, *The Fateful Triangle: Race, Ethnicity, Nation* (Cambridge, MA: Harvard University Press, 2017).

70. Césaire, *Discourse on Colonialism*, 23.

71. Fanon, *The Wretched of the Earth*, 235.

72. Fanon, *Black Skin, White Masks*, 206.

CHAPTER 3

1. Michela Wrong, *It's Our Turn to Eat: The Story of a Kenyan Whistleblower* (London: Fourth Estate, 2009).

2. Koigi wa Wamwere, *Negative Ethnicity: From Bias to Genocide* (New York: Seven Stories Press, 2003).

3. The Greek original text is Μετὰ ταῦτα εἶδον, καὶ ἰδοὺ ὄχλος πολύς, ὃν ἀριθμῆσαι αὐτὸν οὐδεὶς ἐδύνατο, ἐκ παντὸς ἔθνους καὶ φυλῶν καὶ λαῶν καὶ γλωσσῶν, ἑστῶτες ἐνώπιον τοῦ θρόνου καὶ ἐνώπιον τοῦ Ἀρνίου, περιβεβλημένους στολὰς λευκάς, καὶ φοίνικες ἐν ταῖς χερσὶν αὐτῶν. However, the reader is advised that, in this chapter, no judgment is being made regarding which English translation is more faithful to the Greek text than another. Also, for purposes of this analysis, it should not matter whether the words in English are in singular or plural form since the essential sense depends on other elements in the same sentence; for example, both "from every nation" and "from all nations" communicate a plurality of nations.

4. Richmond Lattimore, "Practical Notes on Translating Greek Poetry," in *On Translation*, ed. Reuben A. Brower (Cambridge, MA: Harvard University Press, 1959), 48–56, at 53–54.

5. The same four words appear again in Rev 5:9 and 14:6, but on every occasion in a different order.

6. The contents of the 1380 version of the Wycliffe Bible can be viewed at https://textusreceptusbibles.com/Wycliffe/66/7. (Last accessed May 16, 2022).

7. [William Tyndale], *The Newe Testamente* (Monastery B.M.V. in Schontbal, 1526). Tyndale's spelling is sometimes inconsistent, but not to the extent of obstructing recognition of the actual words he is using.

8. See "nation" in *The Oxford English Dictionary: Being a Corrected Re-issue with an Introduction, Supplement, and Bibliography of A New English Dictionary on Historical Principles Founded Mainly on the Materials Collected by the Philosophical Society*, 12 vols. (Oxford: Clarendon Press, 1961), 7:30–31. (Hereafter this source will be abbreviated as *OED*); see also Eric Partridge, *Origins: A Short Etymological Dictionary of Modern English* (London: Routledge, 1966), 2099–101.

9. *The Bible and Holy Scriptures Contained in the Olde and Newe Testament. Translated According to the Ebrue and Greke, and Conferred to the Best Translations in Divers Languages* (Geneva: Rouland Wall, 1560).

10. Ayumi Hira, "Influential English Translations of the Bible in the Sixteenth Century," CORE, https://core.ac.uk/download/pdf/230281522.pdf (published in 2016, last accessed on May 16, 2022), 161–73, here 169.

11. Robert McCrum, "How the King James Bible Shaped the English Language," *Guardian* (2010), https://www.theguardian.com/books/2010/nov/21/king-james-bible-english-language. (Last accessed May 16, 2022).

12. James Hedges, "The Influence of the King James Bible on English Literature," (2011), https://www.apu.edu/articles/the-influence-of-the-king-james-bible-on-english-literature/. (Last accessed May 16, 2022).

13. Daniel Mace, *The New Testament in Greek and English, Containing the Original Text Corrected from the Authority of the most Authentic Manuscripts: And a New Version Form'd agreeably to the Illustrations of the Most Learned Commentators and Critics: with Notes and Various Readings, and a Copious Alphabetical Index*, 2 vols. (London: for J. Roberts, 1729).

14. See "tribe" in *OED*, 11:339.

15. See Eric Partridge, *Origins: A Short Etymological Dictionary of Modern English* (London: Routledge, 1966), 3552.

16. See "tribe" in *OED*, 11:339.

17. *The Holy Bible*, Douay-Rheims Translation, Challoner Revision, 1749–1752, at https://www.ccel.org/c/challoner/douayrheims/dr.html. (Last accessed May 16, 2022).

18. William Gilpin, *An Exposition of the New Testament…* (London: Printed for R. Blamire, in the Strand, 1790), 652.

19. Noah Webster, *The New Testament in the Common Version with Amendments of the Language* (New Haven, CT: S. Babcook, 1839).

20. *The New Testament of Our Lord and Savior Jesus Christ* (Salt Lake City: The Church of Jesus Christ of Latter-Day Saints, 1971).

21. From "Editor's Foreword to the Readers' Edition," *The Jerusalem Bible: Reader's Edition* (Garden City, NY: Doubleday & Company, Inc., 1968).

22. See https://www.easyenglish.bible/about-easyenglish/. (Last accessed April 30, 2022).

23. Michla Pomerance, "The United States and Self-Determination: Perspectives on the Wilsonian Conception," *The American Journal of International Law* 70, no. 1 (1976): 1–27, here 17.

24. Pomerance, "United States and Self-Determination," 3.

25. See "race" in *OED* 8:87.

26. See "race" in *OED* 8:87.

27. See "race" in *OED* 8:87. In the last example, reference is made to Johann Friedrich Blumenbach (1752–1840), German anthropologist and one of the earliest proponents of a classification of humans into different races. See his *Decas Collectionis Suae Craniorum Diversarum Gentium Illustrata* (Cottingae: Apud Ioann. Christ. Dieterich, 1790), 10–12, and passim.

28. Cf. Eric Allina, "The Zimba, the Portuguese, and Other Cannibals in Late Sixteenth-Century Southeast Africa," *Journal of Southern African Studies* 37, n. 2 (2011): 211–27, here 220.

29. Nancy Stepan, *The Idea of Race in Science: Great Britain 1800–1960* (London: The Macmillan Press Ltd., 1982).

30. Alfred R. Wallace, "The Origin of Human Races and the Antiquity of Man Deduced from the Theory of 'Natural Selection,'" *Journal of the Anthropological Society of London* 2 (1864): 158–87, here 164. Wallace was an authority on his own, but, in this publication, he clearly states that he is applying Darwin's theory of natural selection. See 158–59.

31. Stepan, *Idea of Race in Science*, xii.

32. See Pauline Kleingeld, "Kant's Second Thoughts on Race," *The Philosophical Quarterly* 57, n. 229 (2007): 573–92.

33. Immanuel Kant, *Observations on the Feeling of the Beautiful and Sublime and Other Writings*, ed. Patrick Frierson and Paul Guyer (Cambridge: Cambridge University Press, 2011), 61 (2:255).

34. Stepan, *Idea of Race in Science*, xii–xiii.

35. Étienne Balibar, "The Nation Form: History and Ideology," *Review (Ferdinand Brandel Center)* 13, no. 3 (1990): 329–61, here 29.

36. Balibar, "The Nation Form," 29; see also Étienne Balibar, "The Nation Form," in *Becoming National: A Reader*, ed. Geoff Eley and Ronald Grigor Suny (Oxford: Oxford University Press, 1996), 132–49; and Manu Goswami, "Rethinking the Modular Nation Form," *Comparative Study of Society and History* 45, no. 1 (2002): 770–99.

37. Cf. Elie Kedourie, ed., *Nationalism in Asia and Africa* (London: Frank Cass, 1974), 52–53; Thomas Hylland Eriksen, *Ethnicity and Nationalism: Anthropological Perspectives* (London: Pluto Press, 1993), 5, 12.

38. As reported in [Eric] J. Hobsbawm, *Nations and Nationalism since 1780: Program, Myth, Reality*, 2nd ed. (Cambridge: Cambridge University Press, 1992), 63.

39. M. Ana María Alonso, "The Politics of Space, Time and Substance: State Formation, Nationalism, and Ethnicity," *Annual Review of Anthropology* 23 (1994): 379–405, here 391.

40. Balibar, "National Form," 140–44.

41. Anthony D. Smith, *The Ethnic Origins of Nations* (Oxford: Blackwell Publishers, 1986/1999), 3.

42. Yves R. Simon, *The Ethiopian Campaign and French Political Thought*, ed. Anthony O. Simon, trans. Robert Royal (Notre Dame, IN: University of Notre Dame Press, 2009), 94.

43. Julia Gaffield, "The Racialization of International Law after the Haitian Revolution: The Holy See and National Sovereignty," *American Historical Review* 125, no. 3 (2020): 840–68, here 842.

44. Matsepane Morare, "The Power of Identity" (BA Synthesis Paper, Arrupe College, Harare, 2000), 5.

CHAPTER 4

1. Cf. *Constitution of Italy*, Art. 3 par. 1.

2. Jean-Luc Richard, "Les catholiques, l'immigration étrangère et les tentations racistes en France. Quelques apports d' enquêtes d'opinion et de données macro-sociales," *Migrations Sociétés* 1, no. 139 (2012): 253–66.

3. Second Vatican Council, Pastoral Constitution on the Church in the Modern World, *Gaudium et Spes* 29, https://www.vatican.va.

4. John Paul II, Address to Members of the Special Committee of the United Nations Organization against Apartheid, July 7, 1984, https://www.vatican.va.

5. La controverse entre l'épiscopat Français et M. Le Pen sur le racisme, publié par le Monde, le 25 septembre 1996.

6. Cf. Commission des Migrations: "Vivre ensemble dans la différence," Conférence épiscopale Française, Paris, December 20, 1983.

7. Statement of His All-Holiness Ecumenical Patriarch Bartholomew, for the Forthcoming United Nations Durban World Conference against Racism, Racial Discrimination, Xenophobia, and Related Intolerance in Durban, March 17, 2001.

8. Francis, General Audience, Library of the Apostolic Palace, June 3, 2020, www.vatican.va.

9. Cf. United States Conference of Catholic Bishops, "Brothers and Sisters to Us," U.S. Catholic Bishops Pastoral Letter on Racism, 1979.

10. Cf. Ion Bria, Philippe Chanson, Jacques Gadille et al., eds., *Dictionnaire oecumenique de Missiologie: Cent mots pour la mission* (Paris, Genève, Yaoundé: Cerf, Labor et Fides, CLE, 2001).

11. Martin Bulmer et John Solomos, eds., *Ethnic and Racial Studies Today* (New York: Routledge, 1999).

12. Cf. General Secretary of the Synod, A Synodal Church in Mission: Synthesis Report, XVI Ordinary General Assembly of the Synod of Bishops, First Session, Vatican City, October 4–29, 2023, no. 19 (a).

13. Laënnec Hurbon, "Racisme et théologie missionnaire," *Présence Africaine* 71, no. 3 Hommage à Jean Price-Mars (1969): 35–47.

14. Jean-Pierre Jacque Min, "Le racisme continent obscur: ciblés, stéréotypes, fantasmes à propos des noirs dans le royaume de Belgique," Coopération par l'éducation et la culture (CEC), Bruxelles, (1991): 28–77.

15. For the Holy Father, reparation is a question of justice. Forgiveness must lead us to reintegrate excluded people and groups into society. Cf. John Paul II, Message for the World Day of Peace, January 1, 1997, no. 5.

16. Pontifical Council for Justice and Peace, *The Church and Racism: Toward a More Fraternal Society* (Vatican City: Dicastery for Promoting Integral Human Development, 1988, updated 2001), n. 3.

17. Wanda Deifelt, "La metanoia," in *Faisons route ensemble. Rapport officiel de la Huitième Assemblée du Conseil OEcuménique des Églises* (Genève: WCC Publications, 1999), 28.

18. John Braithwaite, "Restorative Justice and a Better Future," *Dalhousie Review* 76, no. 1 (1996): 9–31.

19. Willie Esterhuyse, "Truth as a Trigger for Transformation: From Apartheid to Transformational Justice," in *Looking Back Reaching Forward: Reflections on the Truth and Reconciliation Commission of South Africa*, ed. Charles Villa-Vicencio and Wilhelm Vervoerd (London: University of Cape Town Press and ZED Books, 2000), 149.

20. Cf. T. S. Maluleke, "Truth, National Unity and Reconciliation in South Africa," *Missionalia* 25, no. 1 (1997): 66–67.

21. United Nations, Declaration of the UN World Conference against Racism, Racial Discrimination, Xenophobia and Related Intolerance, Durban, 2001.

22. Cf. Barney Pityana and Charles Villa-Vicencio, *Being the Church in South Africa Today* (Johannesburg: South African Council of Churches, 1995).

23. *Racism in Theology and Theology against Racism, rapport d'un colloque organisé par Foi et constitution et le Programme de lutte contre le racisme* (Genève: COE, 1975), 13–14.

CHAPTER 5

1. "The issue of identity lies at the heart of the process by which the Christian theological enterprise is actually carried forward." See Kwame Bediako, *Christianity in Africa: The Renewal of Non-Western Religion* (Maryknoll, NY: Orbis Books, 1996), 256.

2. The founding of the Black Lives Matter (BLM) movement predated the George Floyd murder in May 2020. In the wake of George Floyd's murder, BLM protest campaigns against incidents of police brutality and all racially motivated violence against Black people took on extra urgency and momentum. For a helpful history of the Black Lives Matter movement and

its relevancy for the church, see Olga M. Segura, *Birth of a Movement: Black Lives Matter and the Catholic Church* (Maryknoll, NY: Orbis Books, 2021).

3. See Anthony Appiah, *In My Father's House: African in the Philosophy of Culture* (New York: Oxford University Press, 1992). See also the first chapter of my *Who Are My People: Love, Violence, and Christianity in Sub-Saharan Africa* (Notre Dame, IN: University of Notre Dame Press, 2022).

4. Appiah, *In My Father's House*, 155.

5. Tsenay Serequeberhan, "Reflections on *In My Father's House*," *Research in African Literatures* 27, no. 1 (1996): 110–18 (116).

6. Kwame Anthony Appiah, *The Lies That Bind: Rethinking Identity* (New York: Liveright Publishing Company, 2018), xvi.

7. John Samuel Pobee, *Giving Account of Faith and Hope in Africa* (Eugene, OR: Wipf & Stock Publishers, 2017), 158.

8. John S. Pobee, "I Am First an African and Second a Christian," *Indian Missiological Review* 10, no. 3 (1989): 268–77.

9. John S. Mbiti, as quoted by Tinyiko S. Maluleke, "Identity and Integrity in African Theology: A Critical Analysis," *Religion and Theology* 8, no. 1 (2001): 26–41 (38).

10. Stephanie A. Lowery, *Identity and Ecclesiology: Their Relationship among Select African Theologians* (Eugene, OR: Pickwick, 2017), 49.

11. Lowery, *Identity and Ecclesiology*, 49.

12. Miroslave Volf, *Exclusion and Embrace: A Theological Exploration of Identity, Otherness, and Reconciliation (*Nashville: Abingdon, 1996), 40.

13. Volf, *Exclusion and Embrace*, 38.

14. Volf, *Exclusion and Embrace*, 39.

15. Volf, *Exclusion and Embrace*, 39.

16. Andrew F. Walls, "The Ephesian Moment," in *The Cross-Cultural Process in Christian History* (Maryknoll, NY: Orbis Books, 2002), 72–81.

17. Walls, "The Ephesian Moment," 76.

18. Walls, "The Ephesian Moment," 76.

19. Walls, "The Ephesian Moment," 76. Involved in this conclusion is the realization that we are all identities—national, racial, tribal, ethnic, cultural identities are "fragments." However, as the Orthodox theologian Alexander Schmemann noted, the tragedy of fragments is that each fragment thinks it is the whole and vehemently tries to exclude the other. See Alexander Schmemann, *Journals of Father Alexander Schmemann 1973–1983* (Crestwood, NY: St. Vladimir Seminary Press, 2000), 92. Such claims for self-sufficiency, however, not only conceal the limits and fragmentary nature of lives, they obscure the goal to which Christian faith is directed, namely "communion," which as Willie Jennings rights notes is the "working and weaving together of fragments and in the forming of life together." See

Willie Jennings, *After Whiteness: An Education in Belonging* (Grand Rapids, MI: Eerdmans, 2020), 44.

20. Walls, "The Ephesian Moment," 78.

21. André Sibomana, *Hope for Rwanda. Conversations with Laure Guilbert and Hervé Deguine* (Eugene, OR: Wipf & Stock, 1999), 131–32.

22. Emmanuel M. Katongole and Jonathan Wilson-Hartgrove, *Mirror to the Church: Resurrecting Faith after Genocide in Rwanda* (Grand Rapids, MI: Zondervan, 2009), 156.

23. Charles Marsh, *The Beloved Community: How Faith Shapes Social Justice, from the Civil Rights Movement to Today* (New York: Basic Books, 2005), 84.

24. Pope Francis, *Fratelli Tutti: On Fraternity and Social Friendship* (Vatican City, 2020), no. 50.

25. Katongole, *Mirror to the Church*, 46.

26. Emmanuel Katongole, *The Sacrifice of Africa: A Political Theology for Africa* (Grand Rapids, MI: William B. Eerdmans Publishing, 2011), 135–47.

27. Pope Francis, *Let US Dream: The Path to a Better Future* (Simon and Schuster, 202), 120.

28. Antonio Spadaro, interview with Pope Francis, 2013, https://w2.vatican.va/content/francesco/en/speeches/2013/september/documents/papa-francesco_20130921_intervista-spadaro.html. See also Emmanuel Katongole, "Field Hospital: Heal Africa and the Politics of Compassion in Eastern Congo," *Missiology: An International Review* 45, no. 1 (2017): 25–37.

29. Pope Francis, *Let Us Dream*, 119.

30. Pope Francis, *Let Us Dream*, 120.

31. Pope Francis, *Let Us Dream*, 121, 128–33.

32. The Spanish word *mestizo* was first used to describe the children of the violent encounter between European fathers and Amerindian mothers; neither European nor Indian, these children belonged to a new people, a people of mixed heritage. See https://www.dictionary.com/browse/mestizo (11/30/19).

33. Virgilio Elizondo, *The Future Is Mestizo: Life Where Cultures Meet*, rev. ed. (Denver: University Press of Colorado, 2000), 26.

34. Elizondo, *The Future Is Mestizo*, 67–86.

35. Elizondo, *The Future Is Mestizo*, 129.

36. Elizondo, *The Future Is Mestizo*, 129.

37. Elizondo, *The Future Is Mestizo*, 129.

38. For a full exploration of the social political implications of Pope Francis' ecclesiology of "field hospital" that informs my understanding here, see William Cavanaugh, *Field Hospital: The Church's Engagement with a Wounded World* (Grand Rapids, MI: Eerdmans, 2016).

39. Spadaro, interview with Pope Francis.

CHAPTER 6

1. Benedict XVI, *Caritas in Veritate* 7.

2. J. Egbulefu, CCE, "Attempts to provide a vision and strategic plan to assist Africa emerge from the misery and marginalization in the overall movement of globalization," in *The Church of Christ Saviour in Africa*, ed. Rev. Fr. Emmanuel M. P. Edeh, vol. 2 (Enugu: Madonna University Press, 2009), 78–157.

3. The Second Vatican Council has rightly defined the Church as "sacrament, a sign and instrument, that is, of communion with God and of unity among all men" since "both Christ and the Church...transcend the distinctions of race and nationality." See *The Church and Racism: Towards a More Fraternal Society*, Pontifical Commission on Justice and Peace, 1988, no. 22. (See also USCCB, "What We Have Seen and Heard," A Pastoral Letter on Evangelization from the Black Bishops of the United States, September 9, 1984).

4. Benedict XVI, *Caritas in Veritate*, On Integral Human Development in Charity and Truth, June 29, 2009, 51.

CHAPTER 7

1. Pontifical Justice and Peace Commission, *The Church and Racism: Towards a More Fraternal Society* (Vatican City, 1988/2001), 37.

2. Pontifical Justice and Peace Commission, *The Church and Racism*, 29.

3. Cf. Carl Linnaeus, *Systema Naturae sive Regna Tria Naturae* (Leiden: Haak, 1735).

4. Cf. Staffan Müller-Wille, "Race and History: Comments from an Epistemological Point of View," *Science, Technology and Human Values* 39, no. 4 (2014): 597–606.

5. Cf. R. M. Dennis, "Racism" in *The Social Science Encyclopedia*, ed. A. Kuper and J. Kuper, vol. 2, 3rd ed. (New York: Routledge, 2004). See also George M. Fredrickson, *The Arrogance of Race: Historical Perspectives on Slavery, Racism, and Social Inequality* (Middletown, CT: Wesleyan University Press, 1988).

6. Cf. Müller-Wille, "Race and History."

7. Cf. Ivan Hannaford, *Race: The History of an Idea in the* West (Baltimore: John Hopkins University Press, 1996), 6.

8. Cf. Nancy Stepan, *The Idea of Race in Science: Great Britain, 1800–1960* (Houndmills: MacMillan, 1984), 140; and Elazar Barkan, *The Retreat of Scientific Racism: Changing Concepts of Race in Britain and the*

United States between the World Wars (Cambridge, UK: Cambridge University Press, 1992), 10–11.

9. Cf. Michael Banton, *Racial Theories*, 2nd ed. (Cambridge, UK: Cambridge University Press, 1998), 4–8.

10. Hannah Arendt, *The Origins of Totalitarianism* (San Diego: New Edition Harvest Book, 1973), esp. 158–221.

11. Michel Foucault, *"Society Must Be Defended": Lectures at the Collège de France, 1975–1976*, trans. David Macey (New York: Picador, 2003).

12. Claudio Pogliano, *L'ossessione della razza: Antropologia e genetica nel xx secolo* (Pisa: Edizioni della Normale, 2005).

13. Jennifer Reardon, *Race to the Finish: Identity and Governance in an Age of Genomics* (Princeton, NJ: Princeton University Press, 2005).

14. Pontifical Justice and Peace Commission, *The Church and Racism*, 29.

15. Cf. https://treaties.un.org/pages/ViewDetails.aspx?src=IND&mtdsg_no=IV-2&chapter=4&clang=_en.

16. Cf. https://documents-dds-ny.un.org/doc/UNDOC/GEN/N79/055/79/PDF/N7905579.pdf?OpenElement.

17. Cf. https://www.un.org/en/conferences/racism#:~:text=The%20second%20World%20Conference%20to,Durban%2C%20South%20Africa%20in%202001.

18. Cf. https://press.vatican.va/content/salastampa/en/bollettino/pubblico/2021/09/23/210923a.htm.

19. Cf. https://news.un.org/en/story/2020/06/1066722.

20. Cf. https://www.ohchr.org/sites/default/files/Documents/Issues/Racism/A_HRC_47_CRP_1.pdf.

21. Cf. https://www.un.org/en/fight-racism/vulnerable-groups.

22. Paul R. Gallagher, "Statement by H. E. Archbishop Paul R. Gallagher, Secretary for Relations with States of the Holy See, at the United Nations High-Level Meeting to Commemorate the 20th Anniversary of the Durban Declaration and Programme of Action," New York, September 22, 2021. Cf. https://press.vatican.va/content/salastampa/en/bollettino/pubblico/2021/09/23/210923a.html.

23. Yusuf Fadl Hasan, "Some Aspects of the Arab Slave Trade from the Sudan, 7th–9th Century," *Sudan Notes and Records* LVIII (1977): 85–106, at 85.

24. Cf. Luiz Felipe de Alencastro, "Traite," *Encyclopædia Universalis* 22 (2002): 902.

25. Cf. Olivier Pétré-Grenouilleau, referring to Ralph Austen, *African Economic Slavery* (1987). See also Clarence-Smith and William Gervase, *Islam and the Abolition of Slavery* (New York: Oxford University Press, 2006), 11–12.

26. For the original video presentation, cf. https://www.youtube.com/watch?v=p9bI_5MKdQ0.

27. The Holy See is a moral entity *sui iuris* whose territorial sovereignty is guaranteed by the Vatican City State. It refers specifically to the central administration of the Catholic Church, constituted by the pope as the overseer of the Church of Rome and the Universal Church, assisted by the Roman curia.

28. Pontifical Justice and Peace Commission, *The Church and Racism*, 1988, 2001.

29. Pontifical Justice and Peace Commission, *The Church and Racism*, 29, see footnote.

30. Pontifical Justice and Peace Commission, *The Church and Racism*, 12.

31. Cf. https://www.Black-inventor.com/dr-philip-emeagwali.

32. Cf. Lilit Marcus, "All-Black Group Makes History by Summiting Mount Everest," CNN.com, May 12, 2022, https://www.cnn.com/travel/article/full-circle-everest-Black-mountain-climbers-intl-hnk/index.html.

33. Cf. "History of Slavery in the Muslim World," in Wikipedia, nn133 and 134. It is reported that in 2003, Shayk Saleh Al-Fawzan, of Saudi Arabia's Senior Council of Clerics, claimed in a fatwa that "slavery is a part of Islam. Slavery is part of jihad, and jihad will remain as long as there is Islam." In 2016, the same Shayk Al-Fawzan, regarding the taking of Yazidi women as sex slaves, affirmed that "enslaving women in war is not prohibited in Islam" and that those who forbid enslavement are either "ignorant or infidel." Although Shayk Al-Fawzan's fatwa did not reflect the official Saudi laws against slavery, its authority was certain among the Salafi Muslims. That is why the jurist and author, Khaled Abou El Fadl, commented that it "is particularly disturbing and dangerous because it effectively legitimates the trafficking in and sexual exploitation of so-called domestic workers in the Gulf region and especially in Saudi Arabia." (Khaled Abou El Fadl, *The Great Theft: Wrestling Islam from the Extremists* [San Francisco: Harper, 2005], 255).

34. Bertolt Brecht, *The Resistible Rise of Arturo Ui*, ed. John Willet, ed. and trans. Ralph Manheim (New York: Arcade Publishing, 1981). Original text: *Der aufhaltsame Aufstieg des Arturo Ui* (Frankfurt: Suhrkamp, 1969).

35. Fortunatus Nwachukwu, ed., *One Faith: Many Tongues: Managing Diversity in the Church in Nigeria* (Abuja: Paulines, 2017), 103.

36. Pontifical Justice and Peace Commission, *The Church and Racism*, 37.

CHAPTER 8

1. Cf. Edouard Cothenet, *La première encyclique. Actualités de la Première Lettre de Pierre* (Paris, Salvator, 2017).

2. *Post-synodal Exhortation on the Vocation and Mission of the Laity in the World*, Rome, 1988, no. 14.

3. Cf. David G. Horrell, "Race, Nation, People: Ethnic Identity-Construction in 1 Peter 2:9," *New Testament Studies* 58, no. 1 (2012): 123–3.

4. Cf. Jacques Schlosser, *La Première épître de Pierre* (Paris, Cerf, 2011), 35–37.

5. Cf. Paul Bony, *La Première épître de Pierre. Chrétiens en diaspora* (Paris, Cerf), 2004.

6. Cf. Marie-Louise Lamau, *Des chrétiens dans le monde. Communautés pétriniennes au 1er siècle* (Paris: Cerf, 1988), 49–79.

7. Cf. Paul Bony, *La Première épître de Pierre. Chrétiens en diaspora* (Paris: Cerf, 2004), 75–96.

8. John H. Elliot, *The Elect and the Holy: An Exegetical Examination of 1 Peter 2:4–10 and the Phrase Basileon hierateuma* (1966; repr., Eugene, OR: Wipf & Stock, 2006), 217.

9. Nestle-Aland, *Novum Testamentum: Graece et Latine* (Stuttgart: Deutsche Bibelgesellschaft, 1993), 601. Against most witnesses, Papyrus 72 does not have the pronoun αὐτοῦ before the noun φῶς. Admittedly, the pronoun does not impose itself when the meaning is obvious. But because of the weight of the witnesses, we retain the variant with the pronoun αὐτοῦ omitted by P. 72.

10. Cf. "βασίλειον ἱεράτευμα [priestly kingdom] and ἔθνος ἅγιον [a holy nation]" in Exod 19:6.

11. Cf. The books of the Maccabees, Judith, Josephus, Philo of Alexandria.

12. Cf. Ps 12:8; 73, 15; Isa 41:8; 43:5; 44:3; 61:9; 65:23.

13. Cf. Second Vatican Council, Constitution on the Sacred Liturgy, *Sacrosanctum Concilium*, December 4, 1963, 14.

14. In this case, it would literally translate as "toward salvation." The liturgical Bible translates it as "destined for salvation."

15. Cf. *The Protreptic*, 59.3.

16. Horrell, "Race, Nation, People," 142.

17. Benjamin Ndiaye, *Jésus, premier-né d'une multitude de frères. Étude de Rm 8, 28-30* (Dakar, Clairafrique, 1999), 102.

18. Cf. Jean-Bosco Matand, "La solidarité fraternelle de Jésus avec les croyants: Lecture exégético-rhétorique de He 2:5–16," in *The Church-Family and Biblical Perspectives: Proceedings of the 9th PACE Conference*, Pan-African Association of Catholic Exegetes (PACE), vol. 2 (Kinshasa: J. B. Matand Publisher, 2002), 67–88.

19. Cf. Albert Vanhoye, "1 Pierre au carrefour des théologies du Nouveau Testament," *Études sur la Première Lettre de Pierre* (Paris: Cerf, 1980), 97–128.

20. Cf. Enrico Norelli, "Au sujet de la première réception de 1 Pierre. Trois exemples," in *The Catholic Epistles and the Tradition*, ed. Jacques Schlosser (Leuven: Leuven University Press, 2004), 327–66.

21. Cf. Norelli, "Au sujet de la première réception de 1 Pierre," 331.

22. "We, the chosen race, the royal priesthood, holy nation, chosen people, who once were not a people, but are now the people of God" (Clement of Alexandria, *The Protreptic*, 59, 3).

23. Cf. Clement of Alexandria, *Les Stromates*, VII, 7, 35, 2.

24. Clement of Alexandria, *Les Stromates*, VII, 7, 59, 3.

25. Clement of Alexandria, *Les Stromates*, VII, 7, 73, 5.

26. Clement of Alexandria, *The Pedagogue*, I, 6, 32, 4.

27. Racialism is the theory that human races are different from each other. A racialist person considers, for example, that a Black person is different from a white person, both biologically and psychologically.

28. Cf. Love L. Sechrest, *A Former Jew: Paul and the Dialectics of Race* (New York: T&T Clark, 2009).

29. Justin, *Dialogue with Tryphon*, 110, 35.

30. Thus arises the question of the perception of the people of the Bible on the Cushites. What impact on Bible studies and those who do them? Why the lack of importance given to the Cushites in the Bible, compared to other surrounding peoples? Cf. Rodney Steven Sadler, *Can a Cushite Change His Skin?* (1967; repr., New York: T&T Clark, 1967).

31. In the colonial administration in French Equatorial Africa, the term *race* designated the tribe, the custom.

32. The myth of Ham has been widely used to justify slavery and apartheid. Cf. Paulin Poucouta, "Esclavage et mythe biblique de Cham," www.ceafri.net. (5/25/2020, updated 3/6/2020).

33. Second Vatican Council, Decree on the Apostolate of Lay, 3, 18.

34. South African Bishops' Conference, "Pastoral Letter on Christian Hope in the Current Crisis" (May 1986).

CHAPTER 9

1. The definitions of terms in this preliminary section (given as direct quotation) are from the *Miriam Webster Collegiate Dictionary*, unless otherwise stated. A Google search conducted on each of the terms defined is used to collaborate the definitions. Because the project is conversational in nature, emphasis on written resources, in my view, would be minimal.

2. Most Africans have brown skin color, others what we call fair complexion; but there are some Africans who have beautiful black, bronze color. The Albinos, though not many, have another color variation.

3. From Oxford Learners Dictionary: https://www.oxfordlearners dictionaries.com/definition/english/combat_1.

4. Cambridge English Dictionary; https://dictionary.cambridge/us /dictionary/english/combat.

5. The vested interest of the West in Africa is not a baseless assertion as testified, for instance, John Perkins, *The The Secret History of the American Empire: The Truth About Economic Hit Men, Jackals, and How to Change the World* (New York: Plume, 2008). The author, an agent, may be compared to the terrorists in Africa fighting in the interest of their invisible masters; cf. Teresa Okure, "Scriptural Reflections on the Context of Collaborative Mission in South Sudan," in *Collaborative Mission in South Sudan: Towards a New Paradigm*, ed. Lazar T. Stanislaus, SVD and Carolyn Buchs SNDdeN (Rome: Paulines Publications, Africa, 2022), 199–216. The book reveals the complicity of the West in instigating the tribal wars to enable foreigners loot the abundant natural resources of the country; CALAR (Coalition for Africa's Liberation and Restoration) also pointed out the same in its "Statement on Africa Liberation Day, 25th May 2021"; www.afjn.org.

6. Society of the Holy Child Jesus, 28th General Chapter, April 17–30, 2022, Nemi, Italy was on the theme and imperative for the wheat grain that must die to bear fruit: "Unless a grain of wheat falls into the earth and dies, it remains just a single grain; but if it dies, it bears much fruit," John 12:20–26, www.shcj.org.

7. The core issues in sex and race portrayed in Genesis 1—11 apply to humanity, not only the nation Israel.

8. On diversity as grace see Teresa Okura, "Gospel-Based Personal Identity and Life as Recipe for Racism-Free Leadership in the Church," in *One Faith, Many Tongues: Managing Diversity in the Church in Nigeria*, ed. Fortunatus Nwachukwu, 2nd ed. (Abuja: Paulines Publications Africa, 2018), 40–63, where I write of diversity of human beings as flowers in God's garden.

9. A select list of relevant works is given in the bibliography.

10. Pope Francis's call to humanity in *Laudato Si'* to care for the earth our common home or risk perishing with the earth has become a universally acclaimed classic. This call is firmly rooted in Scripture. See further on this, Teresa Okure, "The Use of Scripture in *Laudato Si'*," *Grace and Truth*, Ecological Issue, 37 no. 1 (2021): 6–15.

11. Unsuccessfully, because it does not maintain the word "humankind" for all the instances where the biblical author has *adam*.

12. Cf. Jerome Murphy O'Connor, *St Paul's Corinth: Texts and Archaeology* (Collegeville, MN: Liturgical Press, 1990).

13. "In human genetics, the Mitochondrial Eve is the matrilineal most recent common ancestor (MRCA) of all living human" (a Google search for

mitochondrial DNA, July 5, 2022). The search unveils much information on this issue, including the pictures of what the Mitochondrial Eve looked like.

14. See Teresa Okure, "'God-Word Became Flesh' (John 1:1–3, 14): Index to the Testament Understanding of Humanity," in *Human Beings, Race and the Land*, Acts of the Catholic Biblical Association of Nigeria (CABAN), vol. 13 (2021); https:/www.cabanalive.org.

15. The Greek *hyios* translated "son" in English is rendered by *eyen* (child) in Ibibio language. Child signifies what is begotten by a given species, a human being (*eyen owo*) or an animal; example *eyen edong/erong* (by a sheep).

16. See Teresa Okure "'He Gave Them Power to Become Children of God' (John 1:12–14): Divinization as God's Foundational Gift to Believers; A Survey in John's Gospel," in *The Holy Spirit and Charisms in the Bible*, Acts of the Catholic Biblical Association of Nigeria, vol. 10 (2017), https://www.cabanalive.org.

17. The conquerors of American and South Africa saw themselves as the new Israel, led by God to conquer and rape the lands of the original inhabitants: the native Indians and the peoples of South Africa. America celebrates this conquest today with Columbus Day.

18. "Siblings" is a better word than "brothers" or "brethren" for translating the Greek word *adephos* (pl. *adelphoi*). In Ibibio, it would be neutral: *eyen eka* (pl. *ndito eka*), of the same father and mother. Where one of the parents is different it would be *eyen ete* (pl. *ndito ete*). The NRSV renders the plural "brothers and sisters."

CHAPTER 10

1. I wish to acknowledge, with gratitude, the help of Prof. Pietro Tosato, OFM Cap. at the Salesian Pontifical University for his very useful suggestions and indication of source material.

2. The study of patristic exegesis that flourished on the fertile ground of ancient Christian literature has become a discipline, endowed with its own epistemological status. Cf. Manlio Simonetti and Gian Maria Vian, "L'esegesi patristica nella ricerca contemporanea," *Annuario de Historia de la Iglesia* 6 (1997): 241–67; Charles Kannengiesser, ed., *Handbook of Patristic Exegeses* (*HPE*), vol. 1 (Leiden: Brill, 2006), 23–89.

3. This danger (double-edged sword) was authoritatively denounced twenty years ago, according to Angelo Amato: "Sembra mancare una sufficiente fondazione della continuità genetica esistente tra il momento biblico e quello patristico e della loro stretta interconnessione. La conseguenza è il passaggio spesso arbitrario dalla fondazione biblica alla sintesi attualizzante, mettendo tra parentesi, o accennandolo appena, non solo il momento

patristico ma tutta intera la bimillenaria tradizione della chiesa." ("It appears to lack sufficient foundation of the genetic continuity that exists between the biblical and the patristic periods, and their close relationship. The consequence is an often-arbitrary passage from the biblical foundation to a topical synthesis (or synthesis for application), but which puts in brackets, or barely touches, not only the patristic period, but the whole two thousand-year-old tradition of the Church"), Angelo Amato, "Studio dei Padri e teologia dogmatica," in *Lo studio dei Padri della Chiesa oggi*, ed. E. dal Covolo and A. M. Triacca (Rome: Las, 1991), 90.

4. The Septuagint, the Church fathers' favorite text of the Old Testament, says, καὶ ἤρξατο Νωε ἄνθρωπος γεωργὸς γῆς καὶ ἐφύτευσεν ἀμπελῶνα καὶ ἔπιεν ἐκ τοῦ οἴνου καὶ ἐμεθύσθη καὶ ἐγυμνώθη ἐν τῷ οἴκῳ αὐτοῦ καὶ εἶδεν Χαμ ὁ πατὴρ Χανααν τὴν γύμνωσιν τοῦ πατρὸς αὐτοῦ καὶ ἐξελθὼν ἀνήγγειλεν τοῖς δυσὶν ἀδελφοῖς αὐτοῦ ἔξω καὶ λαβόντες Σημ καὶ Ιαφεθ τὸ ἱμάτιον ἐπέθεντο ἐπὶ τὰ δύο νῶτα αὐτῶν καὶ ἐπορεύθησαν ὀπισθοφανῶς καὶ συνεκάλυψαν τὴν γύμνωσιν τοῦ πατρὸς αὐτῶν καὶ τὸ πρόσωπον αὐτῶν ὀπισθοφανές καὶ τὴν γύμνωσιν τοῦ πατρὸς αὐτῶν οὐκ εἶδον ἐξένηψεν δὲ Νωε ἀπὸ τοῦ οἴνου καὶ ἔγνω ὅσα ἐποίησεν αὐτῷ ὁ υἱὸς αὐτοῦ ὁ νεώτερος καὶ εἶπεν ἐπικατάρατος Χανααν παῖς οἰκέτης ἔσται τοῖς ἀδελφοῖς αὐτοῦ καὶ εἶπεν εὐλογητὸς κύριος ὁ θεὸς τοῦ Σημ καὶ ἔσται Χανααν παῖς αὐτοῦ πλατύναι ὁ θεὸς τῷ Ιαφεθ καὶ κατοικησάτω ἐν τοῖς οἴκοις τοῦ Σημ καὶ γενηθήτω Χανααν παῖς αὐτῶν (Gen 9:20-27 LXX).

5. For a brief overview of the interpretation of the Book of Genesis in the patristic era cf. David Balás and Jeffrey Bingham, "Patristic Exegesis of the Books of the Bible: Genesis," in *HPE*, 278–81.

6. *Biblia patristica: index des citations et allusions bibliques dans la littérature patristique,* (*BP*) vol. 3, *Origène* (Paris, 1980), 46.

7. We have sixteen homilies by Origen on the Book of Genesis, translated by Rufinus, and other fragments taken from homilies that have been lost. These sermons do not contain any commentary on the episode of the curse of Ham. Cf. Maria Grazia Danieli, *Genesi* (scritti esegetici su), in *Origene: Dizionario* (DO): La cultura, il pensiero, le opere, ed. Adele Monaci Castagno (Città Nuova, 2000), 187–90. The homilies that have been passed down to us are probably an anthology of a larger cycle produced by Origen. On this point cf. Manlio Simonetti, "Le Omelie sulla Genesi di Origene: un'antologia?," in *La biografia di Origene tra storia e agiografia: Atti del VI Convegno di Studi del Gruppo italiano di Ricerca su Origene e la Tradizione Alessandrina*, ed. Adele Monaci Castagno (Turin, September 11–13, 2002), Pazzini, Villa Verucchio (RV), 2004.

8. For a short presentation of Origen's *ratio hermeneutica*, cf. Manlio Simonetti, "*Scrittura Sacra*," in *Origene: Dizionario*, 424–37.

9. The cycle of *Homilies on Numbers* is presented by Maria Grazia Danieli, "*Numeri*" (*scritti esegetici sui*), in *Origene: Dizionario*, 289–92.

10. "Propterea fortassis in huius sacramenti figura etiam Chanaan puer, antequam nasceretur, maledicitur. Cham namque peccaverat pater eius et prophetans Noe, cum unicuique filiorum suorum optima quaeque signaret, ubi ad Cham uentum est 'maledictus' inquit 'Chanaan puer' Cham peccavit et Chanaan progenies eius maledicitur et maledicta est. Et ideo acrius nobis intendendum est et prospiciendum, ne forte gigneret aliquid anima quod maledicto dignum sit; etiamsi nondum opere impleuerit, in ipsa tamen voluntate et proposito eius erit huiusmodi maledicta progenies." Origen, *Homiliae in Numeros*, XX,2,3, p. 28. (English translation by Thomas P. Scheck, *Homilies on Numbers*, Ancient Christian Texts Series (Lisle, IL: InterVarsity Press, 2009). With a similar thought process, even Ephrem the Syrian, the poet-theologian of the fourth century, in his commentary on Genesis, examines and solves the same problem of the incongruity of the punishment inflicted on the son for the sins of his father. In fact, according to Ephrem's explanation, Noah prophetically predicted Canaan's future sins. "Noah knew that Canaan would deserve the curse in his old age, or else he would not have been cursed in his youth" (Louth 2003, 207).

11. The centrality of this theme in Origen's writings is briefly explained by Lorenzo Perrone, "*Libero arbitrio*," in *Origene: Dizionario*, 237–43.

12. Allegory in the ancient world was a clever interpretive procedure applied above all to the great mythological narratives of Greco-Roman literature. Founded on Plato's vision of a double level of reality, the sensitive and the intelligible, it was used extensively by the Stoic philosophers who, while professing a holistic cosmic vision, through allegorical explanations grasped the intimate connections existing in the world, in historical events, in human experiences. The allegory was adopted by Alexandrian Jewish-Hellenistic thought and through this mediation was received by the great Christian exegetes, especially Origen and his followers, in the East and in the West. On allegory in ancient thought cf. Jean Pépin, *Mythe et allégorie. Les origines grecques et les contestations judéo-chrétiennes* (Paris: Éditions Montaigne, 1976 [1958]). On allegory and its relationship with "historia" cf. Thomas Böhm, "Allegory and History," in *HPE*, 213–27.

13. Cf. Annewies van den Hoek, "Etymologizing in a Christian Context: The Techniques of Clement and Origen," *Studia Philonica Annual* 16 (2004): 122–68.

14. The cycle of *Homilies on Joshua* is presented by Rosario Scognamiglio, "*Giosuè*" (*scritti esegetici su*), in *Origene: Dizionario*, 195–97.

15. On this concept, typical of Origen, cf. Jean Danielou, *Origène* (Paris: La Table rotonde, 1948), 272–73.

16. "Sed et Iaphet simili modo dilatatio interpretatur, qui utique et ipse formam populi huius ferebat, qui salvatur *ex gentibus*, et Chanaan puer servus ei subicitur a patre et fratri suo Sem, qui formam gerit eorum, qui ex circumcisione salvantur. In quo admiranda est benignitas et providentia Dei, quio volens peccatori Chanaan praestare remedium et conferre ei salutem, servum eum fecit fratribus suis, sicut et Esau factus est ut serviret fratri suo Iacob, non utique periret, sed ut salutem melioribus oboediendo conquireret. Praestatur enim malis plurimum et peccatoribus, qui semet ipsos regere nesciunt, ut non sibimet ipsis committantur, sed ut servi fiant sanctorum et subiaceant melioribus, ut non suo sensu malo, sed illorum bono regantur." Origen, *Homiliae in Iesu*, III,4, p. 138 (English translation by Barbara J. Bruce, *Homilies on Joshua*, Fathers of the Church Patristic Series (Washington, DC: Catholic University of America Press, 2002).

17. On the "philosophy" professed by Origen cf. Gilles Dorival, "*Filosofia*," in *Origene: Dizionario*, 171–77.

18. Cf. Adele Monaci Castagno, "Maestro," in *Origene: Dizionario*, 247–53.

19. "La Scrittura è simile a un albero che si sviluppa di più o di meno a seconda del maggiore o minore impegno e capacità dell'interprete, il che significa che il significato della Scrittura, parola di Dio, è inesauribile e sta all'interprete mettere in luce quanto più di esso gli riesce possibile" ("Scripture is similar to a tree that develops more or less depending on the greater or lesser commitment and ability of the interpreter, which means that the meaning of Scripture, the word of God, is inexhaustible and it is up to the interpreter to highlight as much of it as he can"), Manlio Simonetti, "*Scrittura Sacra*," 434.

20. In this sense, we speak of a "reader-disciple collaborator" of the *didáskalos*: cf. Lorenzo Perrone, "Metodo," in *Origene: Dizionario*, 276–81, at 279.

21. "Ceterum quam multa sint divinarum testimonia Litterarum, quae parentum peccatis obligant filios, numerare quis possit? Cur enim peccavit Cham, et in eius filium Chanaan vindicta prolata est? Cur pro peccato Salomonis filius eius diminutione regni punitus est? Cur peccatorum Achab regis Israel in eius posteros poena dilata est? Utquid legitur in sanctis Libris: *Reddens peccata patrum in sinum filiorum eorum post eos*; et: *Reddens peccata patrum in filios usque in tertiam et quartam progeniem* ? Qui numerus etiam pro universitate accipi potest. Numquid haec falsa sunt? Quis hoc dixerit, nisi divinorum eloquiorum apertissimus inimicus? Sed carnalis generatio etiam populi Dei pertinens ad Testamentum vetus, quod *in servitutem generat*, parentum peccatis obligat filios": Augustine, *Contra Iulianum*, VI,25,82, 978–79. English translation by Matthew A. Schumacher,

Against Julian, The Fathers of the Church series, vol. 35 (Washington DC: Catholic University of America Press, 1957).

22. Cf. Vittorino Grossi, "Giuliano di Eclano," in *Nuovo Dizionario Patristico e di Antichità Cristiane*, ed. Angelo di Berardino, vol. 2 (Genova/Milan: Marietti, 2006–2008), coll. 2309–11. For a more in-depth knowledge of this character and his work cf. J. Lössl, *Julianum von Aeclanum. Studien zu seinem Leben, seinem Werk, seiner Lehre und ihrer Überlieferung* (Leiden: Brill, 2001).

23. There have been attempts to rehabilitate Julian of Eclanum at the expense of Augustine himself, but we do not consider them convincing: cf. Aldo Marandino, "Agostino di Ippona e Giuliano di Eclano. Attualità di una controversia, in Humanitas Nova," *Rivista internazionale di cultura umanistica* I (2020): 69–94.

24. In his *Letter to Demetrias* Pelagius explains his anthropological doctrine: "To do good and enter upon the path of virtue....First you ought to measure the good of human nature...having made (man) seem unarmed outwardly, (God) provided him with a better armament inside, that is, with reason and wisdom....It was for this reason that 'he left him free to make his own decisions' (Sir.15.14) and set before him...good and evil, it is on this choice between two ways, on this freedom to choose either alternative, that the glory of the rational mind is based....It is from this that its dignity is derived." Pelagio sembra essere rimasto troppo legato alla concezione della paideia antica, trasmessa dalla scuola e basata su tre requisiti di ogni educazione artistica: le doti naturali, l'esercitazione e la dottrina con l'esempio, lasciando poco spazio alla dirompente novità cristiana, costituita dalla vita sacramentale e dall'azione interiore dello Spirito nei credenti" ("Pelagius seems to have remained too tied to the concept of the ancient *paideia*, taught in school and based on three requisites of every artistic education: natural gifts, practice and doctrine by example, leaving little room for Christianity's disruptive innovation, based on sacramental life and on the Holy Spirit's action in believers" [Cf. English translation: https://epistolae.ctl.columbia.edu/letter/1296.html]): Nello Cipriani, "Pelagio," in *Letteratura Patristica*, ed. Angelo di Berardino, Giorgio Fedalto, and Manlio Simonetti (San Paolo: Cinisello Balsamo (MI) 2007), 978–79.

25. "I sei libri diretti contro Giuliano di Eclano, scritti nel 421 o poco dopo, rappresentano la terza opera composta da Agostino nel corso della discussione che egli condusse con Giuliano—discussione che era stata avviato dallo stesso Giuliano, il quale, nei suoi quattro libri *Ad Turbantium*, aveva attaccato il primo libro de *De nuptiis et concupiscentia* di Agostino. Una copia dell'opera di Giuliano era stata inviata ad Agostino da un vescovo di nome Claudio. Quando lesse l'intero testo di Giuliano, Agostino si accorse che non tutte le citazioni scelte dal conte Valerio erano accurate in modo

tale che il secondo libro del *De nuptiis et concupiscentia* aveva rappresentato una risposta all'anonimo trascrittore, più che allo stesso Giuliano. A quel punto perciò Agostino elaborò questa replica in sei libri ai quattro libri di Giuliano. Il punto di partenza dell'attacco di Giuliano era la tesi secondo la quale la concezione di Agostino circa la trasmissione del peccato originale mediante la concupiscenza era una dottrina manichea contraria alla fede cattolica." ("The six books directed against Julian of Eclanus, written in 421 or shortly thereafter, are the third work written by Augustine in the course of the discussion he had with Julian. The argument was initiated by Julian himself, who, in his four books *Ad Turbantium,* had attacked Book I of Augustine's *De nuptiis et concupiscentia.* A copy of Julian's work had been sent to Augustine by a bishop named Claudius. After reading Julian's whole text, Augustine realized that not all the quotations chosen by Count Valerius were accurate. Therefore, the second book of *De nuptiis et concupiscentia* became a response to the anonymous transcriber, rather than to Julian himself. At that point, Augustine thus wrote this six-book reaction to Julian's four books. The starting point of Julian's attack was the thesis according to which Augustine's conception of the transmission of original sin through concupiscence was a Manichean doctrine contrary to the Catholic faith"): Gerald Bonner, *Freedom and Necessity: St. Augustine's Teaching on Divine Power and Human Freedom* (Washington, DC: Catholic University of America Press, 2007).

26. "By 'analogy of faith' we mean the coherence of the truths of faith among themselves and within the whole plan of Revelation" (*CCC* 114).

27. "Quaeritur quare peccans Cham in patris offensa, non in seipso, sed in filio suo Chanaan maledicitur; nisi quia prophetatum est quodammodo terram Chanaan, eiectis inde Chanaanaeis et debellatis, accepturos fuisse filios Israel, qui venirent de semine Sem?": Augustine, *Quaestiones in Heptateucum,* I,17, 419.

28. There are two collections of the *Homilies on Genesis.* The second one, which is comprised of 67 sermons, comments on the entire book. The preaching dates to the Antiochian period. The homilies were probably written down in the year 388: cf. Johannes Quasten, *Patrologia II. Dal Concilio di Nicea a quello di Calcedonia* (Marietti 1820, Casale, 1969), 437.

29. Καὶ γὰρ οὐκ ἔλαττον τοῦ παιδὸς ὁ Χὰμ τὴν κόλασιν ὑπέμενε, καὶ τῆς τιμωρίας τὴν αἴσθησιν ἐλάμβανεν. Ἴστε γάρ, ἴστε πῶς πολλάκις ηὔξαντο πατέρες ὑπὲρ παίδων τιμωρίαν ὑποσχεῖν, καὶ ὅπως βαρύτερον αὐτοῖς ἐστιν εἰς κολάσεως λόγον, τὸ τοὺς παῖδας ὁρᾶν τιμωρουμένους, ἢ ἑαυτούς ὑπευθύνους γεγονότας. John Chrysostom, *Homiliae in Genesim,* 29,6 (PG 53, 269).

30. Chrysostom, *Homiliae in Genesim,* 29,6 (PG 53, 269).

31. On his homiletic activity, cf. Alejandro Olivar, *La predicación cristiana antigua* (Barcelona: Herder, 1991), 111–38.

32. "Primum omnium quantam discimus parentibus referre reuerentiam, cum legimus quoniam qui benedicebatur a patre benedictus erat et qui maledicebatur maledictus erat. Ideo hanc parentibus gratiam donauit deus, ut filiorum pietas prouocetur. Praerogatiua igitur parentum disciplina est filiorum. Honora ergo patrem, ut benedicat te. Honoret patrem pius propter gratiam, ingratus pro timore," Ambrose, *De patriarchis*, I,1, 20–21 (Engl. trans. au.).

33. On typology, a key notion of patristic *ratio hermeneutica*, cf. Di Berardino, "*Tipologia*," in *Nuovo Dizionario Patristico e di Antichità Christiane*, vol. III, coll. 5369–70.

34. "Erat Isaac dominum timens, utpote Abrahae indoles, deferens patri usque adeo ut aduersus paternam uoluntatem nec morte recusaret. Ioseph quoque, cum somniasset quod sol et luna et stellae adorarent eum, sedulo tamen obsequio deferebat patri": Ambrose, *De officiis ministrorum*, I, 66, 64–65.

CHAPTER 11

1. Cf. S. Ali, "How Race and Racism Empower a School's Curriculum," *Journal of Research Initiatives* 4, no. 1 (2018): 1–8. See also J. George, "a Lesson on Critical Race Theory," *Human Rights Magazine* 46, no. 2 (2021); R. Kohli, "Breaking the Cycle of Racism in the Classroom: Critical Race Reflections from Future Teachers of Color," *Teacher Education Quarterly* 35, no. 4 (2008): 177–88; M. Pollock, "Everyday Antiracism in Education," *Anthropology News* 47, no. 2 (2006): 9–10; and L. Turney, I. Law, and D. Phillips, "Institutional Racism in Higher Education Toolkit Project: Building the Antiracist" book review, *Higher Educational Institutes* 25, no. 2.

2. Cf. C. Haynes, "Dismantling the White Supremacy Embedded in Our Classrooms: White Faculty in Pursuit of More Equitable Educational Outcomes for Racially Minoritized Students," *International Journal of Teaching and Learning in Higher Education* 29, no. 1 (2017): 87–107, at 95.

3. Cf. P. Freire, *Pedagogy of the Oppressed* (New York: Continuum, 1970).

4. C. G. Woodson, *The Mis-education of the Negro: History Is a Weapon* (1933). Retrieved from https://www.historyisaweapon.com/defcon1/misedne.html.

5. Cf. K. B. Clark and M. P. Clark, "Racial Identification and Preference in Negro Children," in *Readings in Social Psychology*, ed. T. M. Newcomb and E. L. Hartley (New York: Holt, 1947), 169–78.

6. Cf. Clark and Clark, "Racial Identification and Preference in Negro Children."

7. Ali, "How Race and Racism Empower a School's Curriculum," 5.

8. Cf. Woodson, *The Mis-education of the Negro*.

9. D. L. Brown, "How the Founder of Black History Month Rebutted White Racism in a Forgotten Manuscript," *Washington Post*, February 1, 2019, https://www.washingtonpost.com/history/2019/02/01/how-founder-black-history-month-refuted-white-racism-forgotten-manuscript/.

10. B. Joseph, *21 Things You May Not Know about the Indian Act: Helping Canadians Make Reconciliation with Indigenous Peoples a Reality* (British Columbia, Port Coquitlam: Indigenous Relations Press, 2018), 55.

11. J. Shiao and a. Woody, "The Meaning of 'Racism,'" *Sociological Perspectives* 64, no. 4 (2021): 495–517.

12. A. Schleicher, "The Impact of COVID-19 on Education: Insights from Education at a Glance 2020," https://www.oecd.org/education/the-impact-of-covid-19-on-education-insights-education-at-a-glance-2020.pdf.

13. E. Hanson, D. Gamez, and A. Manuel, "The Residential School System: Indigenous Foundations," September 2020, https://indigenousfoundations.art.ubc.ca/residential-school-system-2020/.

14. Cf. L. C. Van Jaarsveldt, M. S. de Vries, and H. J. Kroukamp, "South African Students Call to Decolonize Science: Implications for International Standards, Curriculum Development and Public Administration Education," *Teaching Public Administration* 37, no. 1 (2019): 12–30.

15. Georgetown University, "Baker Trust for Transformational Learning: Progress Report," March 2020, https://futures.georgetown.edu/wp-content/uploads/2021/03/RHBT_Progress-FINAL.pdf.

16. A. Walli, R. Williams, and J. Kelly, "Anthropologists on Racism and the History of Inequality," *Field Museum*, June 18, 2020, par. 5, https://www.fieldmuseum.org/blog/anthropologists-racism-and-history-inequality.

17. C. J. Libassi, "The Neglected College Race Gap: Racial Disparities among College Completers," Center for American Progress, May 23, 2018, https://www.americanprogress.org/issues/education-postsecondary/reports/2018/05/23/451186/neglected-college-race-gap-racial-disparities-among-college-completers/.

18. A. Harris, "The Perverse Pact: Racism and White Privilege," *American Imago* 76, no. 3 (2019): 309–33, at 312.

19. K. Egan, "What Is Curriculum?" *Curriculum Inquiry* 8, no. 1 (1978): 65–72, at 71.

20. M. Young, "What Is Curriculum and What Can It Do?," *The Curriculum Journal* 25, no. 1 (2014): 7–13, at 7.

21. Cf. J. George, "A Lesson on Critical Race Theory," *Human Rights Magazine* 46, no. 2 (2021).

22. George, "A Lesson on Critical Race Theory," par. 2.

23. Cf. R. Kohli, "Breaking the Cycle of Racism in the Classroom: Critical Race Reflections from Future Teachers of Color," *Teacher Education Quarterly* 35, no. 4 (2008): 177–188.

24. Cf. H. Potter and M. Burris, "Here Is What School Integration in America Looks Like Today," the Century Foundation, https://tcf.org/content/report/school-integration-america-looks-like-.

25. S. Ali, "How Race and Racism Empower a School's Curriculum," *Journal of Research Initiatives* 4, no. 1 (2018): 1–8. See also G. Ladson-Billings, "Toward a Theory of Culturally Relevant Pedagogy," *American Educational Research Journal* 32, no. 3 (1995).

26. Ali, "How Race and Racism Empower a School's Curriculum," 3.

27. G. Gay, *Culturally Responsive Teaching: Theory, Research & Practice* (New York: Teachers College Press: Columbia University, 2000), 29.

28. Cf. Turney, Law, and Phillips, "Institutional Racism in Higher Education Toolkit Project."

29. Cf. "University," *Encyclopedia Britannica* (2020), https://www/britannica.com/topic/university.

30. W. J. Jennings, *The Christian Imagination: Theology and the Origins of Race* (New Haven, CT: Yale University Press, 2010).

31. Jennings, *The Christian Imagination*, 222.

32. S. Klotz, "How Native Students Fought Back against Abuse and Assimilation at U.S. Boarding Schools," *The Conversation*, August 12, 2021, https://theconversation.com/how-native-students-fought-back-against-abuse-and-assimilation-at-us-boarding-schools-165222?utm_.

33. Cf. N. Wa Thiong'o, *Decolonising the Mind: The Politics of Language in African Literature* (London: James Curry, 1986).

34. Cf. "University," *Encyclopedia Britannica* (2020).

35. C. Davis, "In the Beginning, There Were Black Catholics," *U.S. Catholic*, https://uscatholic.org/articles/202010/in-the-beginning-there-were-black-catholics/.

36. Davis, "In the Beginning, There Were Black Catholics," par. 78.

37. Cf. "Use of Vernacular in Worship Approved Vatican II: 50 Years Ago Today," *Catholic News Service*, December 10, 2012, https://Vaticaniiat50.wordpress.com/2012/12.

38. Hanson, Gamez, and Manuel, "The Residential School System."

39. Cf. E. Fritz, *The Art of Forming Young Disciples: Why Youth Ministries Aren't Working and What to Do about It* (New Hampshire: Sophia Institute, 2018).

40. Fritz, *The Art of Forming Young Disciples*, 21–22.

41. A. Walli, R. Williams, and J. Kelly, J. (2020, June 18). "Anthropologists on Racism and the History of Inequality," *Field Museum*, June 18,

2020, par. 3, https://www.fieldmuseum.org/blog/anthropologists-racism-and-history-inequality.

42. Turney, Law, and Phillips, "Institutional Racism in Higher Education Toolkit Project," 85.

43. M. Pollock, "Everyday Antiracism in Education," *Anthropology News* 47, no. 2 (2006): 3–4, https://understandingrace.org/pdf/rethinking/pollock.pdf.

44. Cf. Turney, Law, and Phillips, "Institutional Racism."

CHAPTER 12

1. Ijeoma Oluo, *So You Want to Talk about Race* (New York: Seal Press, 2019), 26.

2. United States Conference of Catholic Bishops, *Open Wide Our Hearts: The Enduring Call to Love—a Pastoral Letter against Racism* (Washington, DC: USCCB, 2018), 3.

3. George Floyd was murdered by Dereck Chauvin, a police officer with the Minnesota Police Department.

4. Cf. See https://cruxnow.com/interviews/2020/06/church-must-be-part-of-of-solution-to-cry-of-anguish-from-floyd-killing-priest-says/. See also https://churchlifejournal.nd.edu/articles/one-liners-on-race-from-the-pope-and-other-catholic-officials-wont-do-any-longer/.

5. Cf. Paulinus Odozor, "African Catholics in the United States: Gifts and Challenges," in *Uncommon Faithfulness: The Black Catholic Experience*, ed. M. Shawn Copeland, with LaReine Marie Mosely and Albert J. Roboteau (Maryknoll, NY: Orbis Books, 2009), 197.

6. Cf. Odozor, "African Catholics in the United States," 197.

7. Recall, for example, Hegel's theory of the Universal Mind/Spirit in its incarnations through various historical "realms" on its journey to full and absolute awareness of itself. On this "journey," the spirit incarnates itself in the semitic realm, then the Greek, the Roman, and the Germanic realms. Hegel argues that the Black race could not be a location for the incarnation of the Spirit because the Black race has nothing intellectual to offer. They are only disposed to and capable of physical activity, such as sex and sports.

8. See John T. Noonan, *A Church That Can and Cannot Change: The Development of Catholic Moral Teaching* (Notre Dame, IN: University of Notre Dame Press, 2005).

9. John Connelly, "Catholic Racism and Its Opponents," *The Journal of Modern History* 79, no. 4 (2007): 813–47 at 836.

10. Connelly, "Catholic Racism and Its Opponents," 846.

11. John Langan, "Human Rights in Roman Catholicism," in *Readings in Moral Theology*, vol. 5 , ed. Charles Curran and Richard A. McCormick (Mahwah, NJ: Paulist Press, 1986), 111.

12. See John Langan, "Human Rights in Roman Catholicism," 112–13.

13. Second Vatican Council, The Pastoral Constitution of the Church in the Modern World (*Gaudium et Spes*). The translations used throughout this chapter are taken from Norman P. Tanner, ed., *Decrees of the Ecumenical Councils*, vol. 2, *Trent–Vatican II* (Washington, DC: Sheed & Ward and Georgetown University Press, 1990).

14. Within this category, the Catholic tradition speaks of venial and mortal sin. For a thing to be mortal sin, according to traditional categorization, the object of the act has to be gravely evil, the moral agent has to know it is gravely evil and consents freely to doing it.

15. Peter Henriot, "Social Sin and Conversion: A Theology of the Church's Social Involvement," in *Introduction to Christian Ethics*, ed. Ronald P. Hamel and Kenneth R. Himes (New York: Paulist Press, 1989), 218.

16. Peter Henriot, "Social Sin and Conversion," 219.

17. John Paul II, Encyclical, *Sollicitudo Rei Socialis*, December 30, 1987, no. 36.

18. John Paul II, *Sollicitudo Rei Socialis*, no. 36. Cf. Second Vatican Ecumenical Council, Pastoral Constitution on the Church in the Modern World, *Gaudium et Spes*, 25.

19. Gregory Baum, *Religion and Alienation: A Theological Reading of Sociology* (New York: Paulist Press, 1975), 201.

20. United States Conference of Catholic Bishops (USCCB), Pastoral Letter on Racism: "Brothers and Sisters to Us," 1979, https://www.usccb.org/committees/african-american-affairs/brothers-and-sisters-us.

21. USCCB, Pastoral Letter on Racism: "Brothers and Sisters to Us."

22. USCCB, Pastoral Letter on Racism: "Brothers and Sisters to Us."

23. Benedict XVI/Joseph Ratzinger, *"In the Beginning...": A Catholic Understanding of the Story of Creation and the Fall* (Grand Rapids, MI: Eerdmans, 1995), 43–44.

SELECTED BIBLIOGRAPHY

Appiah, Anthony. "The Uncompleted Argument: Du Bois and the Illusion of Race." *Critical Inquiry* 12, no. 1 (1985): 21–37.

———. "The Uncompleted Argument: Dubois and the Illusion of Race." In *Overcoming Racism and Sexism,* edited by L. Bell and D. Blumenfeld. Lanham, MD: Rowman and Littlefield, 1995.

Arendt, Hannah. *Imperialism: Part Two of the Origins of Totalitarianism.* New York: Harcourt Brace Jovanovich, 1968.

———. *On Violence.* San Diego: Harcourt, Brace, Jovanovich, 1970.

Banton, Michael. *Racial Theories.* London: Cambridge University Press, 1987.

Biko, Steve. *I Write What I Like.* Johannesburg: Picador Africa, 1978.

Blumenbach, Johann Friedrich. *On the Natural Varieties of Mankind: De Generis Humani Varietate Nativa.* New York: Bergman Books, 1969.

Bond, Patrick. *Looting Africa: The Economics of Exploitation.* New York: Zed Books, 2006.

Brabazon, James. *Albert Schweitzer: A Biography.* 2nd ed. New York: Syracuse University Press, 2000.

Brewster, Fanny. "Childhood Innocence: Racial Prejudice and the Shaping of Psychological Complexes." *Psychological Perspectives* 62, nos. 2–3 (2019): 164–75.

Burgis, Tom. *The Looting Machine.* London: Public Affairs, 2015.

Carmody, Pádraig. *The New Scramble for Africa.* Malden, MA: Polity Press, 2016.

Catholic Biblical Association of Nigeria (CABAN). *The Bible on Human Beings, Race and the Land: Acts of the Catholic Biblical Association of Nigeria* (CABAN). Volume 13, 2021. https://

www.cabanalive.org. Relevant articles are listed below according to their numbering in the volume.

Catholic Institute of West Africa. *Becoming Church as the Family of God in Africa: Graces, Challenges and Prospects.* 30th CIWA Theology Week, April 8–12, 2019.

Césaire, Aimé. *Discourse on Colonialism.* New York: Monthly Review Press, 2000.

Cohen, William B. *The French Encounter with Africans: White Response to Blacks, 1530–1880.* Bloomington, IN: Indiana University Press, 1980.

Conrad, Joseph. *Heart of Darkness, Almayer's Folly, the Lagoon.* New York: Dell Publishing Co., 1960.

DiAngelo, Robin. *White Fragility: Why It's So Hard for White People to Talk about Racism.* USA: Beacon Press, 2018.

Du Bois, W.E.B. "Race Friction between Black and White, May 1908." W. E. B. Du Bois Papers (MS 312). Special Collections and University Archives, University of Massachusetts Amherst Libraries. Typed draft with notes and corrections of article discussing Alfred Holt Stone's article, "Is Race Friction between Black and White in the United States Growing and Inevitable," *American Journal of Sociology* 13, no. 5 (1908): 676–97.

Ewans, Martin. *European Atrocity, African Catastrophe: Leopold II, the Congo Free State and Its Aftermath.* New York: Routledge, 2017.

Fanon, Frantz. *Black Skin, White Masks.* New York: Grove Press, 1967.

———. *The Wretched of the Earth.* New York: Grove Press, 1963.

Foucault, Michel. *The History of Sexuality: The Will to Knowledge.* London: Penguin, 1990.

———. "The Subject and Power." *Critical Inquiry* 8, no. 4 (1982): 777–95.

Foucault, Michel, and François Ewald. *"Society Must Be Defended": Lectures at the Collège De France, 1975–1976.* Vol. 1. New York: Macmillan, 2003.

Freire, Paulo. *Pedagogy of the Oppressed.* New York: Continuum 1970. 30th anniversary ed., 2000.

Fyfe, Christopher. "Race, Empire and the Historians." *Race & Class* 33, no. 4 (1992): 15–30.

Galtung, Johan. "Violence, Peace, and Peace Research." *Journal of Peace Research* 6, no. 3 (1969): 167–91.

Gupta, Tania Das, Carl E. James, Chris Andersen, Grace-Edward Galabuzi, and Roger C. A. Maaka. *Race and Racialization: Essential Readings*. Toronto: Canadian Scholars' Press, 2007.

Hegel, Georg Wilhelm Friedrich. *The Philosophy of History*. Translated by J. H. Clarke. Revised ed. New York: The Colonial Press, 1899.

Hochschild, Adam. *King Leopold's Ghost: A Story of Greed, Terror, and Heroism in Colonial Africa*. New York: Houghton Mifflin Harcourt, 1998.

Hudson, Nicholas. "From 'Nation' to 'Race': The Origin of Racial Classification in Eighteenth-Century Thought." *Eighteenth-Century Studies* 29, no. 3 (1996): 247–64.

Hugo, Victor. "Discours Sur L'Afrique (1985), 4:1010." In *Actes Et Paroles*, ed. Fizaine Jean-Claude. Paris: Laffont, 1985.

Huntington, Samuel P. *Political Order in Changing Societies*. New Haven, CT: Yale University Press, 1968.

Idowu, Bọlaji E. *African Traditional Religion: A Definition*. London: SCM Press, 1973.

Kitcher, Philipp. *Preludes to Pragmatism: Toward a Reconstruction of Philosophy*. New York: Oxford University 2012.

Loomba, Ania. *Shakespeare, Race, and Colonialism*. New York: Oxford University Press, 2002.

Mallon, Ron. "A Field Guide to Social Construction." *Philosophy Compass* 2, no. 1 (2007): 93–108.

Mamdani, Mahmood. *Citizen and Subject: Contemporary Africa and the Legacy of Late Colonialism*. Princeton, NJ: Princeton University Press, 1996.

Mandela, Nelson. "Mandela—in His Own Words." *Guardian*. https://www.theguardian.com/world/2001/feb/11/nelsonmandela.southafrica.

Mawuna, Koutonin. "14 African Countries Forced by France to Pay Colonial Tax for the Benefits of Slavery and Colonization." Silicon Africa. http://siliconafrica.com/france-colonial-tax/.

Mazrui, Ali A. "The Re-invention of Africa: Edward Said, Vy Mudimbe, and Beyond." *Research in African Literatures* 36, no. 3 (2005): 68–82.

Mbembe, Achille. *Brutalisme*. Paris: La Découverte, 2020.

———. *Critique of Black Reason*. Translated by Laurent Dubois. Durham, NC: Duke University Press, 2017.

———. "Futures of Life and Futures of Reason." *Public Culture* 33, no. 1 (2021): 11–33.

———. *Out of the Dark Night: Essays on Decolonization*. New York: Columbia University Press, 2021.

Mbiti, John S. *African Religions & Philosophy*. Nairobi: Heinemann Kenya Ltd., 1969.

McLeod, Saul. "Maslow's Hierarchy of Needs." *Simply Psychology* 1 (2007): 1–18.

Middleton, Thomas, Levitt Morris, and Roger Furman. *The Black Book*. 1st ed. New York: Random House, 1974.

Miles, Robert, and Malcolm Brown. *Racism*. 2nd ed. New York: Routledge, 2004.

Montagu, Ashley. *The Concept of Race*. New York: Free Press, 1967.

Morning, Ann. "And You Thought That We Had Moved beyond All That: Biological Race Returns to Social Science." *Ethnic and Racial Studies* 37, no. 10 (2014): 1676–85.

Morton, Samuel George, and George Combe. *Crania Americana, or, a Comparative View of the Skulls of Various Aboriginal Nations of North and South America: To Which Is Prefixed an Essay on the Varieties of the Human Species*. Philadelphia and London: J. Dobson and Simpkin, Marshall, 1839.

Moten, Fred. "The Case of Blackness." *Criticism* 50, no. 2 (2008): 177-218.

Mudimbe, V.Y. *The Invention of Africa : Gnosis, Philosophy, and the Order of Knowledge*. Bloomington: Indiana University Press, 1988.

Naomi, Zack. *Philosophy of Science and Race*. New York: Routledge, 2002.

Nwachukwu, Fortunatus, ed. *One Faith, Many Tongues: Managing Diversity in the Church of Nigeria*. 2nd Edition. Abuja, Paulines Publications Africa, 2018.

Okure, Teresa. "Africa: Globalization and the Loss of Cultural Identity." In *Concilium 2001/5: Globalization and Its Victims*, edited by Jon Sobrino and Felix Wilfred, 67–74. London: SCM, 2001.

———. "Africa, a Martyred Continent: Seed of a New Humanity." In *Concilium 2003/1: Rethinking Martyrdom*, edited by Teresa

Okure, Jon Sobrino and Felix Wilfred, 38–46. London: SCM, 2003.

———. "Biblical Perspectives on Women: Eve, the Mother of All the Living (Gen 3:20)." *Voices from the Third World* 8 no. 3 (1985): 822–92.

———. "Gender in the Church's Teaching and in African Cultures." Gender and Partnership in Development. Caritas Internationalis. First Africa Forum. GIMPA, Achimota, Accra Ghana. September 1–8, 2001.

———. "HIV and Women: Gender Issues, Culture and the Church." Commissioned paper. CAFOD Consultation on HIV/AIDS. Bertoni Center, Pretoria. April 14–17, 1998.

———. "'In Him All Things Hold Together': A Missiological Reading of Colossians 1:15–20." *International Review of Mission* XCI, no. 360 (2002): 62–72.

———. *32 Articles Evaluating the Inculturation of Christianity in Africa*. Contributing coeditor. Kenya: AMECEA Gaba Publications, 1990.

Pope Francis, Encyclical Letter, *Fratelli Tutti* (Brothers and Sisters All). On Fraternity and Social Friendship. Vatican City: Libreria Editrice Vaticana, 2020.

———. Encyclical Letter, *Laudato Si'* (On Care for Our Common Home). Vatican City: Libreria Editrice Vaticana, 2015.

Rabinow, Paul, ed. *The Foulcault Reader: An Introduction to Foulcault's Thought*. London: Penguin, 1991.

Radcliffe-Brown, Alfred Reginald, and Forde Daryll, eds. *African Systems of Kinship and Marriage*. London: Routledge, 2015.

Rodney, Walter. *How Europe Underdeveloped Africa*. Rev. ed. Washington, DC: Howard University Press, 1981.

Satzewich, Vic, and Nikolaos Liodakis. *"Race" and Ethnicity in Canada: A Critical Introduction*. Toronto: Oxford University Press, 2013.

Smiley, Calvin John, and David Fakunle. "From 'Brute' to 'Thug': The Demonization and Criminalization of Unarmed Black Male Victims in America." *Journal Of Human Behavior in the Social Environment* 26, nos. 3–4 (2016): 350–66.

Smuts, Jan Christiaan. *Africa and Some World Problems, Including the Rhodes Memorial Lectures Delivered in Michaelmas Term, 1929*. Oxford: Clarendon Press, 1930.

Solomos, John. *Routledge International Handbook of Contemporary Racisms*. New York: Routledge, 2020.

Thiong'o, Ngugi Wa. *The Decolonization of the Mind: The Politics of Language in African Literature*. London: James Currey 1986.

Valdes, Francisco, Jerome McCristal Culp, and P. Angela Harris. "Battles Waged, Won, and Lost: Critical Race Theory at the Turn of the Millennium." In *Crossroads, Directions, and a New Critical Race Theory*, edited by Francisco Valdes, Jerome McCristal Culp and P. Angela Harris, 1–6. Philadelphia: Temple University Press, 2002.

Weber, Max. *Economy and Society: A New Translation*. Edited by Keith Tribe. Cambridge, MA: Harvard University Press, 2019.

Winant, Howard. *The World Is a Ghetto: Race and Democracy since World War II*. New York: Basic Books, 2001.

CONTRIBUTORS

Edward K. Braxton is bishop emeritus of the diocese of Belleville, Illinois. He earned his PhD and STD from the Pontifical Faculty of the Catholic University of Louvain. He is a former member of the faculties of theology at Harvard Divinity School, the University of Notre Dame, the Catholic University of America, and the North American College in Rome. He is the author of several books and many articles on academic and pastoral theology.

Anthony Egan is a Jesuit priest of the Jesuit Institute of South Africa. He is a lecturer in applied ethics at St. Augustine's College, and professor at Hekima University College, Nairobi. A historian by training (PhD Witwatersrand), he completed undergraduate and graduate studies in philosophy and theology in London (Heythrop College) and at the Weston Jesuit School of Theology (now Boston College School of Theology and Ministry), specializing as a moral theologian.

John Okoro Egbulefu is a Roman Catholic priest from Nigeria, emeritus professor of dogmatic theology at the Pontifical Urban University (1989–2020) in Rome, and the founder of the priestly missionary Congregation of Christ the Emmanuel (CCE). He studied comparative German and English language and literature at the University of Innsbruck, Austria, and dogmatic theology at the University of Münster, Germany, with Habilitation in the same branch of theology at the University of Bonn, Germany. He holds a doctorate degree in each of the two areas of study.

Emmanuel Katongole is priest of Kampala Archdiocese. Formerly an associate professor of theology and world Christianity at Duke University, Fr. Katongole is a professor of theology and peace studies at the University of Notre Dame (Center for Peace Studies). He is a full-time faculty member of the Kroc Institute for International Peace Studies of the Keough School of Global Affairs.

Evelyn Birabwa M. Namakula is an assistant professor at Carleton University in Canada. Dr. Namakula is an interdisciplinary scholar with degrees in theology; ethics; canon; humanitarianism, and international law. She teaches on and does research into race, human rights, natural resource governance, critical minerals, and the transition to green energy.

Dorothy Mensah-Aggrey is from Ghana and holds a doctorate in religious studies (curriculum planning). She is a Certified Online Programmer (CPO, LERN), and a Certified Adult Mental Health Aid, USA. A former director of religious education with the archdiocese of Washington, Dr. Mensah-Aggrey is now a Marianist Educational Associate and a curriculum design specialist and adult faith formation coordinator at the University of Dayton's Institute for Pastoral Initiatives. She is a board member of the National Association for Lay Ministry and a consultant for the USCCB Subcommittee on Certification for Ecclesial Ministry and Service.

Festo Mkenda is a Jesuit priest from Tanzania. He holds a doctorate in history and is currently serving as academic director of the Roman archives of the Society of Jesus. A historian of Africa, Dr. Mkenda holds an MA from the School of Oriental and African Studies, London, and a DPhil from the University of Oxford. Now mainly researching Jesuit history in Africa, his recent publications include *Jesuits in Africa: A Historical Narrative from Ignatius of Loyola to Pedro Arrupe* (Brill, 2022) and *A Splash of Diamond: The Jesuit Presence in Ethiopia from 1945 to the Present* (JHIA and IHSI, 2023).

Pius Ngandu Nkashama was from the Democratic Republic of the Congo and was a professor of literature Sorbonne Nouvelle, Paris III (France, 1997–2000), and lastly at Louisiana State University in Baton Rouge, LA (2000–2023), where he was a distinguished professor of French studies. A renowned novelist, playwright, and author of numerous scholarly studies on African literature, he died on December 19, 2023.

Fortunatus Nwachukwu is a Roman Catholic archbishop. A former apostolic nuncio and permanent observer of the Holy See to the United Nations Offices and other International Organizations in Geneva, Msgr. Nwachukwu is now the secretary of the Dicastery for the Evangelization of Peoples at the Vatican. He studied Sacred Scriptures and specialized in the textual criticism of the Old Testament. He later obtained doctorate degrees in dogmatic theology and canon law.

Paulinus Odozor is a Nigerian priest of the Congregation of the Holy Spirit. He is a professor of Christian ethics and of world religions at the University of Notre Dame, Notre Dame, Indiana, USA. He also pursues interest in African history and culture. Pope Benedict XVI appointed him as an expert to the Second Synod of Bishops for Africa (2009).

Teresa Okure is from Nigeria and is a professed sister of the Sisters of the Holy Child Jesus, a resident professor of New Testament and gender hermeneutics at the Catholic Institute of West Africa, Port Harcourt (Nigeria), and a member of ARCIC III (2011–2018).

Paulin Poucouta is a priest of the diocese of Pointe-Noire (Congo Brazzaville). He holds a doctorate in biblical theology from the Catholic Institute of Paris and a doctorate in the history of religions from Sorbonne. He is an honorary professor at the Catholic University of Yaoundé and the director of the journal *Spiritus*. He is the author of numerous publications including *Quand la Parole de Dieu visite l'Afrique: Lecture africaine de la Bible* (Karthala, 2011), and *God's Word in Africa* (Paulines, 2015).

Peter Kodwo Turkson is a Ghanaian cardinal priest with the titular church of St. Liborio, Rome. He is the former archbishop of Cape Coast, Ghana, the former president of the Pontifical Council of Justice and Peace (Vatican), and the former prefect of the Dicastery for Promoting Integral Human Development (Vatican), and now the chancellor of the Pontifical Academy of Sciences and the Pontifical Academy of Social Sciences (Vatican). He has master's degrees in divinity and sacred theology, and a license in Sacred Scriptures.

Aimé Kameni Wembou is a priest from Cameroun who is incardinated in the diocese of Avignon and holds a doctorate in canon law from the Lateran University in Rome. After working for several years, as the defender of the bond at the Court of the Vicariate of Rome, Fr. Wembou worked as the promoter of justice and "Defender of Bond" at the Inter-diocesan Tribunal of Edéa (Cameroon) in 2001. He is the administrator of the parish of San Nicola de Bari and judicial vicar of the Diocese of D'Avezzano (Italy).